Thinking God Otherwise

Thinking Philosophy of Religion

Entering the stage of philosophy is not a naive endeavor. It requires initiators, those who choose less steep paths to serve as guides for making better progress. This book series, Thinking Philosophy of Religion, aims to do this by introducing the major themes and figures of continental thought, from phenomenology and hermeneutics to metaphysics and spiritualism, with special attention to philosophy of religion. The act of philosophizing always occurs within a community, and while the great works of the philosophical tradition are important, so also is their reception, for it is in dialogue that thought is born. This series will thus strive to reveal in each work its original intuition and internal coherence, even discovering gems that the authors themselves may not have anticipated, recognizing that there is no philosophy without dialogue, and no dialogue without opening oneself to others and the world. Nevertheless, speech often suffers from not being thought through or worked on enough. We have lost the art of conversation—the art that was once practiced in the salons of philosophy and of music, where listening echoed the sounds of the world in others and their own way of living and thinking. This series will thus take the time to meet and question thinkers in the field of continental philosophy. We can only rejoice at the creativity shown by philosophy in Europe, particularly in its dialogue with the American continent. We will relay this exchange here, and in the absence of being able to personally meet the authors, we can always bring them to life, and revive them, when the act of speaking remains an "art" that we pledge to foster and respect. Through the act of introducing and engaging with the masters of continental philosophy, this series will bring to life the living debates that have shaped the formation of contemporary continental thought.

Series Editors

Emmanuel Falque

William L. Connelly

Thinking God Otherwise

Entering into the Work of Emmanuel Falque

ALAIN SAUDAN

Translated by Jacob Saliba
Foreword by Emmanuel Falque
Introduction by David Albertson

CASCADE *Books* · Eugene, Oregon

THINKING GOD OTHERWISE
Entering into the Work of Emmanuel Falque

Thinking Philosophy of Religion

Copyright © 2025 Alain Saudan. All rights reserved. Except for brief quotations in critical publications or reviews, no part of this book may be reproduced in any manner without prior written permission from the publisher. Write: Permissions, Wipf and Stock Publishers, 199 W. 8th Ave., Suite 3, Eugene, OR 97401.

Cascade Books
An Imprint of Wipf and Stock Publishers
199 W. 8th Ave., Suite 3
Eugene, OR 97401

www.wipfandstock.com

PAPERBACK ISBN: 979-8-3852-3012-9
HARDCOVER ISBN: 979-8-3852-3013-6
EBOOK ISBN: 979-8-3852-3014-3

Cataloguing-in-Publication data:

Names: Saudan, Alain, author. | Saliba, Jacob, translator. | Falque, Emmanuel, 1963–, foreword. | Albertson, David, introduction.

Title: Thinking God otherwise : entering into the work of Emmanuel Falque / Alain Saudan ; translated by Jacob Saliba ; foreword by Emmanuel Falque ; introduction by David Albertson.

Description: Eugene, OR : Cascade Books, 2025 | Series : Thinking Philosophy of Religion | Includes bibliographical references and index.

Identifiers: ISBN 979-8-3852-3012-9 (paperback) | ISBN 979-8-3852-3013-6 (hardcover) | ISBN 979-8-3852-3014-3 (ebook)

Subjects: LCSH: Falque, Emmanuel, 1963–. | Christian philosophy—France. | Phenomenology.

Classification: B2430.F424 .S38 2025 (paperback) | B2430.F424 (ebook)

VERSION NUMBER 11/20/25

This English translation, with the permission of the author Alain Saudan, comes from the French text *Penser Dieu autrement: Introduction à l'œuvre d'Emmanuel Falque.* © Éditions Germina, novembre 2013 ISBN: 978-72-917285-46-6. Dépôt légal : 4th trimestre 2013.

Scripture texts in this work are taken from the New American Bible, revised edition © 2010 Confraternity of Christian Doctrine, Washington, DC, and are used by permission of the copyright owner. All rights reserved. No part of the New American Bible may be reproduced in any form without permission in writing from the copyright owner.

To my family, for their unwavering support.
To Mauricia, Fadi, Yelena, and Marie for their love.
To Rachel, for everything.

Contents

Foreword by Emmanuel Falque | ix
Translator's Preface by Jacob Saliba | xi
Introduction: To Defend the Gift by David Albertson | xvii

Ouverture: Thinking God | 1
Part One: Philosophy and Theology in Dialogue | 5
Part Two: Living Finitude | 36
Part Three: Metamorphosizing Finitude | 76
Part Four: The Return to the Body | 93

Epilogue: A Promise Kept? | 129
Appendix: Paul Ricœur—Emmanuel Falque: A Symbolic Confrontation? | 157
Acknowledgments | 173
Books by Emmanuel Falque Translated into English | 175
Bibliography | 177
Index | 183

Foreword

Emmanuel Falque

Penser Dieu autrement is a certain expression of a doctrine yet, above all, of a testimony. It is the very testimony of the author who was a longtime disciple of Paul Ricœur, and who later turned to the present work at hand. We do not choose our interlocutors. Only true creators may know this. It is not the authors who go in search of their readers, but the readers themselves who go to the authors. Because, after all, what counts first and foremost is neither the author nor the reader but the work itself. It makes its way through unexpected twists and turns, and it is always after the fact that we perceive that moment as important.

Such is the meaning, for us, behind the encounter which rests at the core of this book by Alain Saudan. To begin, let us say a few words. Several years my senior, and a certified philosophy professor in his own right, Saudan could very well be seen as the master and me the disciple. This is perhaps the case. For almost two decades, this author and friend has diligently cultivated the present work step by step, he has attended all the courses on which the various written subjects have come from, and has thus remained at the heart of the "workmanship" by assiduously observing an overall progression of thought. It was not simply "from the head" that this work is written, as if to satisfy a simple curiosity. Rather it emerged "from the heart," for the issue is profoundly existential and not just conceptual.

The relationship between philosophy and theology serves as the common thread of this work. Because, as the author very accurately points out, the challenge of Christianity today is to be "credible" (i.e., giving reasons for belief) and not only "believable" (i.e., adhering to the faith). There is, in fact, a cultural dimension of the Christian tradition which we must not forget, and which must necessarily be renewed. Many people today are interested in those "things of faith," including Christian mysteries (e.g., the incarnation, Eucharist, and resurrection), without necessarily believing in them. This is the new situation in which we find ourselves, and which *Thinking God Otherwise* seeks to honor. While the present work at hand has not had the opportunity to follow some of the more recent developments and texts (in particular, in their purely philosophical dimension), Alain Saudan saw, before anyone else, the unity of a thought, even of a person, that the philosophical and theological work has always wished to locate and exhibit. For this we are grateful, and thank him for so much fidelity to a project always in progress.

This book is addressed to all, for all, and in the language of all, and as such it serves as a gateway for the unfamiliar to enter into a thought that some will say is complex, even sometimes impenetrable. It is good that interpreters and commentators can, strictly speaking, "introduce" authors, in the sense of "bringing them in" or "leading them inside" in order to rest there. Once beyond those initial steps, the road always appears easier to meander and explore. It is therefore a path that is proposed here—and likewise *Thinking God Otherwise* certainly leads, in our perspective, to ultimately thinking man differently.

Mettray, February 9, 2025

Translator's Preface
Jacob Saliba

As translator, I have had the unique privilege of knowing personally both the author of this text as well as the thinker on whom the text is based. In many respects, the translation emerged out of not simply an exploration of the written word but also the product of many meetings with Alain Saudan and Emmanuel Falque. When this project first emerged, Falque was giving a course on the philosophy of Michel de Montaigne at the Institut Catholique de Paris, where he is Honorary Dean of the Faculty of Philosophy. It was fitting that one of the most unique French Catholic thinkers of our time would be lecturing on the most creative and sui generis French Catholic thinker of another time. Saudan's book neatly captures Falque's uniqueness, and the reader will no doubt be left with great interest and even greater reflection on an intellectual figure who has only to become even more well known in the United States.

Before speaking directly on Falque's work, though, it is necessary to offer some words on his interpreter, Alain Saudan. Currently a lecturer at the Lycée International de Saint-Germain-en-Laye, one of the highest-ranked international public schools in Europe, Saudan earned *agrégé* in philosophy from the École normale supérieure in early 1968. He was a student and disciple of Paul Ricœur, under whom he wrote his master's thesis on the philosophy of religion in Spinoza. Later, Saudan wrote his doctoral thesis on a topic that few phenomenologists would likely pursue today, about the relationship between philosophy and semiotics. A study of Algirdas Julien Greimas (a founding pioneer of literary theory, second only to his colleague Roland Barthes), this thesis interpreted Hegel's *Phenomenology of Spirit* through the lens of semiotics. As Saudan liked to say on more than one occasion, "C'était une autre époque!" His doctoral project later transformed into Saudan's first two books, *Fonder la loi* in

1998 (now in its second edition) and *Littérature et philosophie: Écrire, penser, vivre* in 2002. Saudan has also published other articles on Hans Jonas and Paul Ricœur. By crossing disciplinary boundaries and playing with the limits of concepts, these texts give readers a helpful framing for seeing the long-term culmination of what would later become his more recent study of Falque's thought in *Penser Dieu autrement: Introduction à l'œuvre d'Emmanuel Falque*.

Published in 2013, *Penser Dieu autrement* is part of a series entitled The Keys of Philosophy that also boasts the publications of esteemed French theorist and public intellectual, Alain Badiou. While coming from vastly different worlds and theoretical models, this juxtaposition with Badiou is not a mere coincidence, for it is also Saudan's intention in *Penser Dieu autrement* to break down the impenetrability of dense philosophical projects and, thus, open them to greater diversity and wider public discussion. In this vein, Sauden's intended audience is not the armchair philosopher. Nor does he seek to speak exclusively to the believing Christian. The book's aim is more modest—and, thus, more powerful—than that. It is intended to rest in conversation with the everyday person, their background reflections and lived experiences, whether it is the Christian who still has questions about their faith or the atheist or agnostic who is fascinated by the language of religion.

For Saudan, part of the significance of Falque's work is that it speaks to the ordinary and oft-forgotten experiences of our lives as well as answers the deeper and more provocative paradoxes that rest at the core of modern thought. Falque's approach is motivated specifically by his creative usage and arrangement of the space between philosophy and theology. In a sense, it mirrors and performs a certain aspect of that special ground that Derrida once referred to as the *khora*, a space of betweenness often taken for granted where truth can breathe and flourish in the absence of borders and limits. As Saudan sees it, this space is organized around the question of "the problem of God," a space that is in need of stimulation and novelty to think anew those perennial ideas of God, philosophical truth, and lived experience. Intended as an "introduction," Saudan takes up Falque's basic premises behind this question as well as how and why theology and philosophy not only work together in answering it but even, in some cases, enter into conflict. Saudan calls it "the problem of God," because, for him, the entire infrastructure behind this question is built on a wager of religious truth's ability to speak to a contemporary culture—whether today's Christian culture that may appear locked in its own dogmatism and traditional apologetics or a secular culture eager to shut down a normative tradition of the past that they see as having no relevance to the present. Rather than take up an explicit position, which Saudan sees as too simplistic and reductive, he argues that Falque's work presses on and productively problematizes the very core of this wager by making thinkable what others see as only unbelievable, and making believable what others see as unthinkable. This approach, in part, is echoed in the introduction to this translation, generously provided by religious scholar David C. Albertson, who draws out and vividly engages with the book's theme by organizing it around what he calls a "defense of the gift." In addition to Albertson's introduction which makes compelling discussion of this proposed framework and its long-standing relationship to the early church, it is necessary to emphasize this concept's deep French roots—hearkening back to the work of Marcel Mauss—in proximity to its deep religious roots too.

Thus, there is no doubt that this book is inspired, in part, by that "theological turn" in phenomenology that was famously the target of criticism by Dominique Janicaud in the 1990s. More than a rejoinder to Janicaud, Saudan takes seriously his critique by placing Falque into conversation with not only religious representatives of phenomenology such as Ricœur, Marion, Michel Henry, Jean-Louis Chrétien, and Jean-Yves Lacoste but also non-Catholic philosophers such as Emmanuel Levinas, Jean-Luc Nancy, Gilles Deleuze, Marcel Gauchet, Michel Foucault, and even Badiou. What Saudan reads into all of these thinkers is a certain commitment to the "language of humanity" that does not necessarily mean the elimination of religion. For Saudan, Falque has built novel concepts into this wider conversation in order to preserve a certain dimension of thinking about God that allows for humanity and religion to coexist and thrive with one another. According to Falque, this coexistence has been taken for granted, either by the theologian content with dry proofs of God's existence or by the secular philosopher who strictly sees the horizons of meaning stop at the limits of the cogito. Here, Saudan places Falque alongside avant-garde Catholic thinkers of the past century such as Maurice Blondel, Henri de Lubac, Étienne Gilson, Karl Rahner, and Jürgen Moltmann. These names appear again and again throughout the text as much as the reader will encounter canonical names in phenomenology and French philosophy.

The ability to creatively traverse and coherently gather together the widest possible range of concepts and thinkers in Western philosophy may be one of Falque's most salient features as a philosopher. And, yet, the category of "philosopher" does not suffice. As Saudan will frequently take notice, Falque also speaks the language of the theologian with numerous texts on medieval and modern theology. In other words, Falque—by crossing back and forth into religious thought—identifies ways in which philosophy can go beyond itself in its very practice. These creative crossings may be the most subtle—and perhaps most important—observation at the core of Saudan's interpretation, and the reader will be interested to pause and reflect on how this model functions and on what texts by Falque they find their basis.

Falque continues to be a highly prolific thinker, the author of more than a dozen books and nearly one hundred articles and essays (many of which have been translated into English, Italian, German, and Spanish). He has been the topic of articles in *Commonweal*, an interlocutor in major journals of continental philosophy in the Anglo-American world, and more recently the subject of collected works forthcoming in English. While Saudan's book provides a window into the basic narrative and structure of Falque's intellectual vision, one point must be made in advance: *Penser Dieu autrement* appeared before a turning point in Falque's project roughly a decade ago. This turning point can be located within a set of more recent texts, including *The Book of Experience: From Anselm of Canterbury to Bernard of Clairvaux* (2017); *Nothing to It: Reading Freud as a Philosopher* (2018); *Hors phénomène: Essai aux confins de la phénoménalité* (2021); and *La chair de Dieu* (2023). In an interview from 2023 in the *Journal for Continental Philosophy of Religion*, Falque suggested that it is through a more focused gaze on contemporary consciousness that this turning point, or "deepening," has reached a certain salience in his thought. For example, it has been through topoi ranging from trauma and illness to the natural environment, embodiment, and social injustice that Falque's philosophy and, by extent, theology remain central for keeping dialogue with pressing concerns in our own time.

Readers will find in *Hors phénomène* and *La chair de Dieu* one of the most striking transformations in Falque's thought since the publication of *Penser Dieu autrement*: the concept of *hors phénomène* (the extra-phenomenal). The "extra-phenomenal" proposes a new philosophical model in which we can penetrate the boundaries of philosophy at large, and phenomenology in particular, without sacrificing those horizons of meaning that are uniquely human. Rather than remain content with a certain style of phenomenology that relies on a principle of preparation with regard to appearance (i.e., "infra-phenomenology") or another style of phenomenology that utilizes the role of excess (i.e., "supra-phenomenology"), Falque isolates those moments of painful exception and trauma as a distinctive type of lived experience that occurs without cause (for the atheist and agnostic) and without sin (for the Christian). Thus, the "extra-phenomenal" illustrates a new type of experience that represents a breakage between the phenomenalizing subject and a presupposed normativity. This question is further addressed in his most recent book, *La chair de Dieu*. In it, Falque identifies a certain rupture in Christian thought and practice as exemplified in the progression of Easter's Holy Week by interrogating the nature of anxiety, suffering, and death. The gaps in meaning—those abysses in our lives—are also deeply reflective of the gospel narrative of Christ's fleshly humanity on earth. These more recent themes of the "extra-phenomenal," "trauma," and "the flesh" that now seem to determine where Falque's contemporary work is going cannot be understood without first seeing where the early stages of his project actually came from. Here, Saudan's book is indispensable.

The language of *Penser Dieu autrement* is simple. As translator, I have preserved this language of simplicity not only to retain the voice of Saudan but also to show the immense skill it takes to repackage dozens upon dozens of texts and thinkers into such an accessible manner for the reader. To weave through Falque's corpus is no small task. Falque has been and continues to be in dialogue with ancient philosophy, the church fathers, Scholasticism, and neo-Thomism, not to mention his productive interventions into twentieth-century phenomenology, post-phenomenology, and psychoanalysis. Saudan helpfully captures and renders in more simple terms these many complexities. Readers of Saudan's interpretation will also find helpful markers and evenly distributed sections that each highlight basic points of change, contention, and evolution in Falque's work. On many occasions, Saudan will retrieve and redeploy the same phrase and quotation. This mode of repetition is not intended to be reductive but rather gives the reader a sense of the many modes, deconstructions, and attitudes that Falque puts into topics that otherwise would appear uninterestingly univocal or uncritically static. On other occasions, it would seem as if Saudan is responding directly to Falque, as though in spoken dialogue and debate. Reading the text in this way is perhaps suggested, for it is in the final pages that Saudan ultimately takes up Falque's wager very directly. This dialogical approach is only further amplified in the appendix, where Saudan has decided to republish a lecture that he gave at the Gregorian on the relationship between Falque and Ricœur—with Falque himself present in the room. *Penser Dieu autrement* is a text of both introduction and intervention, appreciation and disputation, and, therefore, one of the most inviting and stimulating ways to dive into the work of one of today's most innovative French Catholic thinkers.

Introduction
To Defend the Gift

David Albertson

In the early decades of the second century, Justin Martyr crossed back and forth between reason and faith to explain Christian phenomena to the unbelieving. Impressed by Socrates's irenic discourse during his trial in Athens five centuries before, but also cognizant of emerging apostolic traditions, Justin called his project an *apologia*, a speech made to defend one's views. Like Peter before his Jewish community at Solomon's Porch, or like Paul before the Greeks at the Areopagus, Justin proceeds with confidence while presuming some degree of agonistic opposition.[1] His interlocutors find Christianity strange and distasteful, if not morally hazardous. Nevertheless, Justin takes seriously his duty of faith: "Always be ready to give an explanation to anyone who asks you for a reason for your hope, but do it with gentleness and reverence."[2]

Unlike other apologists like Athenagoras, or later Eusebius, Justin does not only reason from abstract Platonism down to earth. He returns again and again to concrete sacramental experience, welcoming the outsider inside the Christian community and sharing its way of life with candor. On baptism Justin promises that "I will also explain the manner in which we dedicated ourselves to God when we were made new through Christ, since if we left this out in our exposition we would seem

---

1. See respectively Acts 3:11—4:4 and Acts 17:16–34.
2. 1 Pet 3:15–16.

to falsify something."³ He explains the water, the bread, and the wine; as if standing alongside the unbelieving he studies the choreography of the liturgy and offers comments like a dramaturg for the benefit of the uninitiated. "This food," he explains, "is called among us eucharist . . . for we do not receive these things as common bread nor common drink."⁴ *Entre nous*, among ourselves. Yet what begins as a eucharistic secret is swiftly introduced by Justin into the agora shared by Greeks and Jews, Romans and Christians. In Justin's peculiar sense of apologia, "defense" means opening up what was closed, giving away to the outsider what the community refuses to hold as its own possession.

As he writes, Justin methodically destabilizes the boundary between apologist and audience. If it is "Christians" who are slandered by their enemies, the philosopher urges caution on both sides, for "by the mere statement of a name, nothing is decided, either good or evil, apart from the actions associated with the name."⁵ Likewise even those who style themselves "philosophers" are not immediately or undeniably such. "For in philosophy, too, some assume the name and the dress who do nothing worthy of the profession: and as you are aware those among the ancients whose opinions and teachings were quite different are yet called by the one name of philosopher."⁶ As Justin points out, Socrates was not celebrated as a philosopher by his peers but condemned as an "atheist" for living without belief in the Greek gods. Now Christians are called "atheists" for living without belief in the Roman gods. "Hence we are called atheists," he admits, as much in protest as in self-congratulation, "and we confess that we are atheists with reference to gods such as these."⁷ It is only in one singular case that Christians are not atheists: the "true God," whom we soon learn is the "God who is called by no given name."⁸

For Justin there is a phenomenon that interrupts reciprocal accusations of unbelief: the materiality of "this food called eucharist," and through that food the whole uncanny animality of the human body in birth and rebirth. The resurrection of the dead is completely incredible, Justin concedes, but truth be told, rebirth is nearly as incomprehensible as conception. "To any thoughtful person what would seem more

3. See Justin Martyr, "First Apology," §61.
4. Justin Martyr, "First Apology," §66.
5. Justin Martyr, "First Apology," §4.
6. Justin Martyr, "First Apology," §4.
7. Justin Martyr, "First Apology," §6.
8. Justin Martyr, "First Apology," §10.

incredible, than if we were not in the body, and someone should say it was possible that from a small drop of human seed, bones and sinews and flesh were formed into a shape such as we see?"[9] The ground of rationality in Justin's apology is neither the eternal forms of Plato nor a natural desire for *agnostos theos*. It is the flesh itself at its most finite, weakest, and yet most glorious. "It is not impossible," Justin concludes, "for the bodies of men and women, dissolved and like seeds resolved into earth, to rise again in God's appointed time and put on incorruption."[10] Theology is strengthened by consulting a philosophy of the body in its organic passage through time. Christians and pagans grasp this horizon together, prior to belief, first in "themselves," Justin says, and then in "the whole world."[11] In the words of Terence: *Humani nihil a me alienum*.

Emmanuel Falque begins from the horizon of embodied finitude, first in ourselves and then in the whole world, inviting Christians to recollect their fleshly solidarity with the unbelieving, shoulder to shoulder, nose to nose, heart to heart. We who have been listening to Falque over the last decade in piecemeal English translations owe a great debt of gratitude to Alain Saudan for this first major survey of Falque's thought. Saudan's immensely satisfying and learned introduction is cartographic in its scope, spanning east and west, north and south, easily taking in the whole in its generous conspectus, yet all the while still measuring with terrific precision the network of lines drawn by Falque across different terrains. Saudan's closing epilogue in particular is a powerful intellectual tribute by a friend whose insights have been won through sympathetic proximity. Like the best intellectual biographers, Saudan tracks the evolving conversations between Falque and a range of voices, not only customary philosophers (Heidegger, Ricœur, Merleau-Ponty) but unexpected theologians (Pascal, Kierkegaard, Bonhoeffer).

As readers can discover for themselves, Saudan outlines the major themes and formulations achieved by Falque in the *Philosophical Triduum* and a few other works, tracing the arguments, interlocutors, and key concepts of each volume in turn. But to his credit, and to our benefit, Saudan also offers a major apologia for Falque's outlook, methods, and priorities. Yet here we find a fold to be unfurled. For at the center of Saudan's apologia is the question whether Falque himself is an apologist. In suturing together philosophy and theology more intimately than

9. Justin Martyr, "First Apology," §19.
10. Justin Martyr, "First Apology," §19.
11. Justin Martyr, "First Apology," §19.

his peers have dared, is Falque engaged in Christian apologetics? More than once Saudan poses this question, this hesitation, this realization. Is Falque's oeuvre an apologia, in the venerable tradition of Justin Martyr, Irenaeus, Tertullian, or for that matter Thomas Aquinas?

Saudan is fascinated by the theme of "Christian philosophy" and by Falque's personal bearing toward Christian faith. As he stresses, Falque's confession of belief is by no means for Christians alone, but offered in the agora shared by all. To seek universality beyond Catholic community is a mode of catholicity, Saudan notes, just as Falque's "bi-disciplinarity" between philosophy and theology is a "guarantee of openness."[12] According to Falque, the experience of God must pass through the experience of human limits, which he calls the "blocked horizon" and Saudan christens the "anchor of finitude."[13] Christian theology can then be understood as the transformation of that horizon, a metamorphosis that can, in Saudan's words, "bear witness to the anthropological fertility of Christianity."[14] Ultimately, this common finitude is unveiled as the domain of the animal body, in birth, suffering, eating, sexuality, and death. As Saudan emphasizes, this means that Falque does not seek to demonstrate the truth of Christianity so much as to describe its choreography before the uninitiated. "The question today is not longer to prove the existence or non-existence of God," writes Saudan, "or even of finding the right way to talk about it, but in finding if we can still talk about it at all."[15]

Is this a Christian apologetics or not? Saudan seems conflicted, perhaps because this antinomy is essential to Falque's project itself. On the one hand, "Falque's goal is not apologetic. For him, the goal is to make Christianity 'credible,' that is, . . . an intelligible and coherent system of thought."[16] He is not prosecuting a "defense" of Christianity.[17] "We do not find in his work the slightest attempt at or sketch of apologetics," Saudan insists.[18] It is "not really (not directly at least) apologetic."[19] On the other hand, Saudan acknowledges that Falque does pursue an "apologetic" in the sense that he appreciates the "necessity for a believing philosopher to be

12. See this book, p. 130.
13. See this book, p. 64.
14. See this book, p. 43.
15. See this book, p. 3.
16. See this book, p. 4.
17. See this book, p. 6.
18. See this book, p. 8.
19. See this book, p. 135.

understood by his contemporaries" by adopting a common "grammar."[20] "One of Falque's objectives is to make Christianity 'credible' and intelligible for those for whom it is 'incredible.'"[21]

After thanking Saudan for this book, we can thank him a second time for this puzzling question, valuable because not easily resolved. To be sure, Falque strives to interpret Christianity in front of an unbelieving audience, in the Areopagus of Nietzsche and Heidegger and Deleuze. "When they heard about resurrection of the dead, some began to scoff, but others said, 'We should like to hear you on this some other time.'"[22] On the other hand, unlike most apologists, especially the impoverished modern ones, Falque's "defense" is entirely lacking in anxious defensiveness. Paradoxically, Falque absorbs the anxiety of Gethsemane in order to drain his apologia of it. Falque listens to Nietzsche with extraordinary patience (one I struggle to match) so that he can purify the apologetic act of resentment. The hand is entirely open, calm, at rest. There are no secrets, no confidence games, no competition. Certainly no enemy, but in a sense not even an opponent. This kind of apologia for Christian faith can be prosecuted, like Socrates, only by abandoning oneself to vulnerability.

It is only in this elliptical sense that Falque is an "apologist" in the twenty-first century, a sense that reverses the meaning of the word since the Enlightenment. Typically, apologists attempt to persuade, to condemn, to distance themselves from the one who needs persuasion, the opponent from whom they must defend themselves, because they pose a threat. Apologetics appeals to reason, an always-contested common ground, and seeks to show that what the opponent has already conceded warrants a further act of faith. Hence an ordinary apology is always a plea, a demand, an act of self-defense, assuaging one's own doubts by rehearsing the reasons one more time, therefore in need of a counterpart to play the role of a silent witness of one's own fear and trembling.

As Saudan makes clear, Emmanuel Falque is not giving a defense; he is, rather, defending a gift. But a gift is a strange object to defend, for if protected in the wrong way it can be lost. A gift is defended only when its donative character is preserved. A gift is protected by dispossession, not possession. To defend a gift as gift, one must give it away. And the ultimate diremption is to give away the secure pedestal of being the

---

20. See this book, p. 34.
21. See this book, p. 142.
22. Acts 17:32.

donor and instead allow oneself to receive. This is ultimately, I think, why Falque listens so patiently to what Nietzsche and Heidegger and Deleuze have to say.

The gift that Christianity defends is finitude. But this is what is least certain, least conclusive, least comprehensible in our human experience: the animal throes of birth, fear, disease, ecstasy, trauma, or the unconscious. This gift is what is held necessarily in common by all, not only by the Christians who strive to tend it. I cannot defend that gift without my neighbor or in separation or alienation from them. I greet them as kin with my guard down, without defenses. That human kinship embraces the fourth and twelfth centuries as much as the twenty-first, such that the defense of the gift is best carried out in the humility of a tradition.

Falque is not simply proposing a more intimate exchange between theology and philosophy, following after Michel Henry, Jean-Luc Marion, and Jean-Yves Lacoste. He not only accepts the church's openness to the modern world after Vatican II, in the footsteps of John XXIII, John Paul II, and Francis, in particular. Even more acutely than others in the same French Catholic milieu, Falque begins from the relatively recent experience of the diminished status of Christian identity. Christianity is a cultural minority in most academic spaces, on the periphery, unburdened of its former cultural authority. For Falque, Christianity should account for itself before the bar of an unbelieving public, but without nostalgia, resentment, or mourning. This irenic affective style is as important a response to Nietzsche as specific conceptual debates.

It is precisely here, in defending the gift, that Falque's apologia remains close to the work of Jean-Luc Marion. Marion's account of revelation responds to a century of multidisciplinary controversy over the "gift" as "given" in anthropology, phenomenology, deconstruction, and fundamental theology.[23] These often-abstract debates were never far removed from controversies over the status of apologetics, which is to say, over the nature of Christian particularism. Can apologetics ever be legitimate, or should Christian theology proceed confidently from the "given" of revelation? After Friedrich Schleiermacher's epochal reply to Kant and Hegel, Protestant theology increasingly doubted that it could be. Albrecht Ritschl and Wilhelm Herrmann sought to transfer systematic theology entirely out of the realm of the metaphysics of nature and

---

23. See Marion, *Revelation Comes from Elsewhere*, 98–108. Cf. Marion, *Being Given*.

to proceed from interior faith.[24] Marburg neo-Kantians turned to the category of the "given" as a model for revelation, which profoundly influenced Karl Barth's theological method.[25] Hans Urs von Balthasar thought that Barth's rejection of philosophy was a major mistake, not because it frustrated the enterprise of Christian apologetics but because it defaulted on the Christian responsibility to defend the gifts of being, nature, and ultimately sacramentality.[26]

Marion seeks a way between Barth and Balthasar, with the assistance of Husserl and Heidegger, and with him Falque steps into the conversation on the gift. In his study of Anselm of Canterbury, Falque quotes Paul Ricœur, who is commenting on Marcel Mauss: "The counterpart to the gift in fact, is not receiving but giving in return, giving back."[27] Falque adds, however, that such gift exchange does not take place at a threshold, but indeed is a threshold. The gift is a threshold inside which, so to speak, God intervenes theophanically in the mode of kenosis. In this sense, "the gift sends us back to our own limits or thresholds."[28]

Marion has invoked the example of Justin Martyr to connect apologetics with the divine Word. Jesus is the Logos, and in gratitude for receiving the gift of the Logos we return the debt of our reasoning.[29] "This figure of reason forces Christians to take up apologetic work again—this time in the best sense of the term, that of the apologetic Fathers, of whom the 'martyr and philosopher' Justin remains the emblematic figure," he writes. "In order to guard reason, in all the senses of the term, it is necessary henceforth to receive it from the Word. A certain poverty is thus required."[30] Falque's approach parallels Marion, but with a difference, as is often the case. For Falque the gift received is not simply the Logos but the Word made flesh, the finitude of flesh itself. The debt of the flesh is owed not only to the Creator but to fellow humans in the animal solidarity that

---

24. See Sockness, *Against False Apologetics*; and Zachhuber, *Theology as Science in Nineteenth-Century Germany*.

25. See Fisher, *Revelatory Positivism?*; and McCormack, *Karl Barth's Critically Realistic Dialectical Theology*.

26. See Balthasar, *Theology of Karl Barth*.

27. Ricœur, *Memory, History, Forgetting*, 482. See Mauss, *Gift*; Derrida, *Given Time*; and Milbank, "Can a Gift Be Given?"

28. Falque, "Debt for the Gift," 49–50.

29. Marion, *Believing in Order to See*, 4–5.

30. Marion, *Believing in Order to See*, 29.

the young Karl Marx called *das Gattungswesen*.[31] In the search for a universal, Falque offers a philosophy of the body to supplement, or perhaps replace, Neoplatonist metaphysics. In this he repeats the gesture of Justin Martyr, who explains Christianity to his unbelieving peers through the Eucharist, as the gift of Jesus's body, and in time through his martyrdom, as the gift of his own. As Marion writes, to defend the gift of reason, a certain poverty is required. As our world sinks deeper into a nihilistic poverty of spirit, the access to that gift is found within a wound stretching ever more open.

Marion himself counsels modern Christian intellectuals to remember that nihilism is a situation, not a sin, and that it is as much a mistake to condemn it as to try to overwhelm it with force. Instead, Christian reason should recollect its obligation to revelation and calmly ask, "What model of rationality do we have available in the situation of nihilism?"[32] His words of encouragement, first published in 1992, are worth citing at length:

> Please allow me to suspect a level of immaturity in a number of Catholics (or else an ambiguous nostalgia for "Christendom," which probably never existed as imagined). They would almost think Revelation to be threatened or definitively destroyed just because they can exercise neither the intelligence, nor the culture, nor above all the work and the courage sufficient for convincing their contemporaries of that of which they themselves are often deep down and to begin with so little convinced. Catholics, my brothers, my fellows, have we not in recent history committed enough follies to have merited this minority position a bit? Maturity would mean first that we notice our mistakes, and then that we work toward providing society with arguments and useful analyses to face the problems that confront us all—a society that expects these arguments and analyses more than it fears them (or fears them because it expects them). The common good requires that we offer to all what Revelation has given us—and has given us to comprehend.[33]

Humani nihil a me alienum. In the twenty-first century, this wisdom takes on a more ominous shade. The multiple, compounding crises, the deprivations and sufferings just appearing on the common horizon of

---

31. Albertson, "Limits of Earth."
32. Marion, *Believing in Order to See*, 20.
33. Marion, *Believing in Order to See*, 28.

our shared finitude, are another basis for solidarity. This is the poignancy of Falque's most recent philosophical efforts on non-phenomenality, or experiences of radical absence. Such crises cast us all into nights of chaos and isolate us from each other: terminal illness, divorce, the death of a child, natural disasters, and pandemic.[34] To these we can add the deadly fires and floods of the Anthropocene; the disorientation of the *humanum* itself through generative AI; and the ongoing devastation of democratic belonging at the hands of plutocratic oligarchies.

These exigencies make Falque's work, and Saudan's valuable guide, only more timely. They point us toward a twenty-first century Christianity that preserves the gifts it has been given by holding them out with an open, scarred hand. Thus, a third round of thanks is due to Jacob Saliba, for giving us this English translation of Alain Saudan's book at a fitting moment as the crises grow more acute by the day. A wise Christian apologia will face our situation of nihilism not with histrionic despair, nor the will to power to impose a nostalgic Christendom, but with the vulnerability of the flesh, as Justin knew well: the witness of martyrdom. Defending the gift requires strength—not the strength of the *tyrannos*, but the strength to endure even a "martyrdom of unintelligibility."[35]

---

34. Falque, *Hors phénomène*.
35. Kierkegaard, *Fear and Trembling*, 70.

Ouverture
Thinking God

WE LIVE IN A time that might be described as paradoxical. "God is dead." For many, doubt on Nietzsche's famous proclamation no longer seems permitted. And, yet, a peculiar indifference towards God has now replaced that revolt against a divinity incompatible with the existence of evil. Atheism is no longer as virulent as it once seemed. According to Emmanuel Falque, it is a "surpassing and relinquishing of God rather than a combat with God."[1] As for the so-called "return of religion," it has no doubt become susceptible to its own transmutations: the development of *religion à la carte*, of triumphant "holy" ignorance, of fundamentalism, and even of integralism.

In the context of these ironies, it must be said that we also see a certain number of renowned intellectuals, unbelievers, agnostics, or atheists devoting themselves to deep reflections on Christianity. Motivations and objectives certainly vary. Marcel Gauchet analyzed the relationship between democracy and Christianity, "a religion for departing from religion."[2] Alain Badiou undertook the work of Saint Paul, and Jean-Luc Nancy tackled a "deconstruction" of Christianity. We cannot deny that we witness, through these many approaches, an attempt to rethink Christianity and the Christian model. These attempts attest, in a certain way, that Christianity is still and always will be a perennial source of curiosity and insight. In another context, perhaps in a more precise and technical manner, a certain number of philosophers who have called themselves believers (or who are described as such) appeal to theological concepts or highlight religious issues in their own philosophical ways. The names of

1. Falque, *Metamorphosis of Finitude*, 35.
2. Gauchet, *Disenchantment of the World*, 4.

Jean-Luc Marion, Michel Henry, Jean-Yves Lacoste, Jean-Louis Chrétien immediately come to mind. The controversy, born rightly or wrongly from the denunciation of a "theological turn in phenomenology," clearly demonstrates that Christianity remains a lively topic of debate. The situation is peculiar, as Emmanuel Falque himself notes: "Christian philosophers trained in theology sometimes pride themselves on not doing theology, while non-institutionally educated secular philosophers of theological training do not hesitate to make for themselves a profession in theology."[3] Can we therefore go so far as to repeat the words of Rimbaud, calling Christ the "eternal devourer of life"?

The "problem" of God therefore no longer poses itself today as it did in the past. This point has been observed by believers themselves. We have just mentioned the "abandonment" of God by unbelievers. Certain theologians for their part often deal with the "abandonment" of God, either experienced tragically by Christ on the cross or felt personally by the profoundly silent and distantly felt truth of God's existence in relationship to mankind. To be sure, this existential "abandonment" may be justified theologically and no longer merely in a negative way. It provides for a representation where God ceases to be an idol to satisfy all human needs, whether speculative or concrete. The autonomy of man is affirmed in the face of his Creator. Thus, Dietrich Bonhoeffer averred that we live "etsi Deus non daretur," that is to say, "as if God did not exist."[4] According to Eberhard Jüngel, God ceases to be "necessary."[5] The Almighty God of a certain tradition sometimes leaves room among theologians for a suffering, fragile, and helpless God. It is not certain that every believer recognizes the same problem, but it is certain that by participating in this debate with a creative freedom we will arrive at a more complete understanding of God and his relationship to the human being.

To be sure, theology can take on a joyful and playful tone too. Here we might mention the famous theologian Jürgen Moltmann: when the need for a God who helps then disappears, we are ultimately free to "enjoy" God. He adds, in a work with the evocative title *Essay on the Joy of Being Free*: "The selfless joy that makes us experience God can then replace the use and abuse of God."[6] The anguished perspective of abandonment from God, which Moltmann illustrates at length, leads to the

---

3. See Falque, "Michel Henry théologien."
4. See Bonhoeffer, *Letters and Papers from Prison*, 477.
5. See Jüngel, *God as the Mystery of the World*.
6. See Moltmann, *Seigneur de la danse*, 127.

experience of joy. The passing of the use of God to fulfill his enjoyment is verified in the "new" status of theology which "is no longer necessary for the practice of beneficence . . . , but can ultimately be cultivated for God and the infinite joy he inspires." Furthermore: "We don't study theology because it could be useful . . . , but rather apply ourselves to theology out of an interest and desire for its object."[7] Here, in the milieu of "joy" we inevitably think of Nietzsche and Spinoza, however problematic it may appear in matters of religion.

In this general and briefly iterated context, the figure of Emmanuel Falque seems powerfully relevant to us. Or so I shall argue. The present book is the result of an encounter with Falque's philosophical insights and theological repertoire with the goal of making them more effectively known to wider audiences. Indeed, I might add that, at bottom, my interpretation is also based on a wager: Falque offers us a possibility of thinking about God, as Marcel Neusch recognized, in a world where it sometimes seems to no longer have a place.[8] This lack of space for God—its "u-topic" character—is also the starting point of Jüngel's own reflection in his book *God as the Mystery of the World*. The question today is no longer to prove the existence or nonexistence of God, or even of finding the right way to talk about it, but in finding if we can still talk about it at all. Traditional and modern discourses on God, both theological and philosophical, seem to be powerless in the wake of those pressing challenges experienced by believers and nonbelievers alike. Falque takes up the challenge by starting from what God says of himself, while recognizing that any attempt at understanding takes place in an order of experience and language that remain very much human.

Such a possibility offered by Falque to think God *otherwise* is not simply within the domain of trained philosophers and theologians but a necessary question of the lay public. It will be of interest to those who do not share the same faith commitment as Emmanuel Falque, but nevertheless find themselves pondering and critically reflecting on the heritage of Christianity in the contemporary moment. As Maurice Blondel once reflected, the important thing is not to speak for the souls who believe but to say something for the minds who do not believe.[9] Falque's presentation of Christianity will surprise the minds of those who do not believe, and at the same time will also illuminate for them some foundations of their

---

7. Moltmann, *Seigneur de la danse*, 131.
8. See Neusch, "Dieu, pour penser autrement."
9. See Blondel, *Letter on Apologetics*, 134–38.

own culture with a dynamic language, often forgotten or ignored today. And, it may very well lead them to a better and more fruitful understanding of their own personhood too.

Falque's goal is not apologetic. For him, the goal is to make Christianity "credible," that is, not simply a "believable" object of faith but rather an intelligible and coherent system of thought for our time. His presentation of Christianity, while drawing from a rich tradition over many centuries, is geared towards an understanding of and promise for culture today. It is left to the reader to freely decide on the fate of this question as it concerns their own worldviews. The attempt to answer the wager mentioned above animates the core purpose of this book. It seeks to introduce and make more accessible the thought of Falque. Nonspecialists should not be disheartened. This is of course an inevitable challenge on my part but I hope that my approach successfully demonstrates that Falque's religious arguments and philosophical observations are part of a larger tapestry—however complex—of self-reflection and contemporary understanding. In short, the present work identifies those essential themes in Falque's work as well as restores a sense of direction on the path towards rethinking God, a path that we are all invited to follow.

Part One

Philosophy and Theology in Dialogue

SECTION ONE: A FACE UNMASKED

A PHILOSOPHER AND CHRISTIAN, Falque neither masks his philosophical views nor conceals his religious beliefs. The prefaces of some of his works are quite revealing in this respect. We will simply mention from *The Guide to Gethsemane* the question of whether or not contemporary philosophy is able to shed light on the ordeal of Christ's anguish, his suffering and his death.[1] Or *The Metamorphosis of Finitude* which only further highlights the ambiguities at play, namely, how God does not seem to ask us to necessarily succeed in our question but rather inspires us to work through it.[2] Often self-reflecting on theology-philosophy relationships, Falque embodies the task of both the "Christian thinker" as well as the "believing philosopher."[3] Both the intellectual approach and the personal biography of the author, from the outset, are inseparable from his religious and philosophical enterprise.

We may begin by saying that an initial approach to his work can be seen as that of a "believing philosopher." As Falque admits, he presents himself as a practicing Catholic, faithful to an ecclesial tradition, and even formerly belonging to a religious community, with a certain

---

1. Falque, *Guide to Gethsemane*, 18–19.
2. Falque, *Metamorphosis of Finitude*, 1–2.
3. Falque, "Penser, c'est décider."

mystical imagination. He still teaches today in a diocesan seminary, participating in numerous conferences where he represents, through his personal life, the Christian-Catholic position. Elsewhere, he has served as dean of the Faculty of Philosophy at the Catholic University of Paris. At first glance, we might be tempted to see him as an institutional figure, i.e., a "religious" philosopher, taking up a certain "defense and illustration of Christianity," of which he would therefore be presumed to be held hostage by. We will have the opportunity later to critique those dimensions of his work that seem to qualify this one-way vision. But his characterization as a "believing philosopher" will remain unchanged for the sake of a more holistic study of his thought.

This assumed qualification of a believing philosopher might arouse astonishment, or even a negative reaction among those for whom the domains of faith and reason remain radically incompatible. To give a preliminary idea of the particular issues regarding this last point, let us briefly present three philosophical models on the general relationship between faith and reason: that of complementarity (Thomas and Leibniz), that of separation—either to the benefit of faith (Luther and Pascal)—or to the benefit of reason (Bayle and the anti-religious Enlightenment), and, last, that of indifferent mutuality (Kant, and even before, Spinoza and what we might call the "a-theological Enlightenment").[4] For the moment, we will not situate Falque in direct relationship to these models. Rather, our objective is to propose another model. While maintaining the separation between faith and philosophy, Falque tries to render credible what may in fact seem incredible to his faith. Appealing to both philosophy and theology, he seeks to make the content of the Christian message intelligible, addressing himself to those who do not believe in it as well as those who do believe in it. Indeed, addressing himself to those who do believe is absolutely essential to the extent that believers do not always take into deep consideration the rationality behind Christianity. Falque's project thus concerns overcoming the initial objection or opposition of those who consider faith and philosophy irreconcilable.

Falque, it must be made clear, immediately distinguishes himself from philosophers who are also recognized as believers, following in the footsteps of Paul Ricœur, who defended a philosophy without absolutes. In a certain sense he also follows his doctoral advisor Jean-Luc Marion. Beyond the generational difference, Ricœur and Marion

---

4. Fœssel, "Trois modèles philosophiques du rapport entre foi et raison," 279–80.

declared themselves believers while also always claiming total separation between their philosophical approach and their religious convictions. Even though they were sometimes catalogued by others as in favor of Christianity, insulated by a confessional stance; and even though they did not hesitate to respond to requests from religious bodies and wrote certain texts of a religious nature, they have always defended the distinction of their truly philosophical work against any outside theological force. For them, there was always a clear distinction between theology and philosophy. Later, we will have more space to present in detail the meeting points and confrontations of Falque with Ricœur and Marion. At present, however, some initial remarks are necessary for highlighting the basic methodological distinctions between the religious convictions and philosophical work of these thinkers.

At the Threshold

Ricœur did not deny the importance of extra-philosophical motivations in his personal commitments. But he did create and employ a type of philosophical argumentation capable of being discussed independently of one's own convictions. He recognized an "allegiance" to "sources," and thereby understood "something beyond control,"[5] and which was, according to his famous formulation, "a chance transformed into destiny by a continuous choice."[6] But religious reflection, if it has "an internal critical dimension," essentially concerns "conviction," while the philosophical approach is fundamentally grounded in the order of "criticism" (as the very title of *Critique and Conviction* suggests). As is plain to see, philosophy and religion often do not refer to the same texts. This difference in textuality thus defines specific modes of readings. As he writes, "All my philosophical work, leads to a type of philosophy from which the actual mention of God is absent and in which the question of God, as a philosophical question, itself remains in a suspension that could be called agnostic."[7] Indeed, he himself once admitted at having been tempted towards the point of promulgating a sort of ban on God in philosophy.[8]

---

5. Ricœur, *Critique and Conviction*, 36, 145.
6. See Ricœur, *Critique and Conviction*, 145.
7. Ricœur, *Oneself as Another*, 24.
8. See Ricœur, *Critique and Conviction*, 144–46.

We do not find in his work the slightest attempt at or sketch of apologetics. His position, if forced to be reduced to religion at all, is explained by his belonging to a Protestant tradition, reluctant towards any theological system and animated by a very different intellectual and ideological context of the one we know and experience today. Ricœur was led to affirm, in a somewhat creative formulation, that he had "always walked on two legs,"[9] probably meaning that two pillars of support—essential yet different from each other—were necessary for full development. He also recognized a certain duality in himself: "The philosopher that I am acts upon the apprentice theologian that moves within me."[10] For Falque, this duality, as we will have many opportunities to explore, is assumed clearly and without rough edges, perhaps harmoniously.

Falque will not notice any ambiguity in Ricœur's work—as he will do for Marion's—but ironically that is the very principle which he seeks to contest: the assertion that the philosopher can and must always sit silently "on the threshold" of theology. Ricœur "remains the tutelary figure" of this "threshold" model, reproducing in his Protestantism the gesture of Blondel in his Catholicism. As Falque observes, "The philosopher from Nanterre had many occasions to step across the threshold or brave the prohibition."[11] Falque will show numerous examples in the work of Ricœur where possibilities are opened up for crossing that very threshold without exploiting it. While there are more points of productive confrontation to be discussed between these two authors, a word must now be said on the relationship between Falque and Marion—another philosopher who chooses not to cross the Rubicon.

Leaping Over

We can note a certain evolution in the approach of Jean-Luc Marion, that is, in his conception of theology-philosophy relationships. Marion long defended the principle of a segregation between the two disciplines. His latest works are now more nuanced. In some respects, he shares Ricœur's strong concern for separating the disciplines, but he has come to observe more openly the practice of the "leap" from philosophy to theology than of a simple obedience to the "threshold" of theology.

---

9. Ricœur, *Critique and Conviction*, 139.
10. Ricœur, *Critique and Conviction*, 152.
11. Falque, *Crossing the Rubicon*, 140.

We can also recall a fact which is more than anecdotal: Ricœur and Marion have always taught in public universities. In contrast, Falque has preferred to teach within the Catholic university system and has openly accepted to be identified in this way. The common concern by Ricœur and Marion in not mixing theology and philosophy, faith and reason, has been evaluated by Dominique Janicaud in an attempt to show that they were in fact performing the work of religious philosophy. As may be well known by now, Janicaud distinguished Ricœur from Marion in their positions on theology and ultimately concludes that Ricœur narrowly escapes the final accusation of a "theological turn." Falque, for his part, wonders if Marion's desire to carefully separate philosophy and theology does not end up harming the fertility of his enterprise. Certainly, Marion distinguishes within his corpus: *The Idol and Distance, God Without Being*, and *Prolegomena to Charity*, on the side of theology; works such as *Descartes's Gray Ontology, Pale Theology, On Descartes's Metaphysical Prism*, as well as *Reduction and Givenness* or (from it) *Being Given* in phenomenology, all on the side of philosophy. Thus, Marion intends to pass as a philosopher with philosophers and possibly as a theologian with theologians, but he does not wish to be seen as a theologian among philosophers. And, yet, to be sure, the distinction is not always so clear. Marion, according to Falque, resembles Descartes, who proceeds with a "masked advance" and thus ultimately exposes the deeper reality that "he who is masked cannot mask the fact *that he is masked* from himself."[12]

In fact, Falque supports Marion on the accusation of a "theological turn," and will do so "almost unwillingly," as he himself says. He does this to affirm the legitimacy of the association between a "philosophical enterprise" and a "theological revelation."[13] He pushes Marion's approach to the limit in order to highlight certain ambiguities as well as critically engage and self-reflexively oppose his own position in an attempt to remove his own mask. As Falque writes of Marion: "It falls upon philosophy to take up the 'theological task' and upon the theologian to summon the 'philosopher's stone.' At this juncture, the past opens onto, at the very least, another mode of thought which we must take up in order to respond to the urgent questions of today's age: *non larvatus sed 'detecta fronte'* (like Ovid) *prodedo* (I no longer make a masked advance, but proceed with bare-faced honesty)."[14]

12. Falque, *Loving Struggle*, 127.
13. Falque, *Loving Struggle*, 133–34.
14. Falque, *Loving Struggle*, 140.

But the greater question still remains: What is the true face of this "believing philosopher"? Falque defends a "differentiated unity" between philosophy and theology, of which he himself recognizes will not seem obvious to everyone, since he is compelled to "propose it to others" in hopes that they will also share "the risk of thought."[15] It is therefore appropriate to interrogate the de facto existence of this original unity, ensure its legitimacy, and also to specify the real nature of this "believing philosopher." As already stated, Falque is not a philosopher or a believer, but philosopher *and* believer, in the sense that Thomas Aquinas in the *Summa Theologica* deals with human acts (*seconda pars*), with the Trinity (*prima pars*), and with Christ (*tertia pars*).

A Personal and Existential Unity

This recognition of an original theology-philosophy union may seem entirely compatible with the institutional dimensions of Falque's project. It is also immediately visible in the books and numerous articles that he has devoted to patristic and medieval thinkers, throughout which theology and philosophy mingle closely. His thesis, "Saint Bonaventure and the Entrance of God into Theology," and *God, the Flesh, and the Other: From Irenaeus to Duns Scotus* seem to suggest that a reading of these authors allowed him to transcend his conception of theology-philosophy relationships. Or, is it a certain conception of these relationships which is actually at the origin of this decision to take up this study at all?

This union of theology and philosophy is shown in a striking way in the writing of Falque's "triptych," which contains particularly evocative titles: *The Guide to Gethsemane*, *The Metamorphosis of Finitude*, and *The Wedding Feast of the Lamb*.[16] The titles alone would certainly shock some philosophers, to whom these formulations may seem foreign to a common and traditional conception of philosophy. Indeed, the official organs of the secular French academy are very reluctant with regard to scriptural references, in many cases, considered anathema to philosophical argumentation and which has only just seen a minor softening in recent times.

While these preliminary considerations move us well in the direction of an understanding of the union between theology and philosophy,

---

15. Falque, "Penser, c'est décider."
16. See Falque, *Triduum philosophiques*.

they also imply a serious responsibility to think through this union in a culturally relevant way. On the one hand, it obligates us to draw faithfully from the teachings of the Catholic intellectual tradition; on the other hand, it is necessary to place these readings in the light of the here and now. For Falque himself already anticipates this twofold obligation: "There is no atemporal philosophy, at least in the sense of a totally and definitively disembodied way. We always use the categories of our time, if only to reconstruct the old ones."[17]

The problem is very much twofold. Falque is a "believer" compelled by a double challenge. On the one hand, he must engage loyally with philosophy, which according to some can be misguided by a reliance on faith and religion. He will have to specify, in particular, the relationships he keeps with his theological discourses on God which he necessarily lives out as a "believer," and which, associated with his philosophy, are always presented as a risk in minimizing his autonomy from it. On the other hand, he will also need to respond to possible criticism from theologians themselves, who may worry about the place taken by philosophy throughout. Can Falque cease to be a philosopher? And, does he not risk using theology only for the benefit and services of philosophy? Faced with these challenges, decisions will be necessary in the exercise of Falque's thought. Not unlike Heidegger, he observes: "To think is to decide."[18] This maxim is true in more ways than one for the meaning, development, and implications of his work.

SECTION TWO: A CHRISTIAN THINKER

The Falquian conception of the relationship between theology and philosophy is in fact not as obviously shared or common, as initially seems. He describes himself as "the leader who goes out in front, climbs the wall alone, even if it means taking risks, but always ensuring the fruits of his labor."[19] The image will no doubt call to mind many commentaries. For now, we will remember that the emphasis rests on the difficulty of the undertaking itself, both individual and collective, at once bold and rigorous.

For building this specific unity between theology and philosophy, and before entering into the precise analysis of their articulation, it is

---

17. Falque, "Penser, c'est décider," 78.
18. See Falque, "Penser, c'est décider."
19. Falque, "Penser, c'est décider."

necessary to discuss the general character of the two terms themselves. In the first place, the relationship does not concern simply the "believing philosopher" and the "Christian philosopher," on the one hand, and the "religious philosopher" and "philosopher of religion," on the other hand. Indeed, it is worth noting that, if Falque wants to be a "believing philosopher" with a "religious philosophy," nowhere does he explicitly proclaim himself as a "Christian philosopher" but rather a Christian thinker. The apparent paradox and the specificity of this particular position are succinctly summed up as follows: "The more that we theologize, the better we philosophize, even though the thesis of a 'Christian philosophy' as such can no longer be maintained."[20] Thus, theology and philosophy are closely linked in a common practice but not directly caught within "Christian philosophy."[21] Now, does this mean that such a formulation no longer contains anything scandalous, as though the affirmation of a wholly Christian identity has lost its previous virulence and threatening character?

A Christian Philosophy?

To help in clarifying this position on a "Christian philosophy," it is worth reexploring the positions at stake from a debate in 1931. There, Emile Bréhier defended the thesis of the de facto nonexistence of Christian philosophy because, for him, Christianity had little influence on Greek philosophy. He also contested the relationship in terms of the grammar of philosophy itself. Associating the qualifier of "Christian" destroyed any sense of the noun "philosophy" which, as a result, lost its productive autonomy. The contestation and instability of Christian philosophy was also neatly reflected in the words of Karl Barth, "The more man knows of God, the more He is yet to be known."[22] This thesis will later be taken up by Heidegger, who evokes a concept of God who cannot be the object of any prayer. Étienne Gilson, for his part, strongly defended a radically opposed thesis. Leaning on the history of philosophy, he affirmed the reality of a Christian philosophy. For him, the many works of Aquinas, Saint Augustine, Saint Bonaventure, Duns Scotus, among others, testify to this. Christianity has over the centuries considerably enriched philosophy. Furthermore, a philosopher who holds religious convictions

---

20. Falque, *God, the Flesh, and the Other*, 16.
21. See Falque, *Crossing the Rubicon*, 139–40.
22. Barth, *Epistle to the Romans*, 73.

cannot think independently of them, and revelation is for him, as Gilson observes, "an indispensable auxiliary of Reason." Gilson therefore practices a philosophy that is "Christian" because of the very tools he uses. Some neo-Scholastics also participated in the 1931 debate and criticized Gilson: if there can in fact be an influence of revelation on philosophy, it must be considered accidental rather than constituting a positive norm. As will be seen, none of these positions satisfy Falque. But this confrontation, however briefly described, is perhaps more meaningfully understood when juxtaposed alongside the work of Maurice Blondel, who differed from all preceding positions.

For Blondel, philosophy is naturally led to recognize its incompleteness and its necessary surpassing towards faith which implicitly reveals itself to be "Christian." Blondel's claims follow a rational approach, which does not trace its origin from a dependence on revelation. Rather, it stems from an analysis of human action that reflects a lived incompleteness, a lack, that Christ will come to fill. The hypothesis may be thus formulated as a possible opening upwards. His entire approach aims to show that there is, from the very beginning, the immanence of the transcendent within us. A careful analysis of human experience demonstrates that the reasons which seem to make an act possible in the first place are, in fact, powerless in defining its true determination. They represent a call for their own surpassing. In Blondelian terms, the "willing will," what pushes us to go always further, underlies and animates the "desiring will," what is limited to particular objectives. When seen together, we find a fundamental recognition that the true will of man is oriented towards a greater divine will.

Paradoxically, though, Blondel can fall under a double criticism, that of restricting the role of philosophy to an outdated model as well as not having given philosophy its full measure before too hastily making it "Christianized." Blondel's approach pronounces too soon the transgression of finitude, perhaps forgetting the existence of an "open question," while Falque tries to remain firmly aware of a "blocked horizon" in need of deeper investigation.[23] As for the function and place of theology, that too needs more elucidation.

We may note that those authors, who more or less defended the expression of "Christian philosophy," were keen to distinguish theology from philosophy—separating them more radically than Falque would

---

23. Falque, *Crossing the Rubicon*, 140–41.

dare. Falque will maintain the autonomy of philosophy and theology but only in order to identify and illustrate the fruitfulness of a true meeting place between the two. On the status of "Christian philosophy," as Merleau-Ponty once observed, "neither Christians nor non-Christians were agreed."[24] These different attitudes, however quickly mentioned, help to clarify Falque's position, which should not to be conflated with any of the previous models. Following Maurice Nédoncelle, we might observe three interpretations of the notion of "Christian philosophy" as follows: "It can be a propaedeutic to Christianity, or at least a philosophy on some level which inherits revelation; or perhaps even a philosophy which is constituted under the indirect influence by a Christian faith; or finally a philosophy which proclaims the insufficiency of human nature to resolve the entire problem of man, discerning and delimiting in some way a supernatural gift which may resolve the original tension but cannot replace it."[25]

Yet, none of the above-mentioned approaches fully satisfy Falque. He refuses the analysis that insists that Christianity has nothing to give to philosophy, and theology to philosophy. His erudite studies of medieval and patristic thinkers contradict such a presumption, as they also show that Greek thought constructively enriched the development of Christian thought over time. But the thesis according to which philosophy, for various reasons, would necessarily lead to its own surpassing or would seek to postulate its own surpassing is also not a demand. To make God a being or a concept in order to fill our lack is a double error, in theology as in philosophy. Philosophy according to Falque gives all its weight and value to the "all-encompassing person," as theology does the same for the incarnation.

Catholicity and Universality

A preliminary paradox may be noted as follows: Falque seeks to closely associate philosophy and theology but without claiming to be "Christian philosophy." Would it, then, be excessive to call him a "Catholic philosopher" rather than a "Christian philosopher"? Though certain to bring some reluctance, this question has a heuristic value. In the first place, we must highlight Falque's manner in affirming his convictions on theological, philosophical, and ecclesiastical levels. From there, we can distinguish Catholicism from Protestantism. For example, Falque does

---

24. Merleau-Ponty, *Signs*, 140.
25. Nédoncelle, *Existe-t-il une philosophie chrétienne?*, 115.

not hesitate to distinguish himself from Ricœur for specifically philosophical reasons (Ricœur favors hermeneutics and textuality, though to the detriment of life, flesh, and phenomenology) which at the same time, as we will recall, is tied to a distinction from Ricœur's Protestant faith as well. It is not a question of marking oppositions or confessional divides, but simply of recognizing differences in intellectual positioning.

But the term "catholic" having a connotation of universality, *catholica*, would also indicate, when applied to Falque's enterprise, that Christianity fully accounts for the human condition. Falque assumes that dimension, while also opening it to its greatest possible metamorphosis. In that regard, this meaning of the term "catholic" is not really the object of Falque's reflection per se; however, it clearly reflects a kind of productive tension, a paradox, even a wager, which makes the philosophical stakes all the more fertile. This is true to the extent that the identity of Christianity and of Catholicism is located, affirmed, and described with the greatest clarity. Paradoxically, as we will see, "the more we theologize, the better we philosophize."[26] That is, the more we affirm our catholic identity, the better we can take into account the fullness and diversity of the human condition. In doing so, we are also able to dialogue more with other forms of thought, in particular, those very forms which are critical of a religious faith.

Falque maintains the need to think about one's faith in its radicalness, in its specificity, but also in its universality which helps to make possible its revelation in a credible manner. This may be summed up in Falque's creative statement on the resurrection: "For, however unbelievable it may be, the resurrection will not become 'credible' unless it has to some extent become intelligible."[27] Such an observation appears to be lucid, prudent, and even bold. Though, from this point of view, we must be sure to mention that Falque still differs from Ricœur, who came to de-absolutize Christianity in recognizing that "religion does not exist anywhere in universal form."

Paralleling this line of thought, Falque, too, recalls that modernity sometimes testifies less to the refusal of God than to the quest for new gods, "and nothing ensures the deployment of the sacred, in its dimension that is both neutral and diffuse, in a more enviable situation for the Christian tradition than that of the pure and simple negation of God."[28]

26. Falque, *Crossing the Rubicon*, 139.
27. Falque, *Metamorphosis of Finitude*, 139–40.
28. See Falque, "Mystique et modernité."

Thus, the task of the "believing philosopher" is to fight against the vagueness of certain spiritual aspirations, by showing that the conceptual can in fact account for the existential; and that Christianity can be lived and spoken for at the same time. Falque seeks to help the believer to overcome the dilemmas of living as a Christian on earth: on the one hand, a Manichean contempt of the world that separates the good (inside the church) from the bad (outside)—a dogmatism by those who claim exclusive possession of the truth; on the other hand, the risk of collapsing two worlds into each other where the believer tries to balance between a loss of identity and a standardization of values leading to an empty syncretism. It is by affirming specificity and difference that Falque may respond to the spiritual aspirations of our time. In this manner, Falque defends a "theology of difference" which accounts for "the four mystifying traits of all Christian discourse," the Trinitarian identity, the mysticism of the other, the incarnation of the Son, and the resurrection of the body.[29] By highlighting the "exemplary" (i.e., apparent inexplicability) and not merely the "absurd," each mode of theological discourse provides the conditions for locating a "renewal" of the rationality of Christianity and, from there, its spirituality.

Philosophy of Religion and "Religious Philosophy"

Another paradox lies in the choice of "religious philosophy" as opposed to "philosophy of religion." The second formulation considers religion in all its manifestations, independent of any religious conviction. However, as a formulation of religious philosophy, the parameter of religious belief is explicitly taken into question. Authors like Pascal and Kierkegaard neatly illustrate that model. Falque himself never conceals the "religious" presuppositions (in many respects, a personal dimension) at the origin of his various works, in many places, the study of authors from a point of view which is also that of a historian of philosophy. Furthermore, if he recognizes the nonbeliever's ability to read medieval thinkers independently of any religious faith, Falque may also not be denied the right to read these thinkers by taking into account their lived experiences of faith as a dimension of truth in their work.

---

29. Falque, "Mystique et modernité," 791.

The choice of "religious philosophy" over "philosophy of religion," as exemplified in a disagreement with Jean Greisch,[30] is justified by the relationship that Falque and Greisch both maintain with finitude and the way in which they conceive of its possible surpassing. Without taking sides in the debate, their very confrontation offers an opportunity for analyzing the description that Falque offers of finitude and discussing, in particular, certain philosophical and theological readings. For the moment, it suffices to focus on their impact in generating yet another paradox: "religious philosophy" is better able than "philosophy of religion" to account for finitude. Religious philosophy describes without a too immediate forfeiture, and it illuminates without overstepping; more than this, it unfolds before our eyes a richer idea of finitude's metamorphosis, which it may be said, is only really made possible by the action of God (and, more precisely, of a Trinitarian God). For Falque, without such a "religious" belief, finite overcoming is an illusion. We, of course, assert that such a thesis deserves a careful study of finitude in itself. Yet, paradoxically, philosophy of religion does not think of this finitude in a sufficiently radical way, remaining on a level of unproductive neutrality.

In his latest book, *Crossing the Rubicon*, Falque further radicalizes his position by proposing that we replace the formulation "religious philosophy" with that of "philosophy of religious experience." This modification is, in the first place, based on a concern for precision: "The importance of the kerygma calls for the rediscovery or reestablishment of an act of philosophizing, as proved by Pascal and Kierkegaard in their day, for which the experience of believing is not dismissed as a matter of course."[31] While it is conceivable to read an author without seeing oneself within his belief system, it is nonetheless necessary to locate a shared space of experience, otherwise we miss the heart of religious life. Falque will insist, in other contexts, on this essential point, that is, to favor experience over texts. From this perspective, we find that Ricœur's approach, which stops at the text, remains under critique. This point with regard to Ricœur will be returned to later in more detail.

For now, suffice it so say, that the young Heidegger—who studies Saint Paul and Saint Augustine—seems to follow the logic of Falque.[32] Indeed, as one scholar put it of Heidegger:

---

30. See Falque, *Loving Struggle*, 250–51.
31. Falque, *Crossing the Rubicon*, 121.
32. See Heidegger, *Phenomenology of Religious Life*.

In this way, it is not for Heidegger to carry out an exegesis of the letters of Paul or the "Confessions of Augustine" but rather to identify the structure, origins, and specific dynamics of a singular "situation," that is, of the believer who lives and understands his existence according to the Christian faith. The challenge is to circumscribe what is specific to the experience of religious life which manifests itself out there. Now, this realization resides neither in theological concepts, nor in dogmatic contents, nor even in a profession of faith. It resides, according to Heidegger, in a type of very specific temporal and existential tension which animates, justifies, and guides the life of the individual at every Christian moment. In other words, the properly phenomenological "material" which interests Heidegger is to be found in the testimony that Paul and Augustine offers lived "experience" of the Christian faith.[33]

Overall, and in this vein of brief observations on the status of the "believing philosopher" though not explicitly "Christian philosopher," (that is, "religious," though not "philosopher of religion"), we find that the position of Falque is far more complex than might appear in any initial approach that would have simply conflated him with a tradition of confessional religious thinkers. Thus, one great uniqueness can already be seen and isolated in his method, namely, his conception of the relationships between theology and philosophy—and perhaps more precisely in the emphasis he places on their proper articulation.

SECTION THREE: PHILOSOPHY BEFORE ALL

If according to Heidegger "to think is to decide," a preliminary decision is necessary for those who want to act as a "Christian thinker," that is, to the believer who wants to increase the intelligibility of their faith by means of theology. This means to suspend the immediate intervention of theology by living the patience of philosophy and by accepting its necessary mediation. The historical and theoretical associations between philosophy and theology is of course well known, if not traditional. While Falque himself belongs to this tradition, he redefines it in an original way.

---

33. Arrien, "Penser sans Dieu, vivre avec Dieu," 69.

The Experience of the Human and the Experience of God

As Falque observes, "At first, we have no other experience of God than the human's."[34] This judgment, frequently iterated and reiterated throughout Falque's work, echoes what Ricœur once said of religious language in its ability to redescribe human experience: "In this regard, the allegories, metaphors, and parables that punctuate prophecies produce an effect similar to the one brought about by the poetry of the Psalms and the Song of Songs. . . . What we have is the whole distance between announcing and showing, making seen."[35] The kinship with Ricœur is, however, only partial due to the fact that Ricœur gives language a privileged place. In Ricœur, we see a resistance to experience as represented in the long path of passing through symbols and texts. In contrast, Falque pursues the short path directly inscribed in the carnal world.

The idea that the experience of God is first and foremost connected to the experience of the human suggests that philosophy bears a certain relationship to God. That is, if by philosophy we understand a discourse of the human, including its theological horizons which remain sustained by the human. To state this neither rejects theological truths nor the truths of lived experience. Although a difficult theoretical hurdle, the close connection between philosophy and theology provides a critical lesson. It demonstrates a necessity for theology to pass through philosophy in the mode of philosophizing as *practice* (it is significant that Falque himself is trained as a phenomenologist). God reveals himself first of all only through humanity, that of the human in general and the Son in particular. It is precisely the vocation of philosophy to account for this humanity. We might say, not unlike Feuerbach, that anthropological experience reflects the teachings of theology. However, this need not be a negative observation. For the theologian to refuse it would be counterintuitive. If theology's passage through philosophy is well founded, it may also very well be justified theologically. The deepest justification for recourse to philosophy will be found in the status of finitude, that is, in the human as a *being*—a philosophical qualification—and in his nature as a *creature*—a theological qualification. On several occasions, Falque has analyzed both categories at length, particularly in his study of Aquinas.

---

34. Falque, *Crossing the Rubicon*, 122.
35. Ricœur, *Thinking Biblically*, 172.

The Return to the Things Themselves

As we saw above, "to think is to decide." And, it is here that we confront the depth of a decision. For many, theology cannot be reduced to a philosophical approach. Yet, the question absolutely deserves to be posed. In the case of Falque, we find a response articulated through the practice of phenomenology. The choice of this method comes from his training. Falque himself has spoken of his reading of Husserl's *Crisis* in his preparatory class,[36] of Merleau-Ponty in his philosophy aggregation program, and last of the firsthand teachings of Marion.

It perhaps goes without saying that phenomenology constituted a true revolution in philosophy, expressed in Husserl's famous injunction "to return to the things themselves." As Gaston Berger famously put it: "Phenomenology first supposes a reduction of prejudgments. It wants to lead us to a vision of things. But to see clearly, you must not have in advance the image of what you want desperately to discover, that is, the second feature of phenomenology. This is so because it is based on a most comprehensive analysis. It is necessary to talk of what we know and not only from what we know theoretically, verbally, conceptually, but from what we have experienced, . . . from what we know from experience. . . . But these concrete examples that we take and analyze in detail, they help us to see. And, on occasion thus we see essences. All phenomenology is a theory of vision. . . . Phenomenology only makes sense if it relates things to man and to their consciousness."[37] Against the natural attitude of naïveté which believes in things as data, already constituted independently of us as though with real objectivity (realistic attitude), and against the idealist position, which posits that reality is a construction of the knowing subject, phenomenology aims to grasp things as they appear to us—within our experience. The gift of the world and the constitution of consciousness are thus inseparable. Consciousness in fact cannot exist independently of the world; "all consciousness is consciousness of something," as Husserl so often would state. But, the world is only revealed to us through the experience we have of it. We only ever fully grasp them in their unity. It is therefore a question of locating ourselves within the horizons of understanding in which things are given. In response to the question of classical metaphysics, "What is that?," which aims to grasp the essence of things, phenomenology replaces the question of "How?"

---

36. See Husserl, *Crisis of European Sciences and Transcendental Phenomenology*.
37. Berger, *Philosophe dans le monde moderne*, 140.

How do things appear to us? We cannot therefore claim to describe and apprehend reality as it is, but as we grasp it, live it, and as it reveals itself to us. We only ever know these things by reaching with and through phenomena. The object is only ever grasped immanently, in my consciousness. Transcendence, likewise, is grasped in immanence. It is therefore impossible to speak of the reality of the object independent of its presence to me; there is no absolute reality outside the constituting power of transcendental subjectivity. The entire phenomenological practice is therefore centered on the experience of consciousness and its theoretical renunciation to a presupposed and independent objectivity.

From the Point of View of Phenomenology

The description of an objectivity and the implementation of a reduction are also demonstrated in a possible conception of God. This phenomenological direction is part of a wider program in Falque's work. God can be grasped only in the experience of our consciousness. God cannot be reached as the destination of reasoning, which lands only at an apprehension of an idol. Such a critical assertion is not only phenomenological but also built into a critique of onto-theology, a conception of God as a most perfect being. This critique denounces the identification of God with a concept of being that cannot be prayed to nor loved. As Heidegger reminds us: "This is the right name for the god of philosophy. Man can neither pray nor sacrifice to this god. Before the *causa sui*, man can neither fall to his knees in awe nor can he play music and dance before this god."[38] Phenomenology always emphasizes the lived experience of consciousness. Merleau-Ponty already noted that we no longer seek to demonstrate the existence of God, as did Aquinas, Saint Anselm, or Descartes; we also place a limit on ourselves in seeking to refute it too.[39] Rather, philosophy, if it may be defined in relationship to religion, seeks a discourse on the phenomenon of God appearing to man. And, this God appears to man in the form of a gift.

A skeptical attitude is warranted. There is perhaps a limit of philosophy and, in particular, of phenomenology, which many will criticize as too soft or excessively neutral on the question of religion. But this critical limit offers a possibility of locating and living a specific experience of

---

38. Heidegger, *Identity and Difference*, 72.
39. Merleau-Ponty, *"In Praise of Philosophy" and Other Essays*, 42.

God, through an awareness that we have of him and the way in which we live, and without needing to judge the metaphysics of its greater reality. Like Falque, we might express it as "by way of a quasi-transcendental deduction of revelation on the basis of the (saturated phenomenon)."[40] This phenomenological scope limited to the study of the "phenomenon" in which God appears, however problematic for some believers, renders the philosophical approach to religion accessible to the unbeliever, even if he qualifies it differently. From a point of view of the history of philosophy, the phenomenological approach constitutes a critique of metaphysics and onto-theology, which at one time were the central subjects of lively debates that, today, Falque considers in need of novelty. For example, in *Crossing the Rubicon*, he recalls that numerous philosophical studies have shown that "we should ask ourselves today, in light of the endless quest, if this putative metaphysics understood as ontotheology—namely, the act of leading being qua being [*ontos*] back to God as the super Being [*theos*]—is not another one of those paradises that is illusory and impossible to find."[41]

Freed from all onto-theology, metaphysics may find its legitimacy and so be able to pursue its true source in transcendence. But this metaphysics must be understood, not as the "after" of physics, nor its "beyond," but as its "crossing," in the experiential sense of its "suffering" and also its ever-moving "passage." Moreover, writes Falque: "This newly queried metaphysics, therefore, does not make us forget the world in which we are rooted, but requires us to cross it without ever being overtaken."[42] In this regard, phenomenological practices within philosophical framings will necessarily have consequences on theology. The latter cannot ignore this experience.

Phenomenology as Style

Phenomenology is not content to denounce things in a purely theoretical manner of the natural attitude. Nor is it satisfied with a philosophical tradition that oscillates between the two poles of realism and idealism. It illuminates the action to take place; and, here, action is no coincidence. Echoing Merleau-Ponty, Falque insists on the fact that phenomenology is

---

40. Falque, *Loving Struggle*, 134.
41. Falque, *Crossing the Rubicon*, 134.
42. Falque, *Crossing the Rubicon*, 135.

not only a philosophical school but a style of life, namely that "phenomenology can be practiced and identified as a manner or style of thinking, that it existed as a movement before arriving at complete awareness of itself as a philosophy."[43]

When translated into a religious context, this position provokes a question of lived experience: "How and in what way is God given to be seen and touched today?"[44] This is the essential question of *God, the Flesh, and the Other*. It runs through all of the works of Falque, and follows from an attention to the theological and philosophical: "To rediscover the meaning of the incarnation in general, whether of man or God, is thus to interrogate the tradition anew and to avoid sinking into a purely 'abstract' mode of thought that contemporary philosophy especially wants to disavow. The course is not primarily confessional, nor even theological. It is above all philosophical inasmuch as the 'carnal mode of the human' is what we must rediscover today."[45] If we have a relationship with God only through the experience of man, if philosophy cannot do without this experience, then we understand that theology can and must work through the passage, proof, and test of philosophy. "*Theologoumena* are translated into a number of *philosophèmes*."[46]

The recourse to phenomenology leads to other questions, beyond the contingencies of personal existence and even happenstance of a philosophical moment. Perhaps phenomenology is the best enterprise for grasping God in experience? Is it because, philosophically, we cannot comment on the effectivity of God in existence unless we limit ourselves to the practice of phenomenology? If understood in this way, we may yet make it possible to establish the credibility of certain theological propositions. Such will be the task ahead.

SECTION FOUR: NEW FRONTIERS

Would Falque take up the advice of Henri Matisse: "Must you always do two things at once?" We also, by extent, may think of Ricœur's metaphor of the "two legs" on the theology-philosophy rapport. As he observes, we cannot be at the same time a theologian and philosopher, as one cannot

---

43. See Merleau-Ponty, *Phenomenology of Perception*, viii.
44. Falque, *God, the Flesh, and the Other*, 7.
45. Falque, *God, the Flesh, and the Other*, 7.
46. Falque, *God, the Flesh, and the Other*, xxi.

be in the same moment *in via* and *in patria*. But the human condition, as it stirs the thought of the "believing philosopher," necessarily requires fulfilling both functions—to seek both states. An initial and significant distinction with regard to Ricœur must again be made in order to shed more light on the position of Falque. Ricœur, a Protestant, primarily seeks to avoid the obstacle, a major one for him, of the confusion between theology and philosophy. Falque, who for his part defends the autonomy of philosophy, expresses a concern as a Catholic, namely, the danger and sterility of a permanent separation between theology and philosophy. Against those who distrust tradition, he avers "the possibility of the philosophical project and the actuality of the theological revelation."[47] Ricœur would no doubt adopt a rather defensive position, understood within the framework of an "age of suspicion." Falque, in contrast, proposes an affirmative attitude that outstrips and positively surpasses critique. Is this a sign of change in the times?

Distinguishing for Unity

The relationship between theology and philosophy is clearly conceptualized by Falque. His approach, which consists of knitting things together, is based on a more fundamental relationship between the concepts of distinction and union. Of the two famous formulations, "unite to distinguish" by Blondel and "distinguish to unite" by Maritain, I propose that the second suits Falque's approach the best, even if he rarely refers to Maritain's philosophy.

Distinction and Union

Philosophy and theology both can have the same content, but they are distinguished by their starting points, that is, the directions of their movement and mode of expression. If their content means the acquisition of knowledge of God and man through an experience, then theology expresses a downward movement (from top to bottom). We often specify this expression as revelation for its *didactic* or, rather, *dogmatic* representation of faith from above. Philosophy manifests an ascending movement, from bottom to top, in a *heuristic* and *interrogative* mode. The Cartesian method, as seen in the metaphysics of the *Meditations*,

---

47. Falque, *Loving Struggle*, 140.

perfectly illustrates such an approach. To be sure, while intelligence opens itself to its own surpassing, as Descartes would have it, the destination is not immediate precisely because it requires mediation. More specifically, the satisfaction of reason involves the intervention of a nonhuman agent. As Falque observes, "The force of theology as a discourse beginning with God does not hinder philosophy as a discourse on the God-phenomenon appearing to the human."[48]

In this presentation of the theology-philosophy relationship, Falque's originality lies first in the recognition of the same content for both approaches. He expands on this similarity by introducing the categories of "possibility" or "effectiveness." Here, philosophy, like phenomenology, can therefore aim at and describe the objects of theology, provided however it adheres, as Husserl observed, "that *everything originally* (so to speak, in its 'personal' actuality) *offered* to us *in intuition is to be accepted simply as what it is presented as being, but also only within the limits in which it is presented there.*"[49] We understand thus why Falque interrogates the stark distinction (especially its principle) made by Marion in his work according to the "content," as either theological or philosophical. Falque proposes another way which does not outright reject Marion but certainly surpasses it in the name of new horizons.

"Théologoumènes" and "Philosophèmes"

For Falque, there are two types of concepts: theological concepts (*théologoumènes*) and philosophical concepts (*philosophèmes*). While often segregated at a distance, as seen with Ricœur and Marion, Falque brings them together. "No *théologoumène* will have any meaning outside of an experience or a philosophical existential which gives it meaning."[50] Falque has affirmed time and again: "We have no other experience of God than that of man."[51] For him, the experience of the human can and must be experienced by God, and, therefore, may be read theologically and philosophically at the same time. Falque provides some examples. In his triptych, he shows that the passion of Christ is understood from the point of

---

48. Falque, *Crossing the Rubicon*, 127.
49. Husserl, *Ideas I*, 44.
50. Emmanuel Falque, "Tuilage et conversion de la philosophie par la théologie," in Falque and Zielinski, *Philosophie et théologie en dialogue*, 46.
51. Falque, *Metamorphosis of Finitude*, 63.

view of anguish in the suffering and death of man, that the resurrection takes on meaning from the analysis of birth, and that the Eucharist refers to the experience of eros. In *God, the Flesh, and the Other*, many more connections are woven between medieval theological terms and modern phenomenological concepts. Thus, we find the "substance" of the Trinity in relation to onto-theology (Augustine), theophany in relation to the appearance of phenomena (John Scotus Erigena), detachment in relation to reduction (Meister Eckhart), the creation of Adam to the visibility of the flesh (Irenaeus), christological incarnation to thickness of the body (Tertullian), conversion of the senses to intercorporeality (Bonaventure), communion of saints to the genesis of the community (Origen), a treatise on angels to intersubjectivity (Thomas Aquinas), and the call of the name to the singularity of others (Duns Scotus).

The list continues into more contemporary philosophy. There, we find Michel Henry on the analyses of the flesh in the incarnation, of the gift and revelation from Jean-Luc Marion, of words and the Word from Jean-Louis Chrétien, and those of the world and the liturgy from Jean-Yves Lacoste. They all attest to what Falque takes to be an overarching paradox, that "the objects of theology are never more clearly brought to light than when they are described with the means of philosophy."[52] He takes this paradox by showing that among them, the place and function of theology are not identical to his work insofar as these thinkers are limited by a "preemption of the infinite." That is to say: "The preemptive right of the infinite over the finite in Cartesian thought seems to have been carried over, like a preferential right gained long ago into a large part of contemporary phenomenology (from Emmanuel Levinas to Jean-Luc Marion or Michel Henry) as well as into theology (from Maurice Blondel to Karl Rahner or Hans Urs von Balthasar): 'In some way I possess the perception (notion) of the infinite before that of the finite, that is, the perception of God before that of myself.'"[53] I will now show the ways in which the point of departure for Falque begins from the blocked horizon of finitude, rather than by the commonly accepted position of the absolute.

---

52. Emmanuel Falque, "Tuilage et conversion de la philosophie par la théologie," in Falque and Zielinski, *Philosophie et théologie en dialogue*, 47. For the Descartes quotation used in that passage, see Descartes, *Meditations*, meditation 3, para. 24.

53. Falque, *Metamorphosis of Finitude*, 16–17.

Liberation of Theology and Philosophy

While philosophy may serve in a certain way the ideals of theology, it may also allow for a liberation, what Balthasar called a "liberation of philosophy through theology." Seen from this way, neither philosophy nor theology exhaust themselves of their content. Philosophy remains close to a descriptive approach to the objects of theology yet remains incapable—by itself—of pronouncing the effectiveness of theology's very source. Falque evokes that this philosophy must "undergo an unexpected and unhoped-for conversion."[54] This "unexpected" and "unhoped-for" conversion attest to the fact that a force intervenes here which is no longer merely human. In *The Wedding Feast of the Lamb*, Falque insists on the contribution of theology to philosophy, on the modification of certain philosophical concepts by theology. And, it will be so for the body, as we will soon see.

Covering Over and Conversion

"Tiling"

The transition from philosophy to theology is described by Falque in terms of transformation, metamorphosis, retrieval, tiling—never in terms of a smooth continuity. Here, the emphasis is no doubt placed on the "content." The movement, however, is seen in the formulation already recalled above: "We have no other experience of God than that of man." To the initial experience, the one which comes "first of all," the possibility of a transformation is offered, at least to the "believing philosopher" who does not hide from it.

It is thus the same content but understood by another dimension. Rather than philosophy which leads by itself to its own surpassing, in the form of a wager as may be seen in Pascal or Blondel, Falque proposes another model. As he writes, if "it is through man that we have access to God," then through mediation of philosophy, the recovery of philosophy by theology is done by "God's initiative," that is, an action of God not man.[55] To the Bonaventurian or Pascalian model of the *relais* of philosophy by theology, we might prefer the Thomistic model of retrieval. "This 'tiling'—namely, the overlaying of philosophy by theology—is thus

---

54. Falque, *Crossing the Rubicon*, 124–25.
55. Falque, *Crossing the Rubicon*, 130.

always borne by the God-man himself, the Word made flesh, and results, in this way, from a decision by God rather than humanity."[56]

Conversion, Incarnation, and Trinity

Here we move from phenomenological "possibility" to theological "effectiveness." That is, the retrieval of philosophy by theology is achieved in and through a transformation of philosophy. This metamorphosis can be described in different ways. At its most basic level, seen throughout the history of thought, theology was able, particularly in the Middle Ages, to transform philosophy methodologically. To take just one example, we will cite Aquinas, who, beginning from Aristotelian premises, transformed Aristotle's idea of God—synonymous with Being—into an act of Being as the first grounding principle, namely, God the Creator. Christian theology not only used philosophy, but radicalized it. As Falque shows in his thesis on Bonaventure, when God "enters into theology," he "resists" and immediately appears under a differentiated form, namely, the "Trinitarian" God, thus leading to radically different philosophical conceptions of divinity.[57] This is all in contrast to what was claimed by Heidegger, who tried to argue that God depended on an overly simplified sedimentation of philosophy, through which God necessarily passes over and covers up. Falque's model offers a novel critique by analyzing the Trinity not necessarily theologically but with an expansive philosophical lens.[58] It is the particular framing of the Trinitarian God which allows us to understand the metamorphosis of man and philosophy, through theology.

Here we also can note a certain evolution in Falque's thought. First, he shows that, with Bonaventure, it is indeed the Triune God who enters into theology, and not into philosophy as Heidegger claims. In a second step, Falque refuses, with Aquinas, to radically oppose the concepts of God as idol or icon, as many phenomenologists claimed to have done in trying to go beyond metaphysics. This conception of a Triune God remains the central place of all *transformations* of God. It also establishes the possibility of the transformation of the human condition and the finitude of "every man." In short, "when the Son passes on to the Father the finitude that he has suffered, not only does the Father receive and

---

56. Falque, *Crossing the Rubicon*, 130.
57. See Falque, *Saint Bonaventure and the Entrance of God into Theology*, 29–35.
58. See Falque, *Saint Bonaventure and the Entrance of God into Theology*, 63–72.

transform this same finitude in the Son, but in return he offers to human beings that we can be transformed, or even given birth."[59] For the Son, as in lived humanity, the resurrection is a transformation of the self by an Other, the intentionality of another in me. The retrieval of philosophy by theology is explained precisely by these transformations, the very infrastructure of Falque's entire approach. The metamorphosis of man occurs through the event of the resurrection in God and made representable in his Trinitarian nature. "Nothing remains outside the Word."[60] The usage of "first" indicates everything. "Just as we have no other experience of God but that of human beings in the phenomenology and theology of 'down below,' similarly we shall not go to God except by God, in the phenomenology and theology of 'on high.' And all this is precisely after the experience of human beings finds itself, and sees itself, radically transformed, in the intra-trinitarian metamorphosis of God."[61]

As a result of the incarnation, everything that man experiences is also experienced by Christ, with the exception of sin. The divinization of man is made possible by the humanization of God. Everything that happens in man thus takes on a different and higher meaning to the extent that God, too, experienced it in his incarnation. The general conversion of the human condition, like the more specific conversion of philosophy into theology, of the "believing philosopher" into theologian is therefore made possible by the action of God, in a certain way by his own conversion. (Again and again, we ask ourselves if Falque ceases to be a philosopher?) The metamorphosis of finitude is first of all "an event intra-divine."[62] This, in part, explains why Falque refers to this event as something "unexpected and unhoped for," outside of the workable tasks of man. As he writes, it is a "break-through, a nullity of all attempts at transformation of the self by the self, when it is imagined as independent of he who is All-Other."[63]

Here, we see the emergence of a central debate in theology, concerning the place of finitude in relationship to the desire for God—namely, a natural desire for the supernatural. For Falque, this desire is the work of God, inscribing it within in us "because it is he alone who inscribes

---

59. Falque, *Metamorphosis of Finitude*, 84.
60. Falque, *Metamorphosis of Finitude*, 82.
61. Falque, *Metamorphosis of Finitude*, 97.
62. Falque, *Metamorphosis of Finitude*, 65.
63. Falque, *Metamorphosis of Finitude*, 63.

in us today this new yearning."[64] Echoing this conception of desire, the theology-philosophy relationship depends on the possibility of there being a knowledge of the divine prior to any revelation. In this way, the philosophy-theology relationship neatly reflects the concepts of union and distinction. The experience of man and that of God appear to be inseparable out of a "common world" of incarnation. However, it is as a result of finitude that any description of experience by the incarnate God can be made possible. And, out of this renewed approach, comes transfiguration, for it is by virtue of being a believer, through the teaching of theology as a depositary of revelation, that philosophy and theology have a shared transformation.

Indeed, the relationship between philosophy and theology is "the place of a meeting of man and God, synthesized in the single figure of the God-man, Christ himself."[65] Briefly put, according to Falque, we find the "philosopher as 'Son of man' and theologian as 'Son of God.'"[66] Commenting on the episode of the disciples of Emmaus who do not immediately recognize Christ (e.g., Luke 24:31–32), he shows that through deciding to travel with them God converts "theologically their philosophical anguish."[67] It is indeed "on the path of man that the disciple there encounters the God-man."[68]

Falque considers, several times, the relationship between philosophy and theology in the mode of a respective liberation. In *Crossing the Rubicon*, he insists on the liberation of theology through philosophy. The inverse relationship, which consists of liberating philosophy by theology, emphasizes the opening of philosophy towards theology, that is, its conversion and transformation by the latter. Methodologically, philosophy thus passes from "possibility" to "effectiveness," a conversion which, as we will see, implies a decision. At present, suffice it to say that the decision to transform demonstrates "its own object according to a heuristic, descriptive—but not actualizing—mode."[69]

---

64. Falque, *Metamorphosis of Finitude*, 109.
65. Falque, "Philosophie et théologie," 205.
66. Falque, "Philosophie et théologie," 206.
67. Falque, "Philosophie et théologie," 206.
68. See "Tiling and Conversion" in Falque, *Crossing the Rubicon*; more specifically, see Emmanuel Falque, "Tuilage et conversion de la philosophie par la théologie," in Falque and Zielinski, *Philosophie et théologie en dialogue*, 51.
69. Falque, *Crossing the Rubicon*, 151.

By tiling over *théologoumènes*, philosophy can give new meaning to its *philosophèmes*. *The Wedding Feast of the Lamb*, a study of the divine body in the Eucharist, provides an innovative conception of the human body. Paralleling *Crossing the Rubicon*, Falque intends to give theology its full and rightful place, no longer wanting to separate radically the exercise of philosophy from it or remain short of the threshold of theology against the judgements of his philosophical contemporaries. It is not a question of confusing the two disciplines, but of thinking about their articulation, of practicing disciplinary flexibility in an overarching sharing of tasks. To do this involves a back-and-forth between the two approaches. It will no doubt, as Falque anticipates, admit a respective shock to reality. The shock is grounding. "Rather than writing theology, I desire to write philosophy, but I will philosophize that much better if I agree also to do theology. The paradox is that precisely where and how philosophy and theology have been separated is now where and how they should properly be united. Only in uniting philosophy and theology can we see that we are consciously crossing the ford at the same time from philosopher to theologian and reciprocally from theologian to philosopher."[70]

Living and Thinking

A "top-down" approach to theology (i.e., based on revelation) and a "bottom-up" approach to philosophy (i.e., purely human) come together in the constitution of a "common world." The link between theology and philosophy is based on a double experience of the very same human being, fixed between the theological and the philosophical. While Blondel starts from his experience as a Christian, and then seeks how to think as a philosopher, we—as belonging to a common world—must rather think as a Christian and live as a philosopher. We see that it is indeed the same human being who lives both. For Falque, thought is not merely the result of the understanding of experience but a mode of experience itself. We think about what we live, and live out what we think. Writing is even a mode of this experience: "To die is to not write."[71] It is the capacity of man to experience an epiphany, which is not always obvious but remains ever central between thought and life. In this way, it is the exercise of reason and the reception of revelation which makes the

70. Falque, *Crossing the Rubicon*, 150.
71. See Falque, *By Way of Obstacles*, 159–60.

philosophy-theology articulation both possible and necessary. This does not solely reflect a concern for academic harmonization but rather an existential requirement.

The believer grants all legitimacy to concepts, a result from the activity of thinking theological revelation. Faith makes this reception possible. But the "believing philosopher" must live as a philosopher in order to locate the expression of concepts which, thanks to the mediation between philosophical and anthropological experience, is always possible to unearth from the life of 'man in general.'

Unlike Blondel, who refused to take charge of strictly theological notions such as the Trinity, the incarnation, and the resurrection (reserving them for theological treatment alone), Falque proposes to make philosophy (in this case phenomenology) work within the corpus of theology. He proposes to translate *théologoumènes* into *philosophèmes*. We have already mentioned several examples of this. For us, at present, how indeed can we understand the Trinity, the incarnation, and the resurrection; and how to make their meaning heard by others, if they are unable to illuminate on their own the very real moments of our life? As Falque observes, we seek to "live the philosopher," a formulation understood well within the practice of phenomenology, which, as Merleau-Ponty states, aims to "inhabit the world" and "to allow oneself to be practiced with and recognized as manner and style."[72]

It is also reasonable to assume that the finitude of the human being in this world, practicing the patience of reflection and philosophical questioning, may very well reach God in crossing through life's tests. This "believing philosopher," to live a fruitful duality as "philosopher-theologian" or "theologian-philosopher" follows the figure of Christ, a philosopher as Son of Man and theologian as Son of God.[73] A this-worldly human foundation of the theology-philosophy union may be taken up in the light of a distinction made by Merleau-Ponty on the essence of Christian philosophy. He writes, "Philosophy is not Christian in its essence but only according to its status, only through the intermingling of religious thought and life."[74] The very same Merleau-Ponty illuminates precisely the challenge that faces Falque, between the philosopher and

---

72. See preface in Merleau-Ponty, *Phenomenology of Perception*. Also, see Falque, *Saint Bonaventure and the Entrance of God into Theology*, xlvii–xlviii.

73. Falque, *Loving Struggle*, 134. Falque admits the possibility of two simultaneous formulations.

74. Merleau-Ponty, *Signs*, 140.

the Christian: "Will there ever be a real exchange between philosopher and Christian (whether it is a matter of two men or of those two men each Christian senses within himself)? In our view this would be possible only if the Christian (with the exception of the ultimate sources of his inspiration, which he alone can judge) were to accept without qualification the task of mediation which philosophy cannot abandon without eliminating itself."[75] Has Falque met this challenge? It is well and good the objective that he has laid out for himself. His enterprise of "mediation," which passes in and through a fully experience finitude, is not meant to reveal exclusivist dimensions of an "unbelieving" sin. Atheism, as a methodological or existential choice, is more than a written drama. True, the "believing philosopher" thinks "as a Christian." But first he must "live as a philosopher," and lead the life of "man in general." Nevertheless, there is an additional resource for seeing the presuppositions of the human condition as a wider expression of the human incarnation of God and transformative power of the Trinity. This so-called acceptance of life before a potential metamorphosis on the part of the "believing philosopher" deserves a critical Nietzschean analysis to reach finitude in its most fundamental mode.

On either side of the believer there are tensions. There is, on the one hand, the believer who too quickly wants to be a theologian as well as the "Christian philosopher"—for whom philosophy necessarily calls for its own surpassing—and who refrains from getting involved in theology. On the other hand, there is the philosopher who defends the principle of a constant separation between theology and philosophy, of the simple "philosopher of religion" whose approach tends towards a distantly agnostic and purely objective pursuit. Falque, for his part, supports the principle of a necessary union between theology and philosophy that, at the same time, guarantees their respective autonomy. Such a conception obviously presupposes a faith in revelation. But Falque's conception of faith aims to leave philosophy free to live out its autonomy, even if this same philosophy can then be illuminated by a revelation through faith.

With these remarks, let us draw out some important conclusions. The theology-philosophy relationship rests upon multiple foundations. It is first experienced through a "believing philosopher" who lives out the double dimension in his thought as well as his existence. It is also based on the anthropological dimensions of religious experience: we have no

75. Merleau-Ponty, *Signs*, 146.

experience of God than through man, an experience which is therefore to be lived fully, almost, one might say, independently of God. We may repeat here Bonhoeffer's famous formulation: "etsi Deus non daretur" (even if God were not given).[76] Without the mediation of this human experience, theological concepts remain empty. This leads to a further connection with Kant. Concepts without intuition are empty; a dove cannot fly in the void without the resistance of the air to hold it afloat. In this manner, we find Falque closer to Rahner (the existential-human dimension) than Balthazar (Trinitarian conversion); God reveals himself by passing through us.

These transcendental conditions of faith within philosophical discourse are also justified theologically. It is the status of man as a creature of God that guides the experience of humanity. Here, Falque defends Rahner against Balthasar's accusation of a heavy anthropological reduction. It is God, not man, who reduced his own condition, through kenosis, to that of this world. Theological teaching establishes the double-role of philosophy, to locate the richest dimensions of incarnation which may also manifest the full transformation of the human condition by God, as well as offer the possibility of an even greater metamorphosis of finitude itself.

Another justification may be found in the apologetic necessity for a believing philosopher to be understood by his contemporaries. Falque aims to "first speak the language of all" in order to locate a "common grammar" of finitude. Recalling the words of Pope John Paul II, Falque writes: "We need a new apologetic, geared to the needs of today.... Such an apologetic will need to find a common 'grammar' with those who see things differently and do not share our assumptions, lest we end up speaking different languages even though we may be using the same tongue."[77] Before claiming to speak about God, we must be present with our fellow beings. *Ecce Homo!* That philosopher must always first approach experience in the mode of its finitude. In the forthcoming pages, it will be necessary to further analyze the description that Falque offers. For now, we may already have an idea that Falque's approach cannot do without a "methodological atheism" in order to preserve a space for "man in general." Atheism, in this regard, is more than a "drama," it is an obligation. To presuppose any manifestation of the divine in our contemporary

---

76. Bonhoeffer, *Letters and Papers from Prison*, 477.

77. Falque, *Crossing the Rubicon*, 133. Cited from John-Paul II, "Address of His Holiness John Paul II to the Bishops of Western Canada on Their 'Ad Limina' Visit," October 30, 1999.

world, we must simultaneously recognize that the greater part of humanity itself holds doubt against that very manifestation.

Part Two

Living Finitude

To ADDRESS A STUDY of finitude in the company of Falque is, above all, to experience a seemingly paradoxical situation, especially concerning his triptych. His words have a strong theological connotation, as seen from the titles of his works. This, no doubt, will perplex a philosopher who tries to preserve separate autonomy of the disciplines. Falque, for his part, does not conceal his presuppositions or his intentions: to illuminate and show how the teachings of Christ account for and radically transform the human condition. He aims to demonstrate how suffering, death, birth, corporeality, finitude—as modes of being human—take on all their fullest meaning and intelligibility through theological concepts. If the overcoming of philosophy has already been announced, and if the operations of transformation and metamorphosis are indeed recognized as "the last word of Christianity," it remains to be seen those modes of critical reasoning and wider conditions that may locate the ultimate ground of both.

While the openings of the three works of the triptych are different, they are all erected on the same ground, that of the experience of finitude. Falque, given his reliance on theological resources, frames finitude as "the first word of Christianity." While a seemingly narrow approach on the surface, I propose that this "first word" of finitude and Christianity paradoxically encapsulates the emphatic reality of death as well as the desire to live, not flee. In a way, it effectively suits an approach that aims to dwell within finitude. How is that possible? Between an atheism which rejects all transcendence and a religious philosophy which tries to take refuge in a transformation through theology, Falque attempts to tease out both while standing on their thresholds. A future metamorphosis will only be accomplished by Christ; only the resurrection is "capable of breaking through the chains."[1] This metamorphosis, following the example of Christ, will be fully human, that is, it takes on its meaning in and through Christ's humanity. To understand this, we turn to immanence as embraced by philosophical and theological discourses.

SECTION ONE: THE CALL OF IMMANENCE

The appeal of immanence, or the call of immanence, is based on an attentive ideality of the human condition. This idea can take different forms. First of all, there is a fidelity to what can be shown to man and the way things appear to him. This is the spirit and method of phenomenology. "If the believer sticks simply to appearances as they appear (immanence), he or she will not run off, or only exceptionally, into the illusions of a discourse of the beyond—a beyond that would have to be quite artificial in that it offered no access to one's own experience (the supposed infinite never being immediately shared out)."[2] In short, it is also learning how to see. But this method of immanence is further based upon a triple-foundation.

The first foundation comes from our contemporaries who, for the most part in the West, live and think without reference to God. For them, transcendence is a horizon clogged with inconsequential meaning. The second foundation comes from Falque's own experience, that of the tragic death of two of his friends (whom he explicitly mentions in *The Guide to Gethsemane*). This point is particularly significant. We are hit by Falque's self-referential tone, by the frequent evocations of work in relationship to his life.[3] Some readers may be surprised, or even annoyed with this personalistic style of exposition. However, we cannot fault him, like Nietzsche, for opening up a mode of life within writing, however painful and difficult to actualize. As Falque ironically puts it: "Nothing is falser than the ideal of transparency, even of the light of *alêtheia* that it would supposedly suffice to let unveil itself . . . no longer being able to depend

---

1. Falque, *Metamorphosis of Finitude*, 22.
2. Falque, *Metamorphosis of Finitude*, 19.
3. Note from the translator: The French Catholic philosopher Gabriel Marcel also wrote in a similar self-referential style (*Being and Having*).

on the pneuma (or the 'breath') that alone can inspire it . . . . No one writes to gaze at himself, and still less to congratulate himself, but to open onto other worlds that are always 'possible' and still 'unsuspected.'"[4] And, yet, this act of writing also testifies to the importance that Falque attaches to existential and personal experiences as ways to legitimize his thought. It resembles a harmonious balance between substance and form. Fidelity, finally and perhaps above all, is the third foundation built on the teachings of Christ and the incarnation. Thus, the philosopher cannot neglect the experience of his contemporaries. Likewise, he cannot consider as insignificant what he lives. Falque, as a believer, must take the testimony of Christ seriously, moreover, in its radicality. These are the three criteria that characterize Falque's enterprise and establish a style for approaching the ultimate question of finitude.

The need to think immanence with finitude confronts philosophical and theological positions which either relativize finitude by a hurried and random teaching of revelation or consider that it wrongly developed within a horizon that is incapable of truly thinking the question of finitude. This necessity to defend the place of finitude reflects a greater need to reach authenticity, as discussed in the first part of *The Metamorphosis of Finitude*.[5] In fact, to establish the need for achieving a lasting and fruitful model of finitude, it is necessary to respond to certain objections, formulated either from atheist authors or believing thinkers. The call of immanence, as Falque sees it, must work through these counterarguments, through the usages and the interpretations of contemporary philosophers and theologians. In this regard, we will arrive at a certain appeal for a revived theological tradition and reinterpretation of the gospel teachings.

As is often the case, Falque's position on finitude is clarified when juxtaposed in dialogue and confrontation with other authors. Here, I will propose the philosopher Martin Heidegger and the theologian Henri de Lubac. Other thinkers are certainly relevant, but these two authors are nevertheless privileged to the extent where they engage with the nature of finitude. It is also significant to note that through them philosophy and theology are also summoned into a productive struggle. The foundation of a privileged status of "man in general" for a believing philosopher must belong to a dual framework with presuppositions that are both

---

4. Falque, *By Way of Obstacles*, 159–60.

5. This text plays a major role throughout Falque's *Triduum philosophiques*.

philosophical and theological. It is not only a question of showing that the passage through finitude is essential and inevitable for thinking about the human condition but of defining human nature itself.

Heidegger is particularly important in the formation and development of Falque's project. The young Heidegger, in his habilitation thesis ("Duns Scotus's Doctrine of Categories and Meaning"), insisted on the importance of medieval thought. The same is true for Falque: "I consider, as particularly pressing, a philosophical study, more accurately a phenomenological study of the mystical, moral, and ascetic writings of medieval scholasticism."[6] On the particular link between Heideggerian phenomenology and medieval philosophy, we find in Falque a central point of inspiration and tension.

The overcoming of Heidegger, that is, the "first" Heidegger of medieval mysticism and *Being and Time*, requires an initial appreciation for his conception of finitude. For Falque, Heidegger successfully distinguishes finitude from faulty conceptions in Christianity. But, in doing so, he raises further questions. Falque thus tries to establish that Christian thought can and must develop in this radicality, contrary to what Heidegger asserts. Heidegger's critique of Christianity—which Falque does not subscribe to but which remains useful nonetheless—is of a triple nature with regard to Christianity's impossibility of thinking finitude. Because, for Heidegger, the infinite preexists what the Christian tries to offer on the question of finitude. We are left with certain conclusions: a) It is impossible for a believer to live fully the anguish of death because this anguish is exceeded by salvation. b) The believer is incapable of asking the question why since he is preordained with a certain response before any real questioning. c) The believer lives a "poor" temporality not from this world but beyond it from eternity.

As for Falque's dialogue with Henri de Lubac, it must be read in continuity with the criticisms and uses of Heidegger. It will also reinforce the importance of finitude through a careful reflection of what the theologian posits on the relationship between nature and grace, on the "desire for God" present in man. More than this, we will find a firm clarification on Falque's views of atheism, as an "existential a priori," like that of Lubac.[7]

---

6. Cited in Falque, *God, the Flesh, and the Other*, 12. Also, see Heidegger, *Duns Scotus's Doctrine of Categories and Meaning*.

7. See Lubac, *Drama of Atheistic Humanism*.

The Finitude of Dasein

To understand Falque's position, we must recall some characteristic features of Heideggerian finitude. Heidegger's interpretation of finitude provides the initial conditions for Falque to specify the nature of finitude as that experienced by the human being, namely, Dasein. It must be described independently of any reference to the infinite or, from a more theological perspective, namely, sin. Finitude does not designate "a limited horizon of human existence."[8] "We must therefore be careful not to confuse the 'finite being' with one who 'lives in finitude.' The former (the finite) requires reference to another—the Infinite—of which he or she regrets being simply a limitation and desires afresh some kind of infinity (conceivable, as we shall see, by the act of the Resurrection rather than by the Creation). The latter (finitude) is happy simply with 'Being-there,' facing death and definitively anchored in an existence that is devoid, at least to begin with, of an elsewhere."[9] The finite must not be considered, as is often the case in theology, from the infinite (the opposite of degradation), and therefore in a depreciative way, but in a much more neutral mode, that simply of the state of the human being living in the world. This conception of finitude is held by our contemporary world, which experiences finitude independently of any implicit or explicit reference to an infinite being, God.

Therefore, the finitude of the human being is in no way caused by sin, even though, for Falque, sin will always be related to a way of experiencing this finitude (i.e., self-closure on oneself and on one's own death). Echoing Heidegger on the being of Dasein, it "must not be conceived as a 'naïve joy of self-abandonment.'"[10] The philosopher, like the theologian, must remain with the description of "the ordinary run of mortals (experiencing the anguish of their Being-there)."[11] This is in fact the first experience that we have of believers and unbelievers alike; moreover, it comes with an "anxiety about being mortal, independently of my value judgment as to the good—or evil—basis of such mortality."[12] Finitude reflects both facticity and anxiety.

---

8. Falque, *Guide to Gethsemane*, 12, 16.
9. Falque, *Guide to Gethsemane*, 16.
10. Falque, *Guide to Gethsemane*, 19.
11. Falque, *Guide to Gethsemane*, 19.
12. Falque, *Guide to Gethsemane*, 17.

We must therefore think about the finitude of "being there," that is, from its contingency in an original horizon of the world as it is. The use of the term of Dasein (being-there) clearly indicates the character of being "thrown there" which defines an original mode of being. But unlike the objects which surround it and which are content to subsist, Dasein is concerned with itself, it has "to be." As Heidegger writes: "The 'essence' [*Wesen*] of this entity lies in its 'to be' [*Zu-sein*]. Its Being-what-it-is [*Was-sein*] (*essentia*) must, so far as we can speak of it at all, be conceived in terms of its Being (*existentia*)."[13] The being of Dasein is its concern, and this concern harmonizes together facticity (being thrown), existence (projection) and "descendance." Dasein is tossed away, it is not brought by itself into its "being there." It is not in a world that exists without it, but truly within the world. It is its own presence that gives presence to things. It is this being that "is there," and from there the world appears. This process of disclosure of the world is played out in and by finitude.

To be sure, Dasein can live this experience of finitude inauthentically, that is, by existing in a mode that does not correspond to the way "to be." This failure mirrors a comparable attitude of dejection that we find in Pascalian amusement. This ejection from authenticity is further rendered in Heidegger by the experience of fallenness, of the "tumble" where Dasein falls, as it were, outside of itself, and thus ceases to be "in" the world. The *existentialities* of chatter, of curiosity, and of equivocation translate into a flight from and closing off of the world. Dasein renounces what it is and its possibilities, to take refuge in the world of "we," of public opinion or of the dominant ideology. This description of decline is not a fall of a human being who had previously known a golden age, however philosophically and theologically determined. We cannot know this human being other than within an anguished and confused finitude. Man does not experience horizons of finitude in a neutral way. It is experienced in the mode of "facticity," feeling the weight of horizons. Indeed, man often experiences it in the mode of anguish and its most radical form, death. The only absolute certainty we have about the future of our existence is, in fact, that of our death. According to the well-known Heideggerian formulation, Dasein is a "being for death" or "a being towards death." Put more ironically, as soon as a man is born, he is old enough to die.[14]

---

13. See Heidegger, *Being and Time*, 67.
14. See Heidegger, *Being and Time*, 23–25.

To further clarify this peculiar condition of man, Heidegger amplifies the anxiety of death with another more fundamental feeling: the fear of death is also the fear of the interruption of my life in this world. This presupposes, in a certain way, a knowledge of the object, for fear is the result of a specific object. Fear can be shared by others, who each seek to retreat from the same fear. Anxiety does not apprehend the object it fears, and therefore it cannot be shared by others. To be sure, it can implicate the entirety of my existence, as it necessarily leads me to question the meaning of my existence. There, death, from this point of view, does not represent the end of life, but a constitutive component of our way of living. The anguish of death should not be confused with the fear of dying but, linked to the feeling of our radical finitude, it reverberates and shocks our present existence—always caught within its horizon. This way of living with and in anguish is specific to the human condition for which we, as a species, are compelled to confront. In light of this description of anxiety, we understand why Dasein seeks to escape anxiety by living its condition in an inauthentic way, by taking refuge in a concern which has the form of mere amusement.

From this Heideggerian analysis, Falque maintains that these dimensions of the human condition necessarily constitute the first word of lived experience. "Only what is assumed will be truly saved," according to Gregory of Nazianzus. But it must be applied first to the human itself, which, if it is to be metamorphosized, it must be recognized in the kind of finitude that constitutes it. Returning to Heidegger's influence, Falque recalls the famous formulation of Michel Foucault: "Our culture has crossed the threshold from which we acknowledge our modernity on that day when finitude came to be thought of as an interminable self-reference."[15] From there, Falque identifies the three essential traits of finitude: insurmountable immanence, finite temporality, and the possible depth of man without God.

Heidegger is content with describing the human condition in his own way. He avers that any religious or theological thought is incapable of truly thinking about this finitude and the experience of anguish that inhabits it. The horizon of the infinite, of eternal life, prevents the believer from truly understanding the nature of the infinite that dissipates in the existence of the believer all existential and authentic anguish. As we have just seen, the latter would fall under the accusation of leading an

---

15. Falque, *Metamorphosis of Finitude*, 14. This quotation stems from the original French text; see Foucault, *Mots et choses*, 323–29.

"inauthentic" existence that seeks to evade the fullness of finitude. The challenge we face is clear. Falque retains the Heideggerian intuition but confronts it with the representations of the Christian and their existential ways of being. Therefore, he tries to establish, contrary to what Heidegger claims, that believers fully assume, or should assume, the facticity of human finitude. It is on this sole condition that a metamorphosis may appear credible. Such a commitment will also be able, at least initially, to bear witness to the anthropological fertility of Christianity, especially on the question of immanence.

It should also be noted that this enterprise remains within a context of paradox. The privilege that many see with regard to the older Christian conceptions of anguish, suffering, and death that ultimately lead to a cultlike mentality of sadness, weakness, renunciation, resentment, and even complacency with regard to misfortune, is now taken up in modern thought. "In particular, meditation upon anxiety, as well as upon lack of suffering, once considered typically Christian and opposed to the impassive ideal of philosophy, has emerged as a key topic in modern and contemporary philosophy, from Hegel and Kierkegaard to Heidegger, Sartre, and Camus."[16] The same philosophy that at one point denounced a complacent mode of existence in Christianity proclaims today its positive influence. What we witness, here, is in fact not a denunciation of Christianity per se, but a betrayal of the inability to think about the full reality of immanence.

Falque's response to Heidegger must therefore be located on different theoretical and existential registers: that of Christian dogmatics and that of the behavior of the believer. Falque clearly recognizes the challenges of the Christian consciousness to think about the finitude of immanence without immediately relating it to transcendence. "The believer, however, doesn't just give up. Today, as yesterday, he affirms that his God is 'already there' in the world, even though he has no immediate experience of God."[17] But on a theoretical level, it must be remembered that Christianity does not really seek to face death, unlike the Greek philosophers. "As opposed to Greeks such as Socrates, Epicurus, or Epictetus, the Bible already symbolically sets up, on different grounds, a universal 'dread of the day of death' that weighs on all the children of humankind."[18] Does the

16. Falque, *Guide to Gethsemane*, 1. Here, Falque also draws on Thévenaz, *Homme et sa raison*, 287–307.
17. Falque, *Metamorphosis of Finitude*, 14.
18. Falque, *Guide to Gethsemane*, 8.

Bible look "death in the face"?[19] Certain philosophical conceptions from Christianity, such as Pelagianism and Origenism, remain mere forms of the concealment of death.[20]

The crux of the Falquian argument lies, as we will see, in the teachings and example of Christ. To accept Falque's understanding of finitude we must recognize its presuppositions from the incarnation of Christ. This incarnation is more than a means of redemption for sin; it embodies a solidarity with the human condition at large. It is, moreover, reinforced in the experience of Christ who, far from adopting a heroic attitude, chose to experience fear, the anguish of death, and despair. Falque's method is suggestive. It also leaves us with lingering questions. It is true that within philosophy and theology we may approach, at any time, the same object. In this regard, Falque may elect to be a philosopher first. With a progressive awareness for the nature of his enterprise, he chooses to engage the truly philosophical—as seen in the *The Metamorphosis of Finitude*—in and against the manner of Heidegger. However, to fully confront what Heidegger says, it is equally necessary to utilize the example of Christ. Here, we arrive at the importance of Henri de Lubac.

Atheism and the Desire for God

Henri de Lubac is one of the most important French theologians of the twentieth century. He is known, on the one hand, for his contrasting views against his theological superiors on church teaching. On the other hand, and perhaps central to the point, is that Lubac introduced two central themes to modern theological discourse: the existence of a "natural desire for God," and the status of "atheistic humanism" which he describes particularly as a "drama."

In *The Metamorphosis of Finitude*, Falque gives certain indications on the conduct that a believing philosopher may take against atheism. Specifically, he tries to locate positive dimensions in order to radicalize and recognize our understanding of immanence. On this point, he enters into dialogue with Lubac, who in *The Drama of Atheist Humanism*, opposes three humanisms (i.e., positivist, Marxist, and Nietzschean) to Christian humanism. His goal is to denounce the bankruptcy of atheistic humanism, which he refers to as "an inhuman humanism." As Lubac

---

19. Falque, *Guide to Gethsemane*, 10, 17.
20. See Falque, *Guide to Gethsemane*, 8–9.

observes: "Atheistic humanism was bound to end in bankruptcy. Man is himself only because his face is illumined by a divine ray."[21] Falque recognizes the positive role played by Henri de Lubac, in his time, for allowing certain believers to discover the thoughts of modern authors as well as to measure the stakes that it poses for Christianity. In this manner, Falque suggests that we should reread Lubac, following Jean-Yves Lacoste, from the horizon of the natural itself. (We will return to this later.) For now, let us recognize that the times have changed since Lubac's original context from more than half a century ago; the problems and issues that shaped Lubac are no longer the same as our own today. We cannot simply begin with the progress of yesterday. For Falque, it is a question of extending the dialogue with Lubac and transforming it into a new concern for a new kind of atheism.

Atheism must, first and foremost, be evaluated by its radicality. According to Falque, the God who died cannot simply be the moral God—a "conceptual idol"—whom we can oppose nor Christ the "icon" of the God who died on the cross—an "unsurpassable" figure called to resurrection. This evokes a recovery death as "an encounter with the divine."[22] Moreover, for our contemporaries, it is God the Father who is dead, and not simply the Son. "In other words, and theologically speaking this time, the definitive agony of God 'remaining dead' points less to the death of the Son resurrected by the Father than to the death of the Father and of his supposed power of resurrection."[23] If atheism must be thought of in its radicality, it is as a result of its contemporary form. Evoking Merleau-Ponty, Falque reminds us that nontheological thought is not necessarily an a-theological denial of God. Moreover, atheism today leads less to denying God, a combat against the persistence of sacramental representation, and more to an attitude of quiet indifference. This is the new way of atheism: "We need to dare to see differently a new mode of being of atheism (the surpassing and the relinquishing of God, rather than a combat with God)."[24]

These considerations form the basis of the real attitude of atheism: an a-combative but confrontational model only to the extent where it risks a believer's way of being, that is, as participating in infinite being. This is the dominant posture of our contemporaries. It constitutes a sort

---

21. Lubac, *Drama of Atheist Humanism*, 31.
22. Falque, *Metamorphosis of Finitude*, 31.
23. Falque, *Metamorphosis of Finitude*, 32.
24. Falque, *Metamorphosis of Finitude*, 35.

of existential a priori. Certainly, it will be a good thing for the believing philosopher, as John Paul II recommends and Falque echoes, "to appeal to a grammar in common is an invitation, proffered to the Christian, of a real comprehension of what there is in this new atheism, an atheism that is less virulent than coherent in its foundations."[25] This is the task before us. Falque continues: "It is a challenge not to destroy this atheism but to learn from it, avoiding definitively this time seeing it only through Christian eyes, and thus condemning it de facto as a 'drama.' ... The supposed certitude of Christianity as a stance of belief for many Christians corresponds then to the no less striking obviousness of atheism, as an existential stance, for many of our contemporaries. The legitimacy of one (the believer) cannot be said to hold the field at the price of a condemnation of the other (the atheist)."[26]

Such a program deserves multiple comments. First, it reveals the basis of the recognition of the thickness of man's existence without God. Faith must not be made the exclusive norm of all truth, in the sense that it would immediately condemn any other way to be or to think. The unbeliever can therefore reach a truth and the believer himself must recognize this common trait of humanity. It is, indeed, what makes dialogue possible at all. Here, we find that finitude is recognized in its universal positivity. Atheism remains an existential a priori in the manner following Bonhoeffer. Does not the believer himself sometimes experience "etsi Deus non daretur" (as if God were not given to us)? This is the precondition for fully experiencing one's humanity. Man, so it is said, has "come of age," and "no longer needs" God. He may very well live a nonreligious relationship with the world. Following Bonhoeffer, this idea of God does not compel us to live with him. On the contrary, God welcomes that we live without him. The God who is with us is the one who has given up.[27] Bonhoeffer does not speak of atheism, but a connection is possible with regard to Falque's approach, namely: "If philosophy is 'fundamentally atheist,' in that it questions the strictly finite modalities of our Being-there (Heidegger), it is in such a position that the believer also must find himself or herself, with the proviso that one accepts, at least from a heuristic point of view, that we come to picture for ourselves first of all

---

25. Falque, *Metamorphosis of Finitude*, 34–41. Also, see John Paul II, "Discours du samedi 30 octobre 1999 aux évêques du Canada," 2.

26. Falque, *Metamorphosis of Finitude*, 33–34.

27. See Bonhoeffer, *Letters and Papers from Prison*, 229, 479.

simply the incarnation of a man rather than the image of a God."[28] Before seeking to live "his aspiration to divinity," he must assume first "his most shared humanity."[29]

For me, it is not certain if Falque would take up all the proposals of Bonhoeffer, but there is certainly no question of his scrutiny of the bankruptcy at work in the "drama of atheistic humanism." It is possible that we can be fully human without being a believer; Christianity passes through humanity and God, even if many would reduce it only to God. Assuming finitude this way also admits that an authentic humanism can exist independently of a reference to God, even if Christian humanism consists not in liberating man but rather to incorporate and transform it into the Trinity. It equally recognizes that man, in living out his humanity, may be called by Christ to surpass it; this is the work of God in its Trinitarian dimension.

Another debate with Lubac must be mentioned regarding the status of a natural desire for God. An age-old problem, which Lubac sought to update in his time, concerns the relationship between nature and grace. On this front, the publication of *The Mystery of Supernatural* aroused much controversy and earned him strong criticism by the church.[30] For Lubac, while man could not think of a true autonomous humanism without God, the desire of God remains inscribed in man by the very fact that he was created in the image of God. The human mind is ordered to a divine source thanks to this natural desire of God. Lubac thus opposed the thesis of a "pure nature," the opposite of the supernatural, which aimed to emphasize the gratuity of grace. Here, the debate thickens. The desire for God is paradoxical because it could testify to an original presence of God in man that would thus risk denying the gratuity of God's grace. (This was in fact the very criticism waged in the encyclical.) Lubac defended himself by claiming to maintain the freedom of the gift of God, without which man could not be called to be with or see God. Lubac's essential concern was to open up the dimensions of the human condition in a mode of divine saving grace, an experience immanent in man and gifted by the divine. The theory of "pure nature," in contrast, had the advantage of defending an anthropological and rationalistic conception, however separated from any historical grounding of the supernatural. Rather than protecting the supernatural from contamination, it had, in

28. Falque, *Metamorphosis of Finitude*, 13–14.
29. Falque, *Metamorphosis of Finitude*, 14.
30. See Lubac, *Mystery of the Supernatural*.

fact, undermined its living spirit in social life, making it vulnerable to the forces of secularism.[31] This assertion by Lubac, though pivotal in its time, was a debate that is no longer current. We, therefore, will not comment on the relevance of criticisms against Lubac but rather the Jesuit theologian's inspiration in clarifying the Falquian conception of finitude.

Without radically opposing Lubac, and moving past any erroneous readings of him, Falque tries to distinguish himself above all from the central objective pursued by Lubac. How, on the one hand, can we "dogmatically" or "didactically" deny the existence of such a desire, if man is indeed God's creature? How, on the other hand, can we not recognize "heuristically" and from the point of view of experience, our finitude? Falque thus takes up the famous Thomistic adage, "Grace does not destroy nature, but perfects it."[32] Yet, he adds: "by transforming it." From this point of view, the idea of a "pure nature" is heresy, yet the aspiration to the supernatural is also not an immediate given. Falque contends that the "desire for God" is not experienced from the outset, in man's condition of finitude. In the light of faith, "didactically," we can wager that its existence will be satisfied at its completion, namely, its transformation. However, "heuristically," this desire is not felt immediately. God is not first known in his essence, not simply because of his infinity but because we are always *in via*, as the saying from Aquinas goes.

To clarify his position, Falque takes up Jean-Yves Lacoste alongside Lubac: "The consciousness of desire does not necessarily belong to the propensity to desire itself. . . . To be sure, the object of desire is always written on the heart of desire itself, but the desirer's consciousness of his desire is never such that he cannot confess it."[33] In other words, it is God who comes to us and makes us discover him. It is the supernatural that is inscribed in nature. Desire for God is put in me by God himself. Man, alone, would have neither reason nor power to overcome these presumably blocked horizons. Falque, for his part, does not take over the position of Maurice Blondel: "Everything within us and outside of us only requires the necessary One."[34] This evidence of the divine absolute alone cannot satisfy us. It is rather as a philosopher that Falque faces the theologian. He is like Deleuze, who recognized the fundamental importance of desire

---

31. See "The Paradox Unknown to the Gentiles," in Lubac, *Mystery of the Supernatural*.

32. Falque, *Metamorphosis of Finitude*, 7.

33. Falque, *Loving Struggle*, 206.

34. Cited by Forte, *À l'écoute de l'autre*, 112.

and who refused to see it as an aspiration to the absolute, a supernatural dimension of man. For Falque, it is necessary that we question our Christian presuppositions to reach "man in general." Yet, to be sure, metamorphosis is only made possible by God himself. It is not nature which opens onto the supernatural but the supernatural which opens onto nature. We must maintain this essential distinction between the "heuristic point of view" which philosophically accounts for the experience of man, and the "didactic point of view," found in theology which illuminates based on revelation.[35] This is where we are confronted with a deep question. To presuppose a desire for God as though it should be experienced by every man, is this not both denying the depth of our humanity and making God inaccessible and unintelligible to our contemporaries?

Thus defined, the idea of a supernatural desire is not contradictory with the description of Heideggerian facticity. The Falquian analysis takes its point of departure from the simple worldliness of man. The theological affirmation of the desire for the supernatural, relating to the "didactic," is supposed to enable us to move with the Heideggerian hermeneutics of facticity and thus amplify the domain of the "heuristic." Because: "What appeared to be intrinsically correct from a didactic point of view (that human beings were created by God and are naturally open to God) is, however, not satisfactory to us from a heuristic point of view (which would emphasize our experience of the closure of the world and of our own existence)."[36] We must remain with philosophy; remain with Heidegger; and remain with a priori atheism. A man without God is not synonymous with a man against God. Perhaps there is a connection to the *Odyssey*? It is because Ulysses decides to remain deaf to the songs of the Sirens that he voluntarily takes the difficult task to continue his journey. Falque, as has already been said and as we will have the opportunity to further explore, will accept to actually be a theologian, unlike Ricœur. Of course, this task imposes on him a risky method.

For now, allow me to conclude by saying that in this dialogue with Lubac and through the reflections on atheism as well as "the desire for God," the place of finitude remains steadfast. The philosophical analysis of finitude, according to Falque, intends to disclose "man in general." The approach, so far as we have seen, highlights the productive means

---

35. Falque, *Metamorphosis of Finitude*, 15.
36. Falque, *Metamorphosis of Finitude*, 15–16.

to recognize a true humanism independent of any religious reference. It does this by granting the status of an existential a priori.

Finitude and the Theological Limit

In the background of the theological debate with Lubac, Falque draws on more resources to legitimize his philosophical approach. He not only draws on a study of man (philosophy) but also on an analysis of the word of God (theology). Moreover, he seeks the grammar and language to describe this God as revealed in the Scriptures. The theological status of finitude, which ultimately seeks transformation, is highlighted by Falque in the work of Aquinas. Let us recall that medieval thought is one of the decisive determinations of a reflection on finitude. As Edith Stein recognized: "At our goal, both what we know *in via* [on our earthly journey] and what we take on faith *in via*, we know in another way. The possible extent of our knowledge *during our pilgrimage on earth* is fixed; we cannot *shift its limits*."[37] As Falque further specifies, we will therefore have to resolve that God is not, in the words of Aquinas, "for us the first object known."[38] Falque has, in fact, devoted a very detailed text to this relationship between Aquinas and phenomenology, entitled "Saint Thomas Aquinas and the Entrance of God into Philosophy."[39] In it, he aims to show the analogies which can exist between Thomism and certain positions within contemporary phenomenology. Aquinas's distinction between man *in via* and man *in patria* is described as "one of those major epistemological ruptures in the history of thought."[40] The theologian of transcendence, Aquinas can also be read as a philosopher of immanence. This particular conception of man, unlike contemporary thought, never excludes the divine reference: it is precisely in the creative project of God that we find finitude inscribed into the human condition of the creature. It is God himself who desires to create man. Where Heidegger calls it a

---

37. "La phénoménologie de Husserl et la philosophie de Saint Thomas d'Aquin (1929)," in Stein, *Phénoménologie et philosophie chrétienne*, 34; cited in the original French text: Falque, "Limite théologique et finitude phénoménologique chez Thomas d'Aquin," 527, 529. This essay is now translated in Falque, *Saint Bonaventure and the Entrance of God into Theology*, 219–57; the translation of Stein's statement is found on p. 225.

38. Falque, *Saint Bonaventure and the Entrance of God into Theology*, 225.

39. See Falque, *Saint Bonaventure and the Entrance of God into Theology*, 219–57.

40. Falque, *Saint Bonaventure and the Entrance of God into Theology*, 226.

"standstill," Aquinas refers to it as a "desire." This should not be confused with any kind of resignation or pessimism. Rather, it concerns how we as human beings refuse to sit in one state and be called upon to be transformed. Is it not so?

Respecting the "limit" is an essential component of Thomist thought. We remain limited even in the beatific vision. At the same time, living with God does not mean a denial of our nature. Nature is transformed but never suppressed. We do not become like God but fully human before God. God wanted the original man to be unique; indeed, to inscribe the human with a fundamental difference reflects the condition of love. This is precisely the reason why Falque will prefer to the formulation of the "divinization of man" that of the "humanization of the divine." It is this particular humanization of the divine that will allow us to speak of humanism with regard to Christianity. As we will see, it will also bring out its specificity at work in Trinitarian love between Father and Son.

Falque recognizes that Aquinas, like Heidegger, takes seriously the finitude of man through the fact of death. "God cannot be seen in his essence by a mere human being . . . *except that he be separated from his mortal life (nisi ab hac vita mortali separetur)*. But our soul, *as long as we live in this life (quandiu in hac vita vivimus)*, has its being in corporeal matter. . . . It is not possible, therefore, that the soul *in this mortal life (quandiu hac mortali viva vivitur)* should be raised up the supreme of intelligible objects, i.e., to the divine essence."[41] Death is certainly not the last word in Aquinas, but it clearly reveals the condition of the finite in the human being. If he cannot manage to grasp his essence, it is less because of the unintelligible character of God and more because of its nature of being finite. Moreover, we must not grab it too soon. We must be ever patient and ever present.

This necessary patience is illuminated by the distinctions in vocabulary that Falque finds in Aquinas and Bonaventure. As Falque writes, it all concerns the "starting point."[42] In other words, the "way" is at first glance a "state" that later appears as a "path" (*itinerarium*), a path which may reflect a "too immediate desire" to leave the condition of man here below. The lesson seems to be clear in that we ought to accept "the detour."[43] Drawing on his doctoral thesis, "Saint Bonaventure and the Entrance

---

41. Cited in Falque, *Saint Bonaventure and the Entrance of God into Theology*, 226–27. Also, see Thomas Aquinas, *Summa Theologica* Ia q. 12.

42. Falque, *Saint Bonaventure and the Entrance of God into Theology*, 220.

43. Falque, *Saint Bonaventure and the Entrance of God into Theology*, 229.

of God into Theology," Falque recognizes the need for a counterpoint through Aquinas as the entry of God into philosophy. In doing so, he distinguishes "the unthought decision for a primacy of the absolute (more Bonaventurian) over necessarily maintaining the point of departure in finitude (more Thomistic)."[44] Aquinas, who seeks to reconcile faith and reason, theology and philosophy, recognizes the concept of time in philosophy and the detours that it can come to embody. Indeed, in terms of the doctrine of philosophy, we study created beings in themselves and, from there, we make our way to "a knowledge of God," where we find an approach that appears to oppose "the doctrine of faith." In philosophy, creatures come first in order to consider them "in themselves."[45]

But if we limit ourselves to a prolonged attention to finitude, one could say that this leads to an impoverished and severed nature. Philosophically, it is a function of the limits of human knowledge, which prohibits any direct access to God. But, can we contend that it is also theological? Even if Aquinas does not question the existence of this God, he works to connect the condition of "being finite" to a desired state of being human in the presence of God. Aquinas, as we have pointed out, is distinguished from Heidegger in the sense that, for Heidegger, the limit is constituted by man, whereas for Aquinas, the limit is actually willed by God and is *not* the consequence of sin. God's desire is first and foremost that we be human. To refuse the limit is, according to Falque, to fall under sin, that is, the absence of our being human. The limit is experienced as a limitation to the extent that we want to be unlimited and thus deny our creature status. This is perhaps the tragedy of the human condition. The possibility of transforming it may be offered to us, but only through the incarnation of Christ. For Aquinas, as for Heidegger, limits of finitude are not the consequence of a fall and sin. They are a constructive desire from God.

Falque's familiarity with medieval thought is extended to another thinker, Duns Scotus. As evidenced in *God, the Flesh, and the Other*, Falque urges for a return to those discourses that recognize the absence of the finite in the infinite. We can see in Duns Scotus a rupture of metaphysics and the theological that requires not the rejection of a natural desire of God as his most natural end, but only the refusal of access to God starting from our nature alone: "I admit that God is the natural end of

---

44. Falque, *Saint Bonaventure and the Entrance of God into Theology*, 236.
45. Falque, *Saint Bonaventure and the Entrance of God into Theology*, 236–41.

man [*concedo Deum finem naturalem hominis*]," says Duns Scotus in the *Ordinatio*, "but this end is not attained naturally, but rather supernaturally [*sed non naturaliter adipiscendum sed supernaturaliter*]."[46] Therefore: "The interdict made by philosophy only reinforces the theological."[47] Access by consideration of our nature alone does not reach the supernatural.

This analysis of finitude, in theological terms, is enriching in more ways than one. On a general level, it demonstrates an important dimension in the Falquian approach: philosophy and theology can work towards the same objects. More specifically, we can locate a movement from philosophy to theology on the question of desire. The legitimacy of such a concept, however theological on the surface, equally recognizes the importance for beginning with and relying on philosophy. In a sense, we are witnessing a kind of reciprocal legitimation. Phenomenological finitude and theological limits are also recognized as positive corollaries. If phenomenological finitude is taken to be the starting point, even the anchoring of immanence, it is at the same time the starting point of a moment in which "we paradoxically fulfill our Creator's desire for the limit." Moreover: "Far from any 'angelism,' we are first caught in our 'humanism,'—not as some current to be overcome or as an era to address, but because 'pure and simple' humanity (*ab homine puro*) is primarily that in which our creatureliness consists. God's desire is there first, and paradoxically, that we 'remain men' and thereby faithful also to his project of creation.'"[48]

SECTION TWO: FINITUDE PUT ON THE CROSS

The necessity and obligation for man to remain in finitude—and its very limit—corresponds to the will and decision of God to appear as an incarnation. This mode of appearing is highlighted by the same method used to analyze human finitude in phenomenology. In the words of Marion, we must "read phenomenologically the events of revelation recorded in the Scriptures, in particular in the New Testament."[49]

The application of the phenomenological method makes it possible to put the specificity of the teaching of revelation en rapport with finitude,

---

46. Falque, *God, the Flesh, and the Other*, 261.
47. Falque, *God, the Flesh, and the Other*, 261.
48. Falque, *Saint Bonaventure and the Entrance of God into Theology*, 246.
49. Marion, *In Excess*, 29.

through the very thematization of the incarnation. In this regard, Falque often echoes Mark the Ascetic: "The Word became flesh as well as the flesh becomes Word."[50] The famous distinction of phenomenology, to which we will return, between the material body as objective (*Körper*), and the lived body as subjective (*Leib*), is particularly illuminating. The living Christ for his part, like every person, holds this double reality. His experience, "Word made flesh" as the Scriptures tell us, represents more than a transition to mere matter. It becomes organic body. This is the case, first of all, in its "incorporation" (*Verköperung*), that of a "becoming-body," and, second, in its "becoming-man" (*Menschwerdung*), "an 'enfleshment' which constitutes him in his own right, even in the pure adequacy of himself to the mode of being of his corporeality alone." Here, Falque draws from a suggestive passage from Tertullian regarding Christ's "ordinary corporeity," in which his flesh evokes a truly human reality of this world: "muscles [*musculos*] similar to mounds of dirt, bones [*ossa*] similar to rocks and even hillocks and gravel, the interlacing of nerves [*nervorum tenaces conexus*] like forking roots, the branching networks of veins [*venarum ramosos*] like winding streams, the downy fuzz [*lanuguines*] like moss, hair [*comam*] like grass, and the hidden treasure of marrow [*medullarum in abdito thesarus*] like the ores of the flesh [*ut metalla carnis*]."[51] Against gnostic excesses, Tertullian poses that life is only given in a body, moreover, that there is no "flesh without body." Such an observation implies the same truth for Christ too.[52]

However, for Tertullian, as for Husserl, Falque remarks that the body becomes "flesh" since "it is aware—or better yet—feels."[53] Moreover, writes Falque: "One would be wrong to see in this 'terrestrial origin' (*terrenae originis*) of all flesh—and therefore in Chris as well (*et in Christo fuerent*)—only the naive portrait of a simple reified metaphor of human corporeity. The composition of the body in muscles, bone, nerves, veins, and so on corresponds to the living and moving and gestating earth (mounds of dirt, rocks with gravel, forking roots, winding streams, etc.)."[54] Christ has hunger and feels thirst. These kinesthetic experiences reveal to Christ his own flesh (*Leiblichkeit*) and not simply his corporeality (*Körperlichkeit*). In this

50. Falque, *Guide to Gethsemane*, 82–83.
51. Falque, *God, the Flesh, and the Other*, 155, 156.
52. And, on this topic, we find a disagreement between Falque and Michel Henry; see "Is There a Flesh with Body" in Falque, *Loving Struggle*, 143–73.
53. Falque, *God, the Flesh, and the Other*, 156.
54. Falque, *God, the Flesh, and the Other*, 155.

incorporation, this "carnality," a double experience of finitude and body come into being. "To put this another way, and this time in the context of theological studies, Christ is revealed to us first of all as 'Son of Man' in that he himself experiences 'in his flesh' (*leiblich*), the same as we ourselves could live through and experience as the world on the basis of our own individual flesh: seeing, talking, hearing, feeding, healing, weeping."[55]

In this description of Christ, which shows to what extent he assumes the dimensions of human finitude, the experiences of suffering and death—of "passion"—is essential. Heidegger's analysis is decisive for Falque. Thus, considering an Heideggerian approach, we may distinguish three stages in *The Guide to Gethsemane*: the fear of dying, the anguish before death, and "the hand-to-hand combat of suffering and death." The distinction between the fear of dying and the anxiety of death is particularly significant: "Fear of decease—which goes from life to death—remains above all psychological (psychoanalysis speaks in this respect of the death drive), while anxiety about death—which reaches back from death toward life—allows an experience that will above all be metaphysical to emerge."[56] Christ lived this double experience of fear and anguish. "He took with him Peter, James, and John, and began to be troubled and distressed [*ekhambeisthai*], and deeply troubled and depressed [*adêmonein*]."[57] In experiencing "fear" at Gethsemane, he also gradually entered into deep anguish which, as a result, tells us something about the nature of his death. It is a death very much within finitude.

"The Fear of Dying"

A question poses itself. Does Christ's incarnation consist of all the traits of fear? "Doesn't becoming-man in his being as the Son (*Menschwerdung*—incarnation) have to proceed as a form of drawing back before a finitude that, properly speaking, is not possible for him to take on?"[58] Echoing the famous words of Christ himself, "Abba, Father, if everything is possible for you, remove this wound." Further, Falque drawing on Péguy, affirms: "This Christ once feared to die."[59] He experienced this fear through the

55. Falque, *Guide to Gethsemane*, 92.
56. Falque, *Guide to Gethsemane*, 30.
57. Falque, *Guide to Gethsemane*, 30; also, see Mark 14:33. The French translation used by Falque includes the word *angoisse* (anxiety) as a translation of *adêmonein*.
58. Falque, *Guide to Gethsemane*, 34.
59. Falque, *Guide to Gethsemane*, 34. Also, see Péguy, *Dialogue de l'histoire et l'âme*, 734.

"double feeling he has, both of the vulnerability of his existence and of his being abandoned to himself (*Überlassenheit*),"[60] that is, in the perspective of "the threat that is the punishment of crucifixion inflicted on all political agitators in a Roman province."[61] This is why he seeks to share this fear with his disciples and earnestly calls to his disciples only to discover that Simon is asleep![62]

Falque's description of human finitude, through the fear of death assumed by Christ, corresponds to Heidegger's position. Heidegger, according to Falque, distinguishes three representations of the end of life (we can also find here a valuable indication of Falque's method of reading other thinkers): disappearance, passage, and completion. The first state refers to the act of disappearing or fading. He who dies, in fact, resigns himself to no longer being there. The second situation presents death as a path that ceases or a road that is blocked. Death, in this regard, is a deviation but one which may also make hope a possibility. The third possibility concerns the one who dies like an artist and, so, completes the painting of his own existence. Faced with these three ways of considering life, three further attitudes emerge: "(1) a resignation in the face of my disappearance, (2) a waiting during this interruption, and (3) a heroism in the accomplishment of death."[63]

If we return to the Gospel texts, we find indications of "the way in which he envisaged the approach of the end—the alarm in his recoil before the cup, the self-abandonment in his sorrow, and the search for help from others before the emerging threat."[64] There, we must be sure to consider a certain question, namely, whether Christ was in a state of ignorance of his situation, or if he had rather given up taking responsibility for his condition altogether by placing it upon the Father. To be sure, we find a textual silence from Christ on the nature of his ending and how to overcome it. This silence has given rise to various interpretations. Three possibilities may thus be considered: either Christ saw himself as the sad resignation of a lamb slain for our sins (and reduced to an expiatory perspective), or he is already in certainty of his resurrection which thus prevents him from experiencing a common death in this world, or last, he heroically longs for the end of his life and, in doing so, foreshadows

60. Falque, *Guide to Gethsemane*, 34.
61. Falque, *Guide to Gethsemane*, 34.
62. Falque, *Guide to Gethsemane*, 35; also, see Mark 14:37–40.
63. Falque, *Guide to Gethsemane*, 36.
64. Falque, *Guide to Gethsemane*, 36.

a "superman." These three interpretations of resignation, certainty, and heroism have often been posed in different forms, but they do not really reflect the finite specificity of the death of Christ. "On the contrary, the death of Christ remains all the more inexhaustible when it is seen first of all as a commonplace and ordinary death."[65] Falque shows how the passion of Christ is unique in its specificity, that is, its capacity to transform the human condition at large. But it is also because Christ fully assumed human finitude through the experience of fear, anguish, and suffering—as first conditions—that this metamorphosis is made possible.

The weight of finitude in the life of Christ beckons us to utilize once again the method of phenomenology. We saw that finitude must be analyzed by the way in which the world (i.e., phenomena) appears to us. Applied to Christ, in particular, it strives to answer the question: How did Christ experience his death? Beyond or below the theological affirmations of the incarnation of God and the kenosis of Christ, we find its truly concrete reality. It shows, in a way, to what extent Christ really experienced this finitude in his existentially grounded flesh. Moreover, it allows us to insist on the greater point of metamorphosis. Christ lived his finitude in a very specific way, namely, that of a God who fully assumed human form. In this first stage, he feels, like any man with a fear of death and the precariousness of his existence; and he seeks to share these moments with others (i.e., his disciples). But he does not seek to overcome this finitude, as man sometimes thinks he can, either in the form of immortality or heroism. Rather, unlike man—and this is the essential message—he knows that he will not be able to overcome finitude without the help of his Father. In some respects, he renounces the desire to evade it all alone, and therefore moves beyond an impossible desire of being, as Nietzsche would have it, "human, all too human."

The Way of Anxiety

If Christ experienced the "fear" of dying, he also experienced this other component of human finitude which is anxiety. In doing so, he reaches into "the depths of his humanity or of all humanity."[66] Here again we may draw from a Heideggerian description in which only certain features are methodologically kept, namely, those susceptible to a theological

---

65. Falque, *Guide to Gethsemane*, 39.
66. Falque, *Guide to Gethsemane*, 39.

interpretation. But, an initial clarification may be necessary. Falque recognizes that Heidegger has clearly identified "a mode of temporality that is particular to 'original Christianity' ... an insurmountable tension between the 'already there' and the 'not yet,' between the first coming of Christ in the flesh and his second coming in glory."[67] For the Christian, it is "concerned with the 'manner of being a Christian before God (*Vollzugzusammenhang mit Gott*)' when the day and hour comes."[68] But Heidegger draws the conclusion that the Christian cannot feel real anguish in the face of death, since it is "always already viewed death together with its interpretation of 'life.'"[69] It is precisely on this point that Falque, as a Christian, but above all as a reader of the Gospels, takes a provocative stand against Heidegger.

The analysis of the passion of Christ shows that Christ did not escape this anguish. On the contrary, he entered into it fully and, from there, transfigured it from the inside. Thus, three characteristics of Heidegger's analysis of anxiety are released from us: its indeterminate character ("anxiety does not know what about which it is anxious"), unlike fear, concerning the "being-in-the-world of man as such"; its extension to all that exists, which makes it an experience of nothingness; last, radical isolation in which the anguished person finds himself immersed.

So, what exactly can we say about the experience of Christ? As Mark 14:33 indicates, he began to be overcome with fear (*ekthambeisthai*) and anguish (*adêmonein*). In this regard, we may "describe here a metaphysical experiment by God in which he shares the extremes of human anxiety in the face of death."[70] Moreover, according to Falque, "to die and be resurrected indeed not only exposes Christ to the meaninglessness of his existence in the face of the reality of his decease (as for a Sartre or a Camus), but also and above all leads him to question whether there is even a possibility of meaning when everything, including himself, plunges into an absence or suspension of meaning rather than into absolute meaninglessness." He thus experiences a real "anxiety of finitude."[71] This is no longer a "fear in the face of one's death" but an "anxiety of his

---

67. Falque, *Guide to Gethsemane*, 41. Also, see Heidegger, *Phenomenology of Religious Life*, 3–42.

68. Falque, *Guide to Gethsemane*, 41. Also, see Romano, "Possible et l'événement (I)," 71–72.

69. Falque, *Guide to Gethsemane*, 44.

70. Falque, *Guide to Gethsemane*, 46.

71. Falque, *Guide to Gethsemane*, 46.

being-in-the-world as such."[72] This is different from certain theological interpretations that speak of anguish against a background of solidarity between Christ and the sinner, and even of a substitution of Christ for the sinner—a Christ who not only dies for us but in our very place. This is not so much a matter of questioning the truth of such conceptions, but rather to note that methodologically they make death a consequence of sin, thus evacuating the thesis of a living Christ in real anguish in the face of death in general. This is an anguish experienced by a man whose finitude is not immediately of a sinful and naturally bound fallenness. Sin, as we will see, will be a way of living finitude.

The indeterminacy of Christ's anguish also lies in the fact that he himself renounces the giving of meaning to his death. As Christ confessed: "If it is possible, let this cup pass from me; yet, not as I will, but as you will."[73] In other words, according to the exact meaning, Christ "no longer knows what he wants," or rather, by relying on the will of another—his Father—he accepts indeterminacy and the radical meaning of his own-most life. The cry of dereliction on Golgotha evokes an "abandonment" by the Father; it testifies to his renunciation of saving his Son. Contemporary theology has commented at length on this "impotence" of God. Falque has been skeptical of such an expression, but he reminds us that it can be best interpreted in relation with human finitude. "The full extremity of His power consists precisely in complying with an original powerlessness. It is such powerlessness that remains always woven into human finitude, with its law of corruptibility to which God himself, right to the end and without ever disposing of it, consents."[74] The entrance of the Son "into Nothing," the second characteristic of anxiety, is confirmed by kenosis. "He who was in condition divine . . . he emptied himself . . . , he lowered himself becoming obedient until death."[75] Christ becomes radically powerless, leaving to his Father and the Holy Spirit the privilege of "power" and thus fully experiences the absence of meaning from all beings, to use an Heideggerian terminology. The whole of creation bends to the law of finitude.

The profound isolation that anxiety generates is expressed by the feeling of abandonment encapsulated in the cry of the Son to the Father on Golgotha. Yet, Falque's interpretation differs from that of Rilke

---

72. Falque, *Guide to Gethsemane*, 46.
73. Falque, *Guide to Gethsemane*, 48. Also, see Matt 26:39.
74. Falque, *Guide to Gethsemane*, 52.
75. Falque, *Guide to Gethsemane*, 52–53. Also, see Phil 2:6–8.

or Moltmann, who see it as an ultimate form of abandonment of Christ, first abandoned by men and now also by his Father. The last words of Christ on the cross invalidates such an interpretation: "Father, into your hands I commend my spirit."[76] Perhaps the isolation was Christ's doing. The real question today concerns how far "will humanity go in its own rejection of God as he is in Jesus?"[77] It is, therefore, through the words of Christ that we find the assumption of his human finitude, that is, in his rejection toward God.

"Being Towards Death"

After the fear of death, after metaphysical anxiety, we turn to the status of "being towards death," the central object of Falque's confrontation with Heidegger. The latter distinguishes three characteristic features of this being towards death. Death is first and foremost a mode of life. Paradoxically, after the "nothing" of anxiety, man experiences the "possibilities" that death offers him. Faced with this, man is not seen as dead per se but as dying. This means that the perspective of death first indicates a way of life. It designates a "current possibility" of my being and no longer just the end of life. This horizon of death requires me, if I want to live in an "authentic" way, to make resolutions regarding my present life. This decision is especially necessary in light of the second specific trait of death, the possibility of annulling all possibilities. As Falque echoes Heidegger, "Death is the possibility of the pure and simple impossibility of *Dasein*."[78] Moreover, Falque writes, "In the light of the permanent possibility of impossibility for my being, I show myself to myself in my manner of living and organizing such an impossible possibility."[79] The third dimension that Heidegger describes is that of the "mineness" of death. "No one can take his death from another."[80] Death designates the most specific possibility of each person: to experience it *particularly*.

In his approach to the experience of Christ, Falque speaks of a total assumption of "the Heideggerian features of death."[81] Christ in fact expe-

---

76. Falque, *Guide to Gethsemane*, 55. Also, see Luke 23:46.
77. Falque, *Guide to Gethsemane*, 55.
78. Falque, *Guide to Gethsemane*, 58. Also, see Heidegger, *Being and Time*, 294.
79. Falque, *Guide to Gethsemane*, 58.
80. Falque, *Guide to Gethsemane*, 58. Also, see Heidegger, *Being and Time*, 284.
81. Falque, *Guide to Gethsemane*, 67.

riences the prospect of his death as "a specific modality" of his existence, refusing to respond to the "when" of the ruin of Jerusalem and the destruction of the temple. Rather, he insists on "how" to behave in the present in order to escape temptation, thus prioritizing "a future that is not simply to come, but possible at any moment—always 'awake and sober.'"[82] He also fully lives the possibility of pure impossibility. In another context, he transforms the corpse of Lazarus as a call to "get up." Finally, he experiences this death as a possibility of his own in a unique relationship with the Father.

But Falque's Christ, though influenced by a Heideggerian approach, assumes the features of death's confrontation in a way that Dasein would not necessarily find authentic. This is explained, in Falque's words, by Heidegger's "neglect of the flesh or of bodiliness in general."[83] This lack also explains, as we will see, why, in the last volume of Falque's triptych, Nietzsche will in some way take Heidegger's path. Such an observation, if it highlights a certain insufficiency of the Heideggerian model, is also significant with regard to the conception of human finitude. Is the lack of control of death within the carnal and corporeal dimensions not the two constitutive traits of man's finitude? A Heideggerian-less Christ is made, from this point of view, even more human in the way of living one's death. Let us add that Christ is not Nietzschean or Promethean in the sense that he would seek to control his life through the resurrection of his death. On the contrary, the human is seen in "the recognition of a bond of free dependence on the Holy Spirit and of filiation with the Father."[84]

The Carnal Dimension of Anxiety

The anxiety of the Son is incarnated in his flesh: "He was in such agony and he prayed so fervently that his sweat became like drops of blood falling on the ground."[85] In light of theology and Scripture, Falque here criticizes Heidegger for "forgetting the flesh," for not taking sufficient account of the incarnation of the anxiety of Christ in his suffering. Christ lives the experience of the passivity of suffering; to "pass" from this world to the Father is, first of all, to "suffer" from this world in its finitude and "not to

---

82. Falque, *Guide to Gethsemane*, 59.
83. Falque, *Guide to Gethsemane*, 67.
84. Falque, *Guide to Gethsemane*, 66.
85. Falque, *Guide to Gethsemane*, 67. Also, see Luke 22:44.

fleeing it in a passage of flight."[86] This weight of the body and its suffering is very true of the passion of Christ, in the sense that we have here the "dead body" which "in these circumstances is to say flesh destined for decomposition (*diaphtoran*) and death (*thanatos*)."[87] It is appropriate "to recognize the total assumption by Christ himself of our corruptible flesh, and at the same time to allow his incarnation to express itself all the way through to its conclusion, even as that is a manifestation of his anxiety and his suffering flesh."[88]

The Gospel stories thus offer a "phenomenology of suffering" which is realized by the fact that the flesh prevails. Christ "resolves ultimately to be nothing but flesh (incarnate and suffering) and silences his speech definitively."[89] In agony, Christ exhibits his suffering through his carnal experience. Suffering always remains silent. No justification is offered. Christ tells us *how* to suffer but never *why* we suffer. This resolution of Christ to the flesh, in conformity to the experience that man has of suffering, brings into focus those distinctions between "I have a body" with "I am my body." It is also evidenced in the transition from "tears of weeping" to "tears of sobbing" which make any distance from oneself impossible and which also reveals the powerlessness of language to articulate the flesh.[90] Through physical suffering, the body offers a silent experience of being. As Balthasar observes, "The word becomes flesh" and it "takes on a way of being that is foreign to speech."[91] In his weeping, Christ fully experiences the excess of suffering. He "breaks down," and offers his suffering in abandonment to his Father.

Because Christ, the "Son of Man," shares the experiences of man as well as of the "Son of God," he passes on to the Father through his flesh the experience of man's suffering. If the Father knows that man suffers, he has not yet undergone the test. This is precisely what brings him in the Trinitarian relationship. There is an abyss, according to Falque, between knowledge and life that does not exclude God. The Father does not experience physical suffering since he is bodiless. But he shares with their experience, which is also that of man, passed to him through his carnal experience. In this regard, we are witnessing a double carnal experience,

---

86. Falque, *Guide to Gethsemane*, 74.
87. Falque, *Guide to Gethsemane*, 81.
88. Falque, *Guide to Gethsemane*, 81.
89. Falque, *Guide to Gethsemane*, 96.
90. Falque, *Guide to Gethsemane*, 99.
91. Balthasar, *Gloire et la Croix*, 124, 132.

between man and God, the Son and the Father. The Son lives both the "corporeality" and the "carnality" of the human condition.

A Radicalized Finitude

This tableau of human finitude, on the one hand, described philosophically by an existential analysis, and, on the other hand, illuminated theologically by a reference to the behavior of Christ, takes its full force by a tension between the two perspectives. This double fertility is confirmed in the last volume of the triptych: *The Wedding Feast of the Lamb*, which we will discuss at greater length when we analyze the Falquian conception of the body and the Eucharist. For now, in our present approach to finitude we must mention that in *The Wedding Feast of the Lamb* corporeality, eros, and animality are components of finitude. They help to newly conceive a carnal dimension that, at the same time, expresses the radicality of a "descent into the abyss." In our contemporary anthropological, philosophical, and artistic mentalities, Falque will not hesitate to speak of a necessary "going beyond." This going beyond will not exclude phenomenology. This is also a serious turning point in Falque's thought.

We can see to what extent the status of finitude (its recognition and its nature) is a determining issue for Falque. The point of focus, at this time, is the descent into the abyss. Moreover, for Falque, this abyss need not be left too soon. It is the new face of finitude full of religious chaos and wandering, not unlike the *sheol*. Philosophically, it would designate a world where the synthesis of sensations would be impossible, something reflected on by Kant, but only to be immediately rejected by him. This abyss would thus be an "existential" (a qualification that Falque prefers to that of unconscious) dimension of man—mute but present, unable to speak on one's experience. It is something entirely obscure.[92] The strength of Christianity is to attest that God, through Christ, shares this condition of obscurity with us.

Falque will thus be led to ask the question of the status of certain phenomena that cannot enter into waking life or language. To realize that, the overcoming of certain principles of phenomenology will be necessary: that of the detours of flesh and body, of the thickening of intentional meaning over chaos, and of passivity over activity. This enterprise

---

92. See Falque, *Wedding Feast of the Lamb*, 1–10.

certainly does not lack ambition. It begins with the recognition of the different faces and qualifications of finitude:

> The abyss makes humankind. It is what humankind is constructed upon: It is what we can never destroy, even if we never recover from it. To borrow a term from the Jewish tradition, there is a *Shéol* (the grave, the pit, the underworld) in humanity. It is not simply a version of the Greek Hades (hell or the abode of the dead), but the etymology of its name points to a "'corruption,' a place of questioning, of interrogation'" (*cheôl*). Chaos, the abyss, the gap, the opening—what Jackson Pollock paints in his work *The Deep*: "A break in the middle of a field of force, something bottomless under the cover of a cloud that immobilizes it." That is what we must now philosophically or, quite simply, humanly try to rediscover.[93]

This is all according to Falque's own terms, which apply to the whole of his enterprise, namely, of the "great crossing" which will later be deployed theologically and philosophically.[94] The term "descent" also warrants comment and will be more evocative of Nietzsche than Heidegger. We will see this "descent" of Christ himself into this abyss, with his full corporeality and animality. There we will locate another anchor of finitude.

SECTION THREE: THE WEIGHT OF LIFE

The Status of Sin

An essential lesson from Falque's reflection on finitude concerns his conception of sin. We can already sense certain aspects of it in light of his conception of human finitude and the importance that he grants them.[95] As such, finitude is in no way the consequence of a fault committed by man. Biological death is not a penalty for sin. Citing Heidegger: the finitude of Dasein is constitutive of its being and "must not be taken as a fall

---

93. Falque, *Wedding Feast of the Lamb*, 6. Also, see "Shéol," in Léon-Dufour, *Dictionnaire du Nouveau Testament*, 62; and Jackson Pollock, *The Deep* (1953), oil on canvas, Centre Pompidou, Paris.

94. Falque, *Wedding Feast of the Lamb*, 6.

95. Note from the translator: For a more recent phenomenological exploration by Falque, see *Hors phénomène*. That text was published by Falque after the original publication of this book, *Thinking God Otherwise*, in French. Also, see Falque, "God Extra-Phenomenal: For a Phenomenology of Holy Saturday."

from a purer and higher primal status."[96] The limit is not the sign of any curse, but a characteristic of the human condition. Falque recalls the determining difference between a "finite being" and the one who "inhabits finitude." The first "requires reference to another—the Infinite—of which he or she regrets being simply a limitation and desires afresh some kind of infinity (conceivable, as we shall see, by the act of the resurrection rather than by the Creation). The latter (finitude) is happy simply with 'Being-there,' facing death and definitively anchored in an existence that is devoid, at least to begin with, of an elsewhere."[97]

This reference helps to clarify the Falquian conception of sin. To commit sin is to refuse the status of "man in general," as a creature experiencing its full humanity; and, we might say, disrupt a certain understanding of Christ in his incarnation and passion. Accepting this limit is to remember that Christ does not come to break our limits. He takes them on and transforms them. We may also consider that this positive connotation of the limit is, at times, not sufficiently taken into account by the believer. It is an essential component of a true contemporary anthropology that seeks to free itself from certain Nietzschean excesses in the desire to always overcome limits. Falque's Christian approach may lead us through that challenge.

Finitude and Providence

This insurmountable character, from the human perspective, of finitude is highlighted in an article by Falque: "Does God Test Us or Must Providence Be Saved?"[98] Starting from a firm belief in the action of God in the world, but also avoiding the contemporary excesses of providentialism, Falque reflects on the meaning of Providence and its impact on human action. We often experience, in a telling way, the mark of our finitude in the experience of evil. We are led to a question of the presence and action of God in our moment of need. The temptation for the believer is to read an action of rescue as an immediate and direct intervention by God in our lives. However, respecting the status of our finitude means, on the contrary, that we must accept that God is not a deus ex machina. There remains, as Aquinas has observed, a certain autonomy in the natural course

---

96. Falque, *Guide to Gethsemane*, 16.
97. Falque, *Guide to Gethsemane*, 16.
98. See Falque, "Dieu nous éprouve-t-il ou faut-il sauver la providence?"

of human affairs. Consequently, a "triple theological drift" is possible on the question of providential intervention: a) "the belief in a watch-making God when an event is answered by our prayers" b) "naive consent to what happens when the event thwarts our aims" c) "the affirmation of an absolute freedom of the divine when we no longer know if what happens still comes from God or elsewhere."[99] We are caught between fideism, fatalism, resignation, or perhaps even an unknowable God.

All these conceptions presuppose a kind of direct or immediate action of God. But "rediscovering the presence of God in all things does not in fact mean identically inserting God into things."[100] We must accept the fact that things do not have immediate meaning in themselves. On the other hand, God can certainly act in such a way as to allow us to find meaning. He does not intervene to modify immediately the laws that govern our finite and contingent world. However, he can enable us to transform our awareness of this unfamiliarity. "There providence is not in the world but only in the way that I interpret the world."[101] It seems that God does not intervene in the objective world but in the subjective consciousness of the world. He operates through our own means for interpreting the world. The God of the Christians, on this point, differs from that of the pagans and the Stoics.

Beyond the theological affirmation, inherited from Aquinas (i.e., secondary causes), we recognize the trace of phenomenology, for which there is no world outside the consciousness of world. "The providential act of God is defined in a certain mode of reading of the world by which God transforms us to combine his own desire and not just ours."[102] Praying to God opens the world. God's response seeks not necessarily to transform natural laws but rather to transform a new means of disclosure within finitude. Thus, "Does God Test Us or Must Providence Be Saved?" ends with the role of the Trinity in this very transformation. It involves the action of the Holy Spirit in allowing us to decipher the world. By virtue of the Bonaventurian adage, according to which "nothing happens in the world that does not first happen in God, apart from sin," we can see that the Father, in his relationship to the Son on the cross, also attests to the same providential relationship to the question of limitations. This

---

99. Falque, "Dieu nous éprouve-t-il ou faut-il sauver la providence?," 75.
100. Falque, "Dieu nous éprouve-t-il ou faut-il sauver la providence?," 71.
101. Falque, "Dieu nous éprouve-t-il ou faut-il sauver la providence?," 85.
102. Falque, "Dieu nous éprouve-t-il ou faut-il sauver la providence?," 75.

is the power of a finite being who recognizes the here and now, and who elects to not disappear before God but disclose the world with him. The human lives with God and, in doing so, finds the transformation of its own vision of the world.

Heidegger and St. Augustine

We initially entered into the study of Falquian finitude through a confrontation with Heidegger. We mentioned the criticisms that he addressed against Christianity. We then saw Falque's response on incarnation and corporeality. It may be useful to once again return to Heidegger. Falque never sought to baptize Heidegger. The break that the German philosopher accomplished with theology at the beginning of his project coheres with his later work. As for Falque's evolution and "turning point," we find a certain resonance with Jean-Yves Lacoste in noticing how Heidegger abandoned atheism in favor of paganism. This, still, was not satisfactory. As Falque writes, "To believe in the 'return of the gods' is not to believe 'in God' in and through an unceasing confession of the 'sacred' and the 'holy.'"[103] Falque considers that the Heideggerian analysis of Dasein is in need of the illumination of the light of faith rather than wrongly assuming, in a contemporary mode, the radical independence of the human subject.

Let us consider this point further. The Falquian approach is distinguished from contemporary philosophy and from Heidegger by their radical and dogmatic closure to transcendence. Heidegger's interpretation, in particular, leaves us with an ambiguity. If Christianity is incapable of thinking finitude a priori, how can modernity conceive of its own way forward? We could certainly try to escape the question as not consequential. But we are reminded of Heidegger's interlocuter, Rudolf Bultmann, who, in his exegetical and hermeneutical approach, served Heidegger's existential analysis as if it constituted a truly decisive existential and anthropological a priori. Falque seeks to enter into this debate.

The Falquian argument aims above all to respond to the accusations made by Heidegger against Christianity. Although perhaps narrow from the point of view of the believer, they nevertheless beckon the believer to question himself. As we have seen, according to Heidegger, Christianity thinks the finite only under an infinite horizon. This prevents the believer from truly experiencing metaphysical anxiety. Heidegger strongly

---

103. See Falque, *Loving Struggle*, 202.

defends temporality. The Falquian response is very clear. Accepting the traits that seem relevant to him in Heideggerian analyses, Falque intends to establish, based on theological teachings and Gospel texts, that God desired humanity so much so that he incarnated himself as a temporally finite man. There, Christ—as the Son of God—experienced truly in his flesh the aspects of this finitude and even the anxiety that Heidegger describes. How, then, poses Falque, does the Christian who seeks to imitate Christ disqualify this finitude? Philosophy and theology therefore follow one another in the same task. Certainly, in "the metamorphosis of finitude" that Falque proposes, theology may proceed to recover and uplift philosophy in order to provide a rich hermeneutics of finitude.

In the confrontation between Heidegger and Falque, highlighted in *The Wedding Feast of the Lamb*, we find a clue. It has often been considered that Heidegger broke with Greek philosophy, which made man a part of the cosmos, by affirming that the being of man was radically distinguished from all beings of nature. It has also traditionally been considered that this radical opposition was found in Christian thought. However, Falque's work, which highlights the corporeality of man understood in an organic sense—his animality, through the conception of an "expanded body" irreducible to the experience of the flesh—develops another perspective. Such an observation shows the importance of the dimension of carnal finitude, as illustrated, as we have seen, by the lived experience of Christ—and insufficiently taken into account by Heidegger.

The Theological Turn

It is in light of the importance of finitude in Falque's approach that we can understand his position in relation to a debate which struck deeply the world of phenomenology, namely, Dominique Janicaud's *Phenomenology and the "Theological Turn": The French Debate*. In it, Janicaud criticized Emmanuel Levinas, Michel Henry, Jean-Luc Marion, and Jean-Louis Chrétien for having broken, each in their own way, from the method of phenomenology and its principle of immanence. The terms of the Other, of the Invisible, of the Gift, and of original revelation used by these authors seemed to demonstrate a theological "turning away." For example, experiences of the "extraordinary" can be seen by "the face" (Levinas), auto-affection (Henry), the saturated phenomena (Marion), the giving of speech (Chrétien). Janicaud thus criticized a phenomenology that deviated towards the verticality of transcendence, as opposed to a "good" phenomenology which remained in the interlacing of immanence. Echoing Merleau-Ponty, this violation ignores a firm "flesh of the world" that is inseparable from corporeality. The issue of the debate could be summarily presented in the following terms: phenomenology wants to be a description of phenomena and therefore claims to remain at the level of what appears. However, the authors in question placed themselves in a phenomenology of the unapparent by describing realities which do not appear.

Janicaud obviously does not contest theology's right to exist. But he reproaches it in the works of these authors who claim to be philosophers and seem to hide under the guise of a philosophical and phenomenological approach whose spirit they seem to betray. He condemns, in a way, as a poor mixture of genres. The phenomenologist who brings about the "theological turn" is not, in Janicaud's eyes, one who is simply interested in theology. He is one who uses phenomenology to make theology, without saying or admitting that he is also a theologian. Yet, as Jean Greisch points out, the question has two layers. Are we dealing with "philosophical discourses contaminated from the start by religious ulterior motives"? Or, "is it, on the contrary, to contest phenomenology's right to invest the field of philosophical theology?"[104]

We need not answer this twofold question now. We could very well reply that there is no more "a theological turn" in phenomenology than there is a "phenomenological turn" in theology.[105] But we can, at least look at the premises in order to gain a glimpse of Falque's position. Two authors will suffice: Michel Henry and Jean-Luc Marion. Overall, Marion seems to share Janicaud's criticism of the preemption of the infinite which fails to take into account finitude as such. Even if Marion experiences the presence of transcendence in immanence, such a presentation does not speak of finitude as such. Falque distances himself from Marion to develop a phenomenology of the extraordinary. In doing so, he interrogates the analysis of the "saturated phenomena," which favors "excess" in human experience and reduces finitude to a simple "residue."

The Heideggerian criterion, according to Falque, is still relevant here: "It is not enough to cite randomly certain human imperfections to define the finitude of mankind . . . this path can only lead us at best

---

104. Greisch, *Buisson ardent et les lumières de la raison II*, 361.
105. Falque, *Loving Struggle*, 197.

to note that man is a finite Being."[106] This also concerns Michel Henry, whose discovery of theology was certainly later than the other incriminated authors, but nevertheless whose late works have revealing titles such as *I Am the Truth*.[107] Falque does not hesitate to affirm that he has written a "*summa* of theology," but at the same time knows that his apologetic enterprise can appear problematic.[108] Does he not in fact write, like Henry, that understanding man from the view of Christ can be done only in this particular way.[109]

We might inquire at what point Falque takes the "necessity of first being a man without God" for it to finally appear as a "more than necessary" mode. Here, we see that the passage through finitude constitutes the first word of an approach. It is not merely the conception of Dasein as "being towards death." There remains an opening. Phenomenology does not prohibit this opening. There is, also, a place for theology. Falque no doubt affirms that the best way to respond to Janicaud's criticism is not to hasten to enter the field of theology but also to recognize that there is no need to hide it either. Why does phenomenology, which, by principle, is an open method, need to prevent itself from reaching to theology, which offers a legitimate interpretation of experience as any experience? From this point of view Falque accomplishes, in his own words, a "crossing of the Rubicon" that other phenomenologists would forbid. Yet, as he indicates: "The paradox is there: we will demand as much better a theological practice of phenomenology when one is also a theologian, than one will forbid oneself when one is only and purely a philosopher."[110] Furthermore, "the metamorphosis of finitude, or the resurrection, will be carried out as a theologian, but not as a philosopher. Neither confuse genres nor advance hidden."[111]

This debate around a so-called "theological turn" allows us to highlight the specificity of the Falquian approach. Falque confirms his conception of the philosophy-theology relationship to clarify and deepen his concept of metamorphosis. He does not jump over or evade the philosophical labors to reach it. It is a patient and careful program that

---

106. See Falque, *Metamorphosis of Finitude*, 17. Also, see Heidegger, *Kant et le problème de la métaphysique*, 276.
107. See Henry, *I Am the Truth*.
108. Falque, "Michel Henry théologien," 525.
109. See "Christian Ethic," in Henry, *I Am the Truth*.
110. See Falque, *Crossing the Rubicon*, 77–99.
111. Falque, *Metamorphosis of Finitude*, 1–14.

evokes the considerations of Lacoste on the patience of the philosopher, for whom "every work of knowledge is a work of patience."

An Inevitable Finitude?

In pursuing finitude, philosophically and theologically, the reader will be aware of the limits that must be admitted to the place and function of finitude. With the debate with Heidegger still fresh, I would like to pose a question that Falque himself has asked in his own discussion with Lacoste: "If finitude as the limiting horizon of existence is the point at which man must begin, then how, conferring so much importance to facticity from the time of its first articulation, can it thus be overcome?"[112] When "the experience of the Absolute takes precedence over the absolute of experience," we may wonder what "then is to become of *the path of experience tout court*, or better, the primordial physicality of finitude?"[113]

This question that Falque raises to Lacoste is also found in relationship to Pascal. Commentators have in fact often questioned the nature of anxiety in Pascal. In a sense, this concept prepared him to make that famous "wager." Did Pascal feel anxiety himself? If not, the reader would certainly doubt his essentially apologetic approach and confer on it a certain inauthenticity. To admit to having experienced it would be, on the other hand, to recognize that uncertainty had erupted in him which also risks weakening his argument. For me, the Falquian approach, though of Pascalian inspiration, slightly differs. Regarding Lacoste and his project, the question concerns the transformation of facticity, the "initial" moment (distinct from the "original") that we live as a "being in the world" (this world distinct from "creation"). In other words, our "being-there" becomes a "being before God."

Beyond comparing the unique qualities of each author, is the question posed by Falque not also necessary in a self-reflexive relation to his own approach? Does his experience identify with that of Aquinas, for whom finitude was not the object of resignation alone, or is it distinct from it, closer—but to what extent?—of experience and its interpretation by our contemporaries? While seeking an answer to that question may lead to a host of complexities outside the scope of the present study,

---

112. Falque, *Loving Struggle*, 205.
113. Falque, *Loving Struggle*, 196.

we receive a certain clue in *The Guide to Gethsemane* on the question of death, at once "passive" and "active."

The Weight of Life: Saint Augustine, Heidegger, and Kierkegaard

In "After Metaphysics? The 'Weight of Life' According to Saint Augustine," Falque analyzes the Augustinian conception of the "weight of life" and sets it against Heidegger. According to Falque, the Heideggerian interpretation is not always ideal to the description of Saint Augustine, while it may allow him to specify the nature of this "weight." In juxtaposing Saint Augustine and Heidegger, we can see a Falquian approach to the conception of life *as* out of and through death.

In *The Confessions*, Augustine describes his experience of the heaviness of life ("I am a weight for me," "I myself have become an immense question"). This provides us with a double lesson: the Augustinian sense of this weight as incontestably sinful in relation to grace. Addressing God, the Doctor of Hippo recognizes: "Not being filled with you, I am a burden to me." Falque extends this thought: "It is not done fully by God that we paradoxically fill up on ourselves. . . . The less we are with God, the more we are with ourselves, and the more we are with ourselves and the more we weigh ourselves, on ourselves."[114] This sinful dimension is a weight and results in a separation from God. Thus, Augustine calls for a "return to oneself through elevation in God and by God." Deploying the Heideggerian rule, we exclude the place of sin and connect it to the "weight of life," that of the sole finitude of "Dasein as such." This is, however, not Augustine's primary intention, and Falque is not satisfied with this radical opposition. We have already seen several times that he does not reduce finitude to its "sinful" component. He therefore proposes an "existential progression."[115] As he writes: "The weight of life, among Augustine, as also with Heidegger, does not derive first or only from the burden of sin. It is also a finitude to exist that the believing as every man must also bear, precisely within the limits of his created being."[116] *The Confessions* help us to further identify this simple weight of life. The loss of a friend, the pain of mourning, and tragic death each represent an experience of this simple finitude of "man in general." The mere fact of

---

114. Falque, "After Metaphysics?," 216–17.
115. Falque, "After Metaphysics?," 209–10.
116. Falque, "After Metaphysics?," 213.

existence becomes a source of worry. Augustine, at another point in *The Confessions*, discusses a dream by Monica, his mother (a believer), who sees herself next to him, still unbelieving; they are "united together in a common humanity." The lesson that Falque draws from this is in line with one of his fundamental claims: "The path of humanization takes precedence over that of divinization, where the encounter with God in the depths of man is more important than the fusion of nature. Man in union with God. He doesn't go there thus, not only of sin in Saint Augustine, but also of pure and simple humanity."[117] The Augustinian approach is able to retrieve and overcome the Heideggerian intuition of grounding finitude in life. Of course, Augustine poses another weight, that of the love of God (*pondus*) to counterbalance the weight of life and death. "The more we weigh 'love,'" writes Falque, "and the lighter the weight of self becomes for me. . . . We paradoxically become heavier when we are alone than when we are two people."[118]

The present Augustinian analysis can be generalized to a discussion of finitude and metamorphosis. Life, in all its forms, truly takes its weight from the love offered in the metamorphosis that God makes possible. We will study, in more detail, this metamorphosis later in relationship to the theme of the resurrection. For now, we rest upon finitude in the existential plane. Following Kierkegaard, Falque states: "We have seen how the Christian carries the heavy burden lightly, Søren Kierkegaard says in *The Gospel of Suffering: Edifying Discourses*, how he doesn't differ from others by being exempted from the burden but shows himself to be a Christian by carrying it lightly. He who, heavily loaded, carries a light burden: He is Christian."[119]

By the end of this initial presentation of finitude, we will arrive undoubtedly to contrasting conclusions. To speak of a "first" presentation is to indicate that this approach needs to be supplemented by a more in-depth study of the carnal and bodily dimension of finitude. Depending on whether the reader is a philosopher or theologian, his judgment may vary. It is difficult, in fact, to find an approach which uses, in full light, both disciplines and puts them face to face with equal legitimacy. If the reader is willing to become both, the question will necessarily arise as to whether or not we can fully deploy the Falquian argument. In other

117. Falque, "After Metaphysics?," 215.
118. Falque, "After Metaphysics?," 217–18.
119. Falque, *Metamorphosis of Finitude*, 118. Also, see Kierkegaard, *Discours édifiants à divers points de vue*, 229–43.

words, we might ask in what sense does the nature of finitude consist as the basis for grasping extraordinary phenomena in the religious domain without sacrificing integrity of method?

We mentioned, at the very beginning of this interpretation, a triple relationality: to contemporary philosophy, to the teaching of the faith, and to personal experience. To hold true, all together, Falque would need to keep the Heideggerian description, share the Christian faith, and recognize one's flesh as a fundamental mode. We can certainly be doubtful about this triple requirement, but we can also, before making a decision, be impressed by this triple conjunction: philosophy, theology, and existence. In this light, we can judge the credibility of this presentation of finitude that Falque wishes to advance.

Let us further ponder the stakes of this thinking. For example, which type of reader requires the greatest effort: the unbeliever, doomed to finitude and perhaps surprised at Christ's capacity to fully assume this finitude; or the believer, who must recognize that philosophy is fundamentally "atheistic."[120] On the latter point, we may further question, with Falque, "the truly initiated modalities of our being there" and accept at least from a "heuristic point of view," to first imagine the incarnation of a man quite simply rather than "the image of a God."[121] Whether believer or unbeliever, we can appreciate the anthropological truth of the entire project to facilitate a fruitfulness in the philosophy-theology confrontation. By the end of this study, we will note the legitimacy in which finitude takes on its full meaning as a limited phenomenon. God "transforms" or "metamorphosizes" the limits of finitude. Because "everything that is not assumed is not saved," only what is "united to God" is saved.[122] Moreover, "such a claim neither reduces God to human dimensions (the anthropological reduction), nor to worldly dimensions (the cosmological reduction) . . . ; on the contrary, it consecrates God himself as Him who makes the choice in his incarnation and his kenosis to take on human, worldly and palatial dimensions in order to communicate with us."[123] We will continue to deepen this analysis of finitude.

Through the above analyses and descriptions of finitude, a problem necessarily arises: that of the incarnation of God and man, of the status of the body and the flesh. These concerns are not foreign to questions in our

---

120. Falque, *Loving Struggle*, 201.
121. Falque, *Loving Struggle*, 202–4.
122. Gregory of Nazianzus, cited in Falque, *Loving Struggle*, 207–10.
123. Falque, *Loving Struggle*, 208.

own time; they also speak to a decisive pivot in Christianity today. Perhaps it is the incarnate mode of Christianity that we find ourselves arriving at. As Merleau-Ponty remarks: "The Incarnation changes everything."[124] The lowering of God is essential, it demonstrates how God takes the body of man. This reversal, so to speak, of God into bodily form beckons an analysis of the status of the body of God through two essential Christian realities: the resurrection and the Eucharist. Here, anthropology and theology come together. We may even argue that they are inseparable.

---

124. Merleau-Ponty, *Sense and Non-Sense*, 174.

Part Three

Metamorphosing Finitude

FOLLOWING MERLEAU-PONTY'S INVOCATION THAT the "Incarnation changes everything," we find Falque urging that "the Resurrection changes everything." The argument is made in the early pages of *The Metamorphosis of Finitude*: finitude is inseparable from its metamorphosis, which does not destroy it but rather transfigures it. After "the philosophical appeal to theology" of Merleau-Ponty, Falque announces a "theological appeal to theology." Albeit this must also be one that works with the tools of philosophy.[1]

Here, we find in Falque's project a fundamental teaching of Christianity that recalls the famous statement of Saint Paul's Letter to the Colossians that if there is no resurrection of the dead, our preaching is empty and so is faith.[2] It is part of a tradition that rang in Paul's time and continues to ring today. Falque, playing the philosopher, even when he feeds on theology, does not hesitate to radicalize finitude as a "metamorphosis." Allow me to point out that Falque, for his part, demonstrates a form of audacity in amplifying the Pauline intuition. The central focus of Paul's epistle is the resurrection, and he attempts to appeal to philosophical arguments to make his case for the resurrection. We know of the reaction: "Some began to scoff, but others said, 'We should like to hear you on this some other time.'"[3]

1. Falque, *Metamorphosis of Finitude*, 63.
2. See Col 1:13–15.
3. See Acts 17:32.

Inspired by the Pauline moment, Falque relies, on the one hand, on scriptural and theological references, and, on the other hand, on philosophical and more precisely phenomenological references. But, to be sure, he develops his thought by distinguishing it from traditional religious interpretations. To put it more precisely, the Falquian method does not so much seek to break with old models as to transform them from the inside. His major concern, for his reader, is to flush out all readings or conceptions of the resurrection which risk bringing us back to a "human, all too human" impulse. As a good phenomenologist, Falque begins with the credibility of his argument.

SECTION ONE: OF THE METAMORPHOSIS

Théologoumènes and *Philosophèmes*

Even if a study of "metamorphosis" makes theological references, like an analysis of finitude, we nevertheless have at our disposal *théologoumènes* rendered intelligible through *philosophèmes* (i.e., a knowledge of God that passes through the mediation of human experience). "We have no other experience of God but that of human beings in the phenomenology and theology of 'down below.'"[4] Finitude is never destroyed but transformed. If aspects of our finitude can make certain traits of God visible, it is as a result of incarnation. We can thus speak of a "good anthropomorphism," of an "anthropomorphosis" of God. While some theologians may disagree, it is this anthropomorphosis of God that leads to the complete transformation of the resurrection of finitude.

An Intra-Trinitarian Transformation

The most original aspect of the Falquian argument probably lies in the fact that it closely links the metamorphosis of man in the resurrection to the transformation that God experiences in himself as a Self-Same. It is not only about Christ, the Son who resurrects, but of what that experience means for the other persons of the Trinity. Falque's argument suggests that man is radically transformed in the intra-Trinitarian metamorphosis of God. The reader will certainly be left wondering what exactly this means. The Father receives the carnal ordeal of the Son, who passes his suffering

---

4. Falque, *Metamorphosis of Finitude*, 97.

towards the Father, and the Spirit, in turn, accomplishes the action of transformation in the Son through the Father. Here again, however, the specificity of the Christian message ought to be made plain.

The Work of God

The prevailing presentation leads to the idea that the resurrection is only the work of God. Is it vain to seek a form of "anthropological" legitimacy for this resurrection, to see it as the simple continuation of existence, carried by a Spinozist *conatus* or a desire for eternity, or even as an "original affirmation," in the terms of Jean Nabert or Paul Ricœur? These certainly translate a human need into rationally grounded propositions, but do they remain only illusory? Falque seems to suggest as much. "We cannot have recourse to God through a simple will to last, to go on and on, even supposing that were required by the rebellion of our own bodies (health as opposed to sickness)."[5] A conception that thinks life as an extension of itself risks depriving the vital power of the resurrection.

Resurrection presupposes death. This rendering is essentially Epicureanist and Stoicist: "We should perhaps remind ourselves simply that for Epicurus it is our lack of experience of death that prevents us from talking about it."[6] Moreover, for Falque, "as opposed to what are in effect falsehoods from Greeks such as Socrates, Epicurus, or Epictetus, the Bible already symbolically sets up, on different grounds, a universal 'dread of the day of death' that weighs on all the children of humankind."[7] The reversal is significant and probably paradoxical for many of our contemporaries accustomed to thinking of religion only as a source of consolation. In a certain way, we might posit that it is Epicurus whose propositions appear reassuring. But the new existence that the resurrection confers is not the extension of our life; it is the work of God. "Similarly, we shall not go to God except by God, in the phenomenology and theology of 'on high.'"[8]

Here, we find an insight already mentioned, that of the desire for God placed in us through the action of God. "It is simply because God himself, by his metamorphosis and by our metamorphosis in him,

---

5. Falque, *Metamorphosis of Finitude*, 65.
6. Falque, *Guide to Gethsemane*, 8.
7. Falque, *Guide to Gethsemane*, 8.
8. Falque, *Metamorphosis of Finitude*, 97.

transfigures the structure of the world, and places a desire for him in us."[9] This paradox may be a challenge to grasp. For Falque, the desire for God would be the same desire for another life in which we would experience metamorphosis of our finitude; this desire is born in us only through the transformation of God himself. "'Becoming man in God' precedes and conditions the 'becoming God in man.'"[10] We must, I argue, insist on this essential point in Falque's project, for it is "at this measure, and at this measure only, can the 'Christian metamorphosis' (resurrection) break through the nullity of all attempts at transformation of the self by the self, when it is imagined as independent of he who is All-Other."[11] A final, essential question is also that of the nature of the resurrection itself. The Falquian intention is very clear. For us, we will organize it into two moments: the analysis of the "conditions of possibility" of the resurrection described by the intra-Trinitarian metamorphosis, and a "phenomenology of the resurrection" which details the nature of the transfiguration.

SECTION TWO: THE CHARACTER OF THE EVENT OF THE RESURRECTION

The Divine Metamorphosis

The expression "conditions of possibility" should certainly not be understood in the sense of a Kantian transcendental by which to deduce the resurrection in thought. It is rather about highlighting the character of the event of the resurrection between God and man. Why was God resurrected? asks Falque in the medieval spirit. He does not exclude the traditional response, that of redemption from sin, but rather he wagers the economy of salvation "not independently of sin, but beyond it."[12] God takes our sinful nature, but takes it as simply alive and therefore mortal. If Christ fully assumes the human condition and its finitude, his resurrection (as metamorphosis) must find its reason within itself. If the finitude of human nature, and the atheism which is often linked to it today, are no longer simply dramas, how can we explain the reasons for their overcoming? Falque rejects the perspective of intrinsicism in Aquinas, who finds

---

9. Falque, *Metamorphosis of Finitude*, 97.
10. Falque, *Metamorphosis of Finitude*, 97.
11. Falque, *Metamorphosis of Finitude*, 63.
12. Falque, *Metamorphosis of Finitude*, 93–94.

these reasons in man himself; he also refuses the extrinsicism of Barth or Bultmann, who make God's intervention that of a deus ex machina. Metamorphosis must be thought of, not as an intervention from within or without God, but as an intra-divine event, a test of God in which we are "trinitarianly taken."[13]

"The resurrection is primarily a matter of God," writes Falque.[14] It seems that the reasons for our metamorphosis and our resurrection are found first of all in what God experiences. Christ lives "the death of God" and "the death of the Son." He remains God while at the same time, asserts Falque, sharing the life of man, that is, he assumes the gap between his humanity (the finite) and his divinity (the infinite). And, in this way, he is intimately involved in the three persons of the Trinity. As Falque states, "The Son suffers from dying, and the Father suffers from the death of the Son."[15] The test that Christ lives out as man also becomes the test of God. "The suffering of the Son then appears as a passage to the Father."[16] More philosophically, the Son, because he is not simply human but also divine, expresses an "apperceptive transposition" to "make the spiritual and eternal Father experience what it is like to experience of his temporal and corruptible flesh."[17] The Son is capable of making the other feel what he feels. We as humans, it may be argued, can never truly live the experience of the other. We remain in the "as if" mode. To be sure, the Son lives in the flesh, that is, corporeal experiences of the body, whereas the Father (as Father) suffers without flesh as spirit. Thus, we find a spiritual meditation of suffering but not necessarily a carnal one.[18]

Following this logic, we must speak of a divine passion on the part of God, who is not "impassible" but also not reducible to human passions. As Falque observes, echoing Origen and even Bernard de Clairvaux, the Father is not impassive, but rather shows himself capable of compassion. Here passions, at once human and divine, come together. Our human passions tend to manifest themselves in our shortcomings, while God's passion voluntarily comes from a positive excess of love. Again, like Bernard, God is not affected, he *is* affection.

---

13. Falque, *Metamorphosis of Finitude*, 93–94.
14. Falque, *Metamorphosis of Finitude*, 93.
15. Falque, *Metamorphosis of Finitude*, 94.
16. Falque, *Metamorphosis of Finitude*, 97.
17. Falque, *Metamorphosis of Finitude*, 67–68.
18. See Falque, *Metamorphosis of Finitude*, 75–80, 99–102, 135–48.

Moreover, with regard to the comprehensive power of the Trinity, we find that the metamorphosis of the Son by the Father is also the work of the Spirit. If the resurrection is a "transformation of oneself by someone other than oneself, then the coming down to receive the form which is inherently tied to God can only be received of the force capable of shaping it."[19] Here, Falque insists, perhaps against certain representations sometimes dominant today of a weak and powerless God, on the first definition of the Spirit as a force that is found in the resurrecting and reviving strength of the Word in the flesh. In theological terms, pneumatology becomes the principle of Christology. We recognize thus the contribution of the Second Vatican Council in the affirmation of the Holy Spirit as a source of Trinitarian strength.

The metamorphosis of finitude is governed in accordance with the essential principle that nothing occurs in man if it is not first produced in God (apart from sin). The transformation of the Son's finitude therefore entails "the transformation of our own finitude in Him (the Word), at the summons of the Father and under the force of the Holy Spirit."[20] More specifically, our corporeality corresponds to God insofar as we understand the nature of the ascension, where it is not only the soul of the man which is carried away with him, but his body whole. "Implanted in God, the body of man is one with [makes a body with] the body of God, and in this 'body-to-body' they are transformed together, or are waiting to be so transformed."[21]

As we will see, it is also a question of the incorporation of man in God in the reality of the Eucharist, not unlike a certain mêlée of finitude. In other words, while eating the bread of Christ, man is in a way "eaten by him" and transformed into another body. The same law governs both the resurrection and the Eucharist. According to Falque: "I do not make God come to me, but God makes me come to him to metamorphose me with him."[22] Any real metamorphosis is above all a divine work, that of an incarnate God, of a transformation of oneself into oneself, by someone other than oneself. This incorporation of man into God, through Trinitarian action, does not however, make him equal to the three persons of the Trinity. Man is incorporated into the Trinity "by grace," while the three persons are united among themselves "in nature."

19. Falque, *Metamorphosis of Finitude*, 125–26.
20. Falque, *Metamorphosis of Finitude*, 83.
21. Falque, *Metamorphosis of Finitude*, 85.
22. Falque, *Metamorphosis of Finitude*, 87.

Human Transformation

The transfiguration concerns the whole of finitude. The philosophical structure of the world is phenomenologically revealed by the metamorphosis of the Risen One. "It is precisely because our finitude shows itself impassable in its immanence, enclosed in its time frame, and obvious to atheists that human beings do not feel the desire to go beyond it in the absence of any other revelation."[23] The key terms at stake in this debate (because it is a question of definition) are therefore those of world, temporality, and flesh. In Falque's approach, we seek to make "credible" what could seem "incredible" to the unbeliever and "believable" to the believer. "The Resurrection will not be 'credible' until it has it has to some extent become intelligible."[24] The difficulty of the undertaking does not, however, escape Falque who recognizes the magnitude of the question. As Falque self-reflects: "But in spite of the enormity of the task, I do not wish to draw back—since up to now I have tried not to avoid or skirt any obstacles."[25] Let us now suppose, with Falque, four modes of the task at hand.

A Transformation of the World: "A World That Has Become Another" and Not "Another World" but "Another Way of Experiencing Our World and Our Time"[26]

The method to follow is that of phenomenology in order to locate a new structure of the world. It is also a question of marking the specificity of Christianity in its refusal of dualism, of any conception posing two separate worlds. Falque thus shows the difference between Christianity and Platonism (to be sure, a Platonism to which Christianity was able to resort to). The two cities of Saint Augustine, terrestrial and celestial, like the two modes of "being the body" in Saint Paul, according to the flesh or the spirit, the terms of earth and sky, high and low, do not designate two places or two different worlds but two different ways of being in the world. These are existential categories of experience through which we let ourselves relate to God. We may always find openness in and through

---

23. Falque, *Metamorphosis of Finitude*, 87.
24. Falque, *Metamorphosis of Finitude*, 139–40.
25. Falque, *Metamorphosis of Finitude*, 75.
26. Falque, *Metamorphosis of Finitude*, 95–96.

him. The comparison between the myth of Aristophanes in Plato's *Symposium* and the story of the creation of Eve in coming to life from Adam's rib in Genesis also highlights the difference in meaning between Platonism and Christianity. Zeus, by separating the female species from the male species, executes punishment; whereas in Genesis it is a matter of benevolent creation. In Christianity, it always emanates from the good, whether it is that of the uncreated to the created, or that of man and woman. The expulsion of Adam and Eve in the garden of Eden is not a Platonic fall from a bright high to a dark, cavernous low. As for Christian death, it does not reflect a purification of the soul from the body, as in Plato, but a real body into a new body that surpasses suffering and death.

"Thinking theologically, this world is conceived not as an 'other world,' but rather a 'world that has become another' which is to say that 'the world in the Gospels,' as in phenomenology, does not indicate (only) a negative concept but also the neutral horizon of all that to which we ourselves are related; that we show finally how the event of the resurrection does not so much take place in the world as it 'makes worldly' the world."[27] As for the resurrection, it "is not an event of the world, or one that is produced in the world, but the event that 'makes worldly the world.'"[28] We might see that the worldly concept of nature has today become rather complicated in philosophy. We tend to favor, alternatively, the concept of the "human condition" compared to that of "nature." Man, in modernity, is not defined by its given nature but by its status of "being in the world," of being thrown into conditions of existence. There, theology must offer its assistance without, however, renouncing this concept of nature which is inherent to it and remains necessary in philosophy. Theology must recognize that the transformation of man does not presuppose a return to a preestablished or predetermined nature. "It is not human nature or nature itself that is to be transformed but transformation or metamorphosis (resurrection) that forms mankind's nature and nature itself."[29] Privileging the concept of the world requires thinking about it beyond the Husserlian "natural attitude." Of course, we know that we are in the world like "the water is in the glass." But phenomenology has shown that the world is not a mold for verification; it is a relationship in which we interact with what surrounds us and is familiar to us. It is what Christianity

---

27. Falque, *Metamorphosis of Finitude*, 103.
28. Falque, *Metamorphosis of Finitude*, 107.
29. Falque, *Metamorphosis of Finitude*, 105.

announced, unlike the Greeks, that this world and another world may both have the same fullness of reality.

As for the resurrection, it is not an event of the world, but an event which makes a world, which transforms the world into which man belongs through his own transformation, that of his way of experiencing the world. The resurrection is an "eventual irruption" which transforms radically my way of "being in the world." As Falque observes, "The world is like this becoming other in that in myself I become other." As opposed to Nietzsche, who asserts "Become what you are," Falque states, "Be what [you] become."[30] It is therefore, not a question of the transformation of the world which may become an "other" world, but my way of living this world, a world which also becomes another. Thus "the (Christian) way of being resurrected to the world will consist less in proclaiming some kind of objectivity for the resurrection and more in welcoming the way in which the believer gets ready to let himself or herself be transformed by him who 'is' transformation itself, and thus to be shaped by him."[31] Certainly, philosophy, as such, is incapable of guaranteeing a full and total disclosure of this world, but it allows us to think about the possibilities of reaching it. Falque gives an example through the communion of saints as explored in *God, the Flesh, and the Other*. How can we conceive the "presence" of the deceased, who no longer inhabit our world? A person objectively present in a room can be much less present for us than a loved one who has left us and who apparently no longer belongs to our world. The transformation thus offered does not transport us beyond our space but leads us to a metamorphosis of our representation of space in terms of a "here" from a "there"—that is, a presence.[32]

A Transformation of Temporality: "From Time to Eternity"

In Heidegger, we can only, in our finitude, go "from time to time." This closure of time remains the truth of man. But God, and he alone, has the capacity to transform the structure of time, as we have just seen with regard to space. This transformation of time will be, for the world, that of our relationship to subjective time. Augustine offers a beautiful illustration of this transfiguration with the description of his conversion. The

---

30. Falque, *Metamorphosis of Finitude*, 108.
31. Falque, *Metamorphosis of Finitude*, 108.
32. Falque, *Metamorphosis of Finitude*, 110.

present moment of conversion which makes him "change his face" and dissolve all hesitations becomes "the instance of all time in every moment of time."[33] The past, the present, the future—all that arrives in the moment—represents the reception of God in one's consciousness. Augustine instantly experiences a radical transformation in his way of experiencing time. It is not about living the Epicurean way of solitary enjoyment of the moment, but rather to be freed from the burdens of the past and future. Three messages from Christ illustrate this transfiguration: to the disciple wanting to bury his (past) father, the injunction to go and announce the reign of God (e.g., Luke 9:60); to the man anxious to collect his harvest (future), the evocation of the next night when his life will be required of him (e.g., Luke 12:20); to the good thief who asks for forgiveness (present) and to whom the Christ speaks in the present tense of the future saying that "today you will be with me in Paradise" (e.g., Luke 23:43). Eternity is not something beyond time but another way of living temporality.

The resurrection brings about a temporal metamorphosis and provides access to "the today of eternity," which is neither the extension of time, nor the enjoyment of the moment, but the place "by which the Son sees himself born (again) of his Father and us in him."[34] Metamorphosis does not produce another time but opens into eternity another way of living the same time. The "moment of eternity is not the making eternal of a moment but the joy of the eternal in the moment of all moments in time."[35] The believer does not flee outside of time. He is fully outside of the linear time of this world. He lives in the act of transformation itself, the mode of being of his new birth, which "does not let us know tomorrow what our future life will be but teaches us today to live our present life otherwise—in the union and the engendering of the Trinity."[36]

The affective mode of a passage, namely, the resurrection, can be compared to a form of joy experienced at the occasion of birth. For the believer, the first lesson of resurrection is birth and no longer death, joy and no longer anxiety. The event of birth is indeed rich in meaning: "In being born to the world, then, one does not simply place a new being in the world but offers in some way a new manner of being 'in the world'—what signifies, for the Christian, a different way of living the world and

---

33. Falque, *Metamorphosis of Finitude*, 117.
34. Falque, *Metamorphosis of Finitude*, 115.
35. Falque, *Metamorphosis of Finitude*, 116.
36. Falque, *Metamorphosis of Finitude*, 124.

time."[37] For the phenomenologist as for the Christian, what makes the weight of existence is not the amount of the load to bear but the ways we bear it. In the light of the resurrection, the believer can carry the load lightly and with joy, for joy is a new way of being in the world. And, we might add that this joy is specific; it is put in us by God. It is not ecstatic, because it does not make me leave myself, nor is it a beatitude, because it is given from today, and neither happiness, because it is not human work but a gift of God, nor even "amusement," because it beckons a self-reflexive turn.[38] In this resurrection, the "joy of the theological" prevails over the "angst of the philosophical."[39] The carefree life, that of the birds of the sky who neither sow nor reap, comes from the ways in which we receive this life. This turning of suffering into joy, enabled by a new birth in the resurrection, is being experienced now.[40]

A Transformation of Flesh: "A Flesh to Be Reborn"

What exactly is resurrected? This is perhaps the central question for the modern mind in trying to imagine the resurrection. Nicodemus already raised it, addressing Christ: "How could a man enter a second time into the belly of his mother and be born? How can this be done?"[41] According to an essential principle in Falque's project, which we have already explored on other occasions, the *théologoumène* cannot be understood unless by the mediation of a *philosophème*. Thus, the resurrection, "birth from above," is explained by the "birth from below" where we actually experience it. "We are not 'born from on high except in the way in which we are 'born from below'—following an analogic, and not a dualist, reading of the body and the spirit."[42] While the act of being born may remain obscure, Falque notes that being reborn exemplifies very precisely a rebirth (*re-naissance*). But what kind of rebirth? As Falque continues, the

---

37. Falque, *Metamorphosis of Finitude*, 117.
38. Falque, *Metamorphosis of Finitude*, 119.
39. Falque, *Metamorphosis of Finitude*, 119–20.
40. See John 16.
41. Also, as Falque writes: "Once the hypothesis of a return has been excluded, in the act of birth ('enter a second time into the mother's womb' as in rebirth (the myth of the Golden Age or the restoration of the unchanged Garden of Eden), the need to restore to life ('You must be born from above' is not a guarantee of its realization)" (*Metamorphosis of Finitude*, 133). Also, see John 3:9.
42. Falque, *Metamorphosis of Finitude*, 128.

"mystery" of the resurrection joins the "darkness" of birth. Birth and resurrection are all received between two kinds of flesh, one that is dark and one that is light.[43] But the resurrection (i.e., renaissance) is neither a mere "return" ("entering a second time in his mother's womb"), nor a rebirth as a "the restoration of the unchanged Garden of Eden."[44] It is essentially a "transformation" in and through "metamorphosis," a transition from one state to another. By being born, as by being resurrected, we ourselves become "other" while remaining "the same."

The resurrection also necessarily refers to the question of its effectivity. Falque distinguishes three figures to illustrate the effectivity-possibility relationship: a) Nicodemus, who questions "How can this be done?" and supposes its lack of possibility. b) The good thief, on his cross, who implores the effectiveness by whatever conditions—"Jesus, remember me when you become king"—and where doubt has no place. c) Mary, who faced the announcement of the incarnation and after posing a question of possibility immediately transitioned to effectivity and acceptance. For Mary, ultimately, "the thing is already done."

The great question, therefore, is that of the relationship we have with the possibility of resurrection and its effectivity. Nicodemus remains in the "conditions of possibility for the realization of an impossible," whereas Mary wonders "only about the methods of realization." May my resurrection become "believable" in and through a consciousness which, previously, found it to be "incredible"? "In the same way, the resurrection in its authentic meaning is what is given to us to believe in, at least as much as it is a resurrection in itself."[45] Believing in the resurrection is, in a certain way, already a resurrecting experience. Once again, we may measure to what extent the theological content is interpreted through a phenomenological practice. The reader may find a motivation but also, perhaps, a certain frustration in this method. We will continue to see, especially in *The Wedding Feast of the Lamb*, a certain significance in utilizing phenomenology but also a certain turning away to capture the true theological meaning of these modes of experience. The specificity of Christianity, of course, lies in its announcement of a resurrection of the flesh. How many Christians reduce the conception of eternal life to, so to speak, a simple immortality of the soul? But simple ignorance, according to Falque, is not the only cause of misrepresentation. "The impossibility

43. Falque, *Metamorphosis of Finitude*, 128–31.
44. Falque, *Metamorphosis of Finitude*, 133.
45. Falque, *Metamorphosis of Finitude*, 135.

of believing this anymore—something we all agree on today when we read Gothic church portals in a strictly symbolic way—is what makes us now come back to the problem, not so much to deny it as to trace out the lineaments of a new conceptualization."[46]

Then, how ought we to think about the body? This question, central to the Falquian approach, arises once again. The answer will be found in a double reference to philosophy and theology. This will concern, on the one hand, the design of phenomenological corporeality, on the other hand, of the testimony offered by the resurrected Christ who reveals himself to his disciples. For present purposes, the distinction between "flesh" and "body" (the carnality) of Christ as not reducible to his physical corporeality is illuminating. By this, two obstacles must be avoided: complete identification of the biological body and the resurrected body, and the negation of the reality of the substantial and material body. *The Metamorphosis of Finitude* emphasizes the first point, and the second point will be found in *The Wedding Feast of The Lamb*.

The flesh-body distinction, which will also be discussed in connection with the Eucharist, is particularly relevant here to grasp the nature of that which resurrects. The resurrection is not about coming out of the tombs (e.g., John 5:20) or "the raising of the biological body," as illustrated by Gothic portals, of a simple material substance, corpses—a design which explains, according to Falque, a silent gap of the resurrection. It first marks the recovery of our way of being in the world and in time through our flesh. Here, we find the Husserlian distinction between "carnal being" and "corporeal being." According to Falque, the "resurrected body" is indeed a "fleshly body," and ought to be seen as the one and the same body, if indeed what we mean by "flesh" as not our bodily substance (*Körper*) but the way in which we live and experience it today as a living body that affects us and by which we are affected (*Leib*).[47] As Husserl himself shows, the idea of carnality obviously does not simply mean to be bodily, but rather refers to those functions which are egological in their own way, such as seeing and hearing, "and of course other modes of the ego belong to this (for example lifting, carrying, pushing, and the like)."[48] It's not the objective body which resurrects but "the subjective

---

46. Falque, *Metamorphosis of Finitude*, 136.
47. Falque, *Metamorphosis of Finitude*, 135–37.
48. Husserl, *Crisis of the European Sciences and Transcendental Phenomenology*, 108.

way" of living and experiencing our body "which constitutes us in our most fundamental experiences (birth, sexuality, death)."[49]

This emphasis on the flesh is not contradictory, as we will see, with Falque's assertion that there is "no flesh without body." It is an obligation to think about the incarnation as incorporation with all the thickness of the body and its "animality." Flesh and body should not be opposed. They constitute two distinct layers, while the flesh constitutes us in its own right.[50] And the challenge of Christ's journey is "not only to show that he 'was a body' like us but also to reveal 'in one's flesh' a certain way of living one's body by which he resurrects and from which we too will resurrect."[51]

True corporeality is neither bodily nor biological substance but ways of living the body. The resurrection is not that of our corpse but that of our way of being in the world. Such a reading is made intelligible by recourse to the concepts of phenomenology, as well as by the testimony offered by Christ in his "apparition-disappearance."[52] Following his death, Christ is not recognized in his resurrected body but in his way of distributing the fish and breaking the bread. He appears, similarly, to more than five hundred brothers, to Mary Magdalene at the tomb, and to the Eleven in Jerusalem; such a set of encounters seems to deny the principle of noncontradiction if we remain at a level of the substantialist conception of corporeality. The perception of Christ passes through a conversion comparable to the passage from the natural attitude, a version of the objective body, to a clever phenomenological *epoché*, reinforced by the experience of flesh.

Such a withdrawal of the body to a manifestation of flesh is also illustrated, according to Falque, by the analysis proposed by Eckhart of the respective attitudes of Martha and Mary during the visit of Jesus in Luke 10. Martha, in some way, foreshadows our mode of being resurrected. Unlike Mary who remains seated at the feet of Jesus, of her "objective body" listening to him, Martha is detached from him, in the kitchen, but still feels the "lived presence." As Falque observes: "We need to renounce objectivity, and therefore renounce what is simply the materiality of our bodies, to reach the resurrected Christ."[53] This is what lies behind the famous injunction of Christ to Mary Magdalene: "Noli me tangere" (Do

49. Falque, "Athéisme moderne et puissance de la resurrection," 22.
50. Falque, "Athéisme moderne et puissance de la resurrection," 21.
51. Falque, *Metamorphosis of Finitude*, 143–44.
52. Falque, *Metamorphosis of Finitude*, 140.
53. Falque, *Metamorphosis of Finitude*, 144.

not touch me).⁵⁴ This illustration also attests to the fact that Christ shows himself in diverse modes of appearing. What therefore matters in the resurrection is not the thing itself, "but the manner or the act by which the resurrected person gives himself to me."⁵⁵ The episode of Thomas, who incredulously asks for tangible signs, is similarly revealing. It is enough for Christ to speak to him, in a certain way, such that Thomas's request loses its meaning and that touching the body becomes useless. A phenomenological analysis and evangelical thematization amplify both the richness of the flesh-body distinction and its meaning for the resurrection of the flesh.

In *The Wedding Feast of the Lamb*, we find the total weight of the question of the body, through the experience of the Eucharist (in philosophical and anthropological terms). The incarnation first gives priority to the body over the flesh, the resurrection favors the flesh, but the Eucharist will restore all its importance to the body: such is the chronological order of the Falquian triptych. Which, we may ask, bears the ultimate rank in the whole hierarchy? Such a question raises a whole host of other concerns and complexities.

Resurrection and the Power of God

A Falquian reading of the resurrection is also an occasion for a passionate and fascinating confrontation with Didier Franck's work *Nietzsche and the Shadow of God* which opposes the resurrection and the thought of the Nietzschean eternal return, the transfiguration of man into a superman, and the metamorphosis of man in God in Christianity.⁵⁶ Such a multipronged confrontation develops out of Paul's epiphany on the path of Damascus and Nietzsche's revelation at Silvaplana. For Franck, Nietzsche's approach is fundamentally "the place for a confrontation with Christianity."⁵⁷

The confrontation is essential for Falque: "Rather he returns to the dogma of the resurrection of bodies, precisely because he cannot accept the idea of the destruction, or putrefaction, of all fleshly matter, of the making eternal of a temporality that dies because it is not eternal, of the giving a chance to the earthly or material body by transforming it into

---

54. Falque, *Metamorphosis of Finitude*, 145.
55. See Falque, *Metamorphosis of Finitude*, 146.
56. See Franck, *Nietzsche and the Shadow of God*.
57. Franck, *Nietzsche and the Shadow of God*, 28.

a celestial or spiritual body. . . . Where the Christian is driven, on the one hand, only by fear—in his will to go on and on—and on the other hand by a wish to escape and make an irresistible leap into another world, the Nietzschean Overhuman shows both courage in his assumption of perishability and an attachment to the earth in his love of the moment."[58] The rapprochement is legitimate to the extent that Paul speaks of the resurrection of the body, opposed to any dualism of the Platonic typification of soul and body. We will briefly recall here that, contrary to what is often stated, the distinction made by Paul between the flesh (*sarx*) and the spirit (*pneuma*) does not overlap with that of Plato between the body (*sôma*) and the soul (*psyche*). For Paul, the flesh and the spirit are two modalities of the same experience of the body and not two opposing substantialist principles.

For Falque, the attack by Franck is radical, like Nietzsche. For them, the Christian resurrection is a false resurrection or a resurrection to false life. Here, Nietzsche makes a triple accusation against the Pauline and more broadly Christian conception: a) The Nietzschean transformation as "self-transformation" of the superman, victory of his active will; whereas, in the Christian resurrection, the subject passively undergoes his metamorphosis. b) The Christian resurrection refers to a desire for an end, to a belief into something lasting, which expresses a fear of death and translates into a flight towards another life. This escape is opposed to the courage of the superman who faces his perishable life and lives the moment as "a unique form of life." c) Finally, the mode of corporeality is also very different; Paul, through his metaphor of the seed, refers to a permanence of the body, to a substrate which makes death only a passage.

Falque opposes such an interpretation and sees in this Pauline-Nietzschean body the opportunity to clarify the true nature of resurrection. Concerning corporeality, he recalls that the Pauline body is not re-instantiated in a pure substantification, but that it is a mode and way of being (like the phenomenological conception). As for the relationship with death and the willpower of the last man, the resurrection that we could oppose to it is not an escapism to another world, but the metamorphosis of this world of ours. Of course, we really must die. However, Falque does not hesitate to affirm: "And so we find the same, or almost the same (along with, as we shall see, major differences) in the vision of the enigma of Zarathustra, and in the resurrection of Jesus: a standing

---

58. Falque, *Metamorphosis of Finitude*, 50.

up and transfiguration of man into an Overhuman on the one hand (Nietzsche); a raising up and metamorphosis of man into God on the other (Christianity)."[59] If it is true that the resurrection is the work of God, we must not see on the part of man a simple passivity. On this point, the opposition with Nietzsche is clear. This observation is also very significant for Falque, who considers, as we have seen, that the conception of a weak, suffering, powerless God (e.g., Hans Jonas in "The Concept of God After Auschwitz" is quite emblematic) must be put into perspective. The God of Christianity, even though he reveals himself in kenosis, in a form of weakness and abandonment, calls man to his metamorphosis and provides the conditions of possibility through his very own metamorphosis. "Where the one (Xenophon or Nietzsche) praises the fleshly power of the gods in a corporality quasi-foreign to man, the other (Christ along with his disciples) recognizes in the weakness of the flesh the true site of the deployment of the force of the Father by the power of the Holy Spirit."[60] It is the mistake of theology to exclusively favor the incarnation and thus reduce the place of the resurrection. Falque, likewise, does not hesitate to show the insufficiency of the Nietzschean position: "a victory of one's own will over death . . . but it raises the ego to the highest degree of its 'all-powerfulness' and its mastery over the self (heroism)."[61]

A further connection could be made here with the work of François Gachoud in *Beyond Atheism*, where the insistence on the sacrificial and suffering dimension of Christ may be observed to contribute to a certain detriment in his power of transfiguration.[62] It is the privilege granted to the crucifixion over the resurrection which explains Nietzsche's condemnation of Christianity, that is, Nietzsche not seeing that the triumph of death over life is a radical victory. Nietzsche and Christianity in fact would take an affirmation of life, though in different modes. Moreover, to be sure, the resurrection, unlike what Nietzsche claims, means, according to Gachoud, "nothing less than the most total identity to the earth." As he observes: "For it is in an earthly body that the Word of life was incarnated, and it was in a fleshly earth that he experienced himself alive and suffering. . . . His resurrection is nothing other than the finally accomplished transfiguration of all that is of this world."[63]

59. Falque, *Metamorphosis of Finitude*, 48.
60. Falque, *Metamorphosis of Finitude*, 102.
61. Falque, *Metamorphosis of Finitude*, 49.
62. See Gachoud, *Par-delà l'athéisme*.
63. Gachoud, *Par-delà l'athéisme*, 157.

Part Four

The Return to the Body

REFLECTION ON THE STATUS of the body, on incarnation, is absolutely decisive in Falque's project. On one level, it testifies to a certain evolution in thought. It allows us to highlight his philosophical originality in relation, in particular, to fellow phenomenologists. It, moreover, shows how innovative and stimulating his theological hypotheses which, however radical with the spirit of its method, are nourished by a creative commitment to the tradition. As *The Wedding Feast of the Lamb* helps to show, we have a strong sense of the fruitfulness of Christianity in our own time to reach audiences far and wide.

The theological component, even if it is from one who remains above all a philosopher, neatly demonstrates a double dimension, *ad intra* and *ad extra*. By this, I mean that *ad intra* concerns a question of renewing philosophical and theological thought from within, and *ad extra* as a dialogue with the "world of our time." Now, we may see in Falque's work a motivation to think about Christianity from the body, that of man and that of Christ, and not simply from the incarnation and resurrection. More specifically, it is a matter of his presence in the host of the Eucharist. Such a body becomes the fundamental issue and perhaps the essential challenge of our modernity as well as for believers specifically imprisoned by a theology or philosophy that devalues the body.

Such a formulation calls for some clarification. Other philosophers and theologians, present and past, have recognized the importance of the carnal dimension of Christianity, if only through the Christian specificity of the incarnation. However, we still need to know what we mean by "the body." Such a requirement for understanding is demonstrated by Falque's relation to other thinkers on the concept of the body. For the time being, we can note here a certain analogy with Ricœur, with which Falque often confronts and deepens in his own way.[1] Falque, for his part, recalls in Ricœur: "Each work responds to a 'determinate challenge'—a notion that could very well describe the relation to my previous books of what I undertake here. 'And what connects it to its predecessors seems to me less the steady development of a unique project than the acknowledgement of a residue left over by the previous work, a residue which gives rise in turn to a new challenge.'"[2]

It is thus with regard to the body, that we further explore the power of Falque's thought. It must be mentioned that the first two books of the triptych—the first part as an analysis of suffering and the death of man, the second part as a question of the metamorphosis and the resurrection of Christ—relate to bodily experiences. The study of man, in *The Wedding Feast of the Lamb*, is dedicated, in large part, to that of animality, corporeality, and a reflection on the Eucharist. The emblematic formulation of Christ, in "this is my body," carries within itself a double revelation, that of the body of man and that of Christ. This is a revelation whose stakes are enormous. The reader will not emerge without a certain shock of positioning and interpretation by Falque's approach. It may very well be a territory of unfamiliarity for many. The description of finitude and the recognition of its importance are common themes in contemporary philosophical thought. To my mind, this approach to the Eucharist and the resurrection is without precedent.

The evolution that we note in the conception of the body, according to Falque, may be explained in different ways. First, it reveals a sense of method, namely, the deepening of personal and existential structures. Second, it offers a productive confrontation with modern thinkers who often do not appear in references to Christians or atheists. Third, it highlights the challenges addressed to Christian thought by modernity writ large, for which very often resurrection and Eucharist has become more and more incomprehensible. To be sure, the contemporary culture, in a way, has acted on certain subconscious zones, as Jean-Luc Nancy recognizes: "*Hoc est enim corpus meum*: we come from a culture where this

---

1. See the appendix ("A Symbolic Confrontation?") which contains a more explicit explanation of this relationship between both thinkers.

2. Falque, *Wedding Feast of the Lamb*, 12. Also, see Ricœur, *Hermeneutics and the Human Sciences*, 32.

cult phrase will have been tirelessly uttered by millions of people officiating in millions of rites. Everyone in this culture, Christian or otherwise, recognizes it."[3] Taking into account the meaning and importance of the cultural dimension of Christianity is, in the same way, a very important dimension in Falque's work. Rather cleverly, he notes that this very same modernity that doubts the framing principles of Christianity also tends to posit the body as the only reality. Falque, however, takes this contemporary felt intuition and goes beyond conceptions of the body as "the only nature." This is precisely the role of religion.

In relation to our own approach for understanding the thought of Falque, an analysis of the status of the body is key. It allows, on the one hand, to specify the nature of human finitude, as assumed by Christ (and of whom we have already considered at length). On the other hand, it renders more thinkable, intelligible, and "credible" the perspective of resurrection. The body is decisive in this regard. And, to perform this move, *The Metamorphosis of Finitude* insists on the difference between the body and the flesh. As we recall from *The Metamorphosis of Finitude*: "The impossibility of believing in the resurrection of the flesh probably stems from the lack of an adequate and contemporary anthropology of the body capable of being transformed."[4] The "incredible" must be subjected to the criterion of the "credible." This is the Falquian method.

We have often spoken of Falque's project in terms of a space-time journey. Regarding immanence, we maintained its rightful place in religious experience. Regarding corporeality, we unearthed its deeper meanings between religious and phenomenological consciousness. We also studied how Falque uses, in *The Wedding Feast of the Lamb*, the metaphor of a chaotic descent into the abyss. The body is indeed the residence of human consciousness, in all its forms. And, we experience it differently—especially in mediation with Christ who also made his descent into the abyss. Approaching the body in the correct manner will allow us to see in what ways theology and philosophy make their foundation and, also, echoing Gregory of Nazianzus, we locate how "whatever is not assumed is not saved."

If we think of man from the point of view of his body—from his animality, in chaos, below—then we may achieve a method of finitude that also affirms the legitimacy of Christ. In this manner, following St.

---

3. Nancy, *Corpus*, 3.
4. See Falque, *Metamorphosis of Finitude*, 149–51.

Irenaeus, our thought becomes "eucharistic." The Eucharist, as discussed in *The Wedding Feast of the Lamb*, represents the place of a bodily transformation, of an incorporation, already proposed by the resurrection. It is a fundamental teaching of Christianity: "This is my body." With it, two types of questions from the Johannine texts are asked: philosophical ("What can a body be?") and theological ("Who is this man who gives his body to eat?"). It is a double question that indicates to us the need to fully appreciate the body and its capacity to reveal and transform. Or, more precisely, the body discloses a metamorphosis from animality to humanity through the sacrifice of Christ.

SECTION ONE: CARNAL AND ORGANIC MAN

The underlying idea of carnality, as introduced by *The Wedding Feast of the Lamb*, is that of "chaos"—of the initial "hustle and bustle" in which man exists. This model exposes the "external" conditions of the "animality" in man, an "animality" which will take on a new meaning in light of the gospel. To reach that stage, a "descent into the abyss" will be necessary. Without this prerequisite, the prospect of metamorphosis is unthinkable. In the Greek world, "first of all Chaos came into being," then came Earth (*Gaia*) and Love (*Eros*)."[5] In the Jewish tradition: "In the beginning when God created the heavens and the earth, the earth was a formless void (*tohu wabohu*) and darkness covered the face of the deep (Genesis 1:1–2)."[6] Hellenism, Judaism, or Christianity all evoke the same original gap. As Falque questions this gap, following Plato, as "surely some terrible, savage, and lawless form of desires."[7] The Last Supper will somehow come to exemplify it, but phenomenology, we will see, fails to really grasp this.

The Falquian conception of the body will make sense if we put it in dialogue with certain representations of the body in past and present. We can thus take note of the innovation within the conceptual infrastructure of Falque's work. In contemporary thought, Falque calls into question the privilege of the soul over the body, and the feeling that we must remain in an essentially dualistic universe. For him, the dualist and spiritualist references often remain hidden in contemporary thinking. This can lead

---

5. Falque, *Wedding Feast of the Lamb*, 16.
6. Falque, *Wedding Feast of the Lamb*, 16.
7. Falque, *Wedding Feast of the Lamb*, 18.

to a vision—materialistic, impoverishing, and reductive—that does not appreciate the body for what it really represents.

Phenomenology distinguishes, as we have seen, two forms of body: "objective" and "subjective," *Körper* and *Leib*. In philosophical terms, the objective represents the "body" (*corps*) as matter whereas in the second place we have the body, as privileged by its "flesh" (*chair*). In an attempt to move beyond phenomenology, Falque investigates what he calls the "organic body." The reader will certainly be left wondering if this "organic body" is simply a reintroduction of the "flesh." To organize it schematically, we begin "from the soul to the body," then "from the body to the flesh," and more particularly in phenomenology, "from the flesh to the body." Ultimately, in the act of the eucharistic moment, we move "from the body to the flesh." Here, Falque intends to disrupt a tradition of dualism that favors the soul; instead, we must learn to recognize the importance of the body. To do so, it is necessary to push against an idea of the body that reduces it only to its physical dimensions. It is about recalling the "carnal, against the excess of the flesh." There, we find the "organic" and "expanded" body. Moreover, in these successive reversals, the body will have renewed meaning.

"Flesh" and "Body"

A Dualist Tradition

Let us begin with a few different conceptions that Western philosophy has made of the body as well as some pivotal distinctions and differences that have arisen over time. Such a schematic is particularly relevant for Greek philosophy and its afterlives in the Christian conception of the body. We should rightly denounce the caricatured reading of Plato, who saw in his work a radical condemnation of the body, based on a vision of a narrow dualism of the world and of man. This reading has undervalued the Platonic strategy of mixing aesthetics and virtue, or the theory of the participation of the sensible and the intelligible. Plato, to be sure, favored the lesson of the *Phaedo*, according to which "the body is the prison of the soul," the body (*sôma*) as a tomb (*sema*). As many of us can recall, "To philosophize is learn to die." We can also recall from *The Republic* and that famous Allegory of the Cave, illustrating the imperative to leave the "sensible" world for the "intelligible" world, the place of truth. This dualistic vision reverberates in Western thought and, therefore, generally celebrates the soul to the detriment of the body. Descartes himself may represent the apex of this dualism.

As for Christian religion, there is an initial difficulty to be considered. In its fundamental dogmatic affirmations of the incarnation, the Trinity, and the Eucharist, we recognize an essentialness of the body, both human and divine. But such assertions were not self-evident in light of Hellenic philosophy, at least Platonic, which could have considered this point scandalous. Once Christianity had met, philosophically, the Greco-Latin tradition, various heresies and questions came to pervade the intellectual climate: that of an incarnation not assimilated to a fall, that of the conciliation of humanity and divinity in Christ, and that of the relationships between the three divine persons. All of these questions center on a conception of the body. This same body, in a more general context of salvation, has often been considered as prey to sin and perceived through the demonization of sexuality, human perdition, pleasure, and an overall obstacle to salvation. The immortality of the soul, in favor of which Plato wagers, thus appeared more convincing than a resurrection of the flesh. We cannot thus deny that our philosophical and religious traditions, at least the *doxa* it has provoked, has been based on an erroneous interpretation of their original meanings. Though, it has, in part, disqualified an image of the human body and insufficiently taken into account that of an incarnate God.

The link between Christianity and Platonism has been the object of much scrutiny by Nietzsche, who called Christianity a "Platonism for the people." If we recall the gap between Platonism and Christianity as the fathers of the church were well aware, then the image of this body as "doubly disqualified" still remains today in other forms.[8] Their evocation allows us to highlight a certain revolution accomplished in modernity on this very concept. Nietzsche even attested to the importance of the status of the body for this modernity by clearly defining the issue in *The Gay Science*: "I have asked myself quite often whether, all things considered, philosophy until then would not have absolutely consisted of an exegesis and a misunderstanding of the body."[9]

So far, we have insisted on an irremediably deprived status of man for contemporary thought. The body, as a measure of finitude, is an essential component of Christianity, according to Falque. Falque seeks to

---

8. See Falque, *Metamorphosis of Finitude*, 50–51.
9. See Nietzsche, *Gay Science*, 34–35.

redeem this relationship. Here again, it is through a confrontation with modern thinkers, such as Nietzsche and Heidegger, as well as phenomenology more broadly that Falque provides a way forward. The relevance of Heidegger's analysis of finitude, as previously discussed, was a helpful resource for demonstrating, against Heidegger, the mode and power of transformation at work in a Christian understanding of finitude. It is now a question, from the current conceptions of corporeality (Nietzsche offering the most radical formulation), to show that Christianity is also able to render intelligible a bodily conception of man and of God.

From the Soul to the Body, and the Body to the Flesh

Regarding finitude, Falque continues a principle within a certain kind of contemporary philosophy, while separating himself from phenomenologists, whom he criticizes for wanting to escape from finitude too soon and for not sufficiently respecting the stage of "the simple in general." Falque takes great advantage of the means and methods of phenomenology; however, he is not satisfied with all of its conclusions. The stakes are high. He intends to truly and absolutely grasp the nature of the body. If ultimately a failed effort, his ideas of transformation and metamorphosis, through the resurrection and the Eucharist, would be unthinkable.

We might briefly provide an interpretation of modernity as that moment when the body took the place formerly occupied by the soul within the philosophical tradition. Nietzsche, in a certain way, would illustrate this reversal through his celebration of "the great reason of body." Freud and Marx could be associated with him, in their criticism of idealism, in their critique of power and the celebration of this-worldly consciousness. We would thus evoke, ever so schematically, the triumph of "materialism" over "spiritualism." But such a presentation remains very incomplete. As shown, in fact, very clearly by Maurice Merleau-Ponty, this formulation is inadequate. Modernity did not stop at this reversal: "Our century has wiped out the dividing line between 'body' and 'mind,' and sees human life as through and through mental and corporeal, always based upon the body and always (even in its most carnal modes) interested in relationships between persons. For many thinkers at the close of the nineteenth century, the body was a bit of matter, a network of mechanisms. The twentieth century has restored and deepened the notion of flesh, that is, of animate body."[10] This text is quite emblematic of what we may call a second reversal. Valéry, too, defined the body from of a triple experience, that of "my" body, that of the body "seen" by others, that of the body "known" by science.[11]

The contribution of phenomenology, as we have had the opportunity to see, passes through new distinctions and definitions of the body. The "flesh" and "body" are well-known concepts. If phenomenology rejects traditional dualism, it also criticizes the approach which makes the body a simple object of scientific knowledge. I don't "have" a body, I "am" my body. True knowledge of the body also passes beyond the sole experience I have of it. What matters is how I live my body. Husserlian phenomenology distinguishes, as we have seen on several occasions, *Leib* my own fleshly body—subjective, phenomenal, privileged object of phenomenology—from *Körper*, the objective body—"object of the world" of matter. Husserl will also speak of *Leib-körper* (body of flesh) to account for the unity between the body that I have and the flesh that I am by the very fact that I experience a certain experience of my body in everyday experience.

But as Falque himself remarks, the verbal indicator of the "body of flesh" is of course not enough to constitute its "unity."[12] Does this mean that in fact the different analyses always end up favoring only one of the two terms, or that phenomenology results in disqualifying the body? As the prevailing discussion has shown, we must do justice to the body. So, the real difficulty—most ironically—consists of thinking of *Körperlichkeit* rather than *Leiblichkeit*, the biological and material body and not simply the lived body. The Husserlian distinction is decisive, but in favoring the flesh, it does not sufficiently account for the body itself. Given this complexity, it is worthwhile to follow and consider the approach of Michel Henry.

Is There a Flesh Without Body?

The question arises: Does Michel Henry amplify and agree with Falque's analysis of the body in contrast to the one that Heidegger poses on finitude? Certainly Henry, a believer, at least at the end of his life, does not hesitate to refer to the Gospels, which Heidegger rejected thoroughly. Falque retained the conception of Heideggerian finitude insofar as it was

---

10. Merleau-Ponty, *Signs*, 227.
11. Valéry, *Poésies. Mélange. Variété*, 923.
12. See Falque, *Loving Struggle*, 143–46.

a resourceful a priori to allow him to clarify his own position. As far as Henry is concerned, he will note all positive aspects of the human and divine body, as contrasted to Heideggerian finitude, in order to reveal more radically the true position of the body and finitude. This step is of particular importance for Falque's method, a *disputatio médiévale*—a performance with a significant interlocutor, who pushes (often) at the end and which allows one to assert their specificity more vividly and clearly. In pursuing this course of dialogical truth, we are better able to locate his framework and aims.

The dialogue with Henry makes it possible to clarify the true phenomenological context that defends the "flesh" against those who would hold to a reductive and objectivist vision of the "body." The difference can certainly offer a productive perspective for an idea of "flesh without body," according to Falque, who appreciates a very clever phenomenological move on the part of Henry.[13] The words seem to speak for themselves. In a sense, the situation of Henry is emblematic, as though representing a culmination vis-à-vis a reversal brought about by modern thought, particularly phenomenology. Henry celebrates the flesh; the body is in some way excluded; our body is not flesh. His thesis is radical: "Body and flesh are thus distinguished through the radicality of an originary phenomenological dualism. The body lacks the power to make manifest; it has to seek its manifestation in the world outside-of-itself and is thus constituted as a mundane body.... The flesh, by contrast, is an auto-impression in the process of the auto-revelation of life. Its revelation is derived from life and from it alone. Bodies are possible in the world, whereas a flesh never occurs elsewhere or otherwise than in life."[14] Falque's approach, at first glance, would seem to accept the exclusivist conception of a flesh which would no longer have any bodily dimension; a doubly criticizable conception from the point of view of anthropology and theology.

Henry seeks to substitute a phenomenology of life for a phenomenology of the world (or being). All living beings are embodied beings, but the body of living beings is not identical to the material body dealt with by quantum physics, biology, or chemistry. For him, the fundamental distinction is to be made between the body and flesh:

> The body is also the seat of originary, immanent movements. They are more than the movements that orient our senses and

---

13. See Henry, *Incarnation: A Philosophy of the Flesh*.
14. See "Incarnation," in Henry, *Michel Henry Reader*, 48.

are indispensable to their effective functioning. This body originally moves itself within itself.... There is no flesh that does not have a Self within itself, such that this Self, which is implicated in the givenness of this flesh to itself, turns out to be the Self of this flesh just as much as it is the flesh of this Self. There is no flesh that would be an anonymous, impersonal flesh: the flesh of the world. There is no such impression either: there is no pain, suffering, or joy that would be the pain, suffering, or joy of no one! ... What the flesh derives from life is precisely its condition as flesh, that is, the auto-impression of suffering and joy that constitutes the pure phenomenological substance of every conceivable flesh.[15]

There, the flesh appears as distinct from the body. They stand apart from each other like feeling and non-feeling. Life, affect, and flesh are all the marks of true a self-consciousness, seized positively in an experience that we cannot distance ourselves from. The true body, according to Henry, is not the objective body but the subjective body which *affects* itself, the "my body," the flesh.

This experience of the flesh, a place where what I am is confused with what I experience (and, so, Henry reinterprets Descartes by showing that thinking is also and first "feeling," "being," and "self-affected"), is opposed to objective and scientific knowledge of the world and the body which presupposes a dissociation of man from himself. He, therefore, refuses the Heideggerian qualification of man as "being in the world." You must protect yourself from the world for the benefit of *real* life. The Gospel of John, according to Henry, articulates the same teaching, as Christ himself affirms that he is not of this world; as the Gospel reads, "The Word is made flesh." Ultimately, this flesh-body distinction is in fact based on a confrontation with the true nature of life. Henry, against other phenomenologists, wants to restore a form of thought fully consistent with life, a philosophy of *pathos*: a being is alive when it is present to itself. He supports the thesis of a carnal subjectivism ("I am through my flesh") against sensual empiricism ("I am through my body").

These few statements bear witness to the originality of Michel Henry's thought. In a certain way he opposes the scientific and objectifying approach to man and the world. His book *Barbarism* constitutes a radical denunciation of such an approach.[16] He refuses the Heideggerian status

---

15. See "Incarnation," in Henry, *Michel Henry Reader*, 50–52.
16. See Henry, *Barbarism*.

of "being in the world," but he also distinguishes, by the importance he gives to "self-affectivity" (echoing Levinas), the dimension of otherness in man. He radicalizes the Husserlian distinction of the flesh and of the body in a true opposition that, in a way, also outstrips and relativizes Husserlian intentionality.

This brief discussion of some of Henry's principal concepts makes it possible to clarify the problem of the body in modern thought. As the emblematic title of one of Henry's own works indicates, it is indeed a question of whether or not to celebrate the "incarnation" of man and God.[17] The ancient dualism of the soul and the body no longer grips so tightly. Importantly, the conception of the "flesh-body," from a certain point of view, no longer distinguishes the body from what we mean by the "soul." His reading of the Johannine Gospel allows him to confirm this importance of the incarnation in a theological context for God as well as for man. This observation also attests to and reinforces the carnal dimension of finitude, and the analogies to be found in Falque's own approach.

To be sure, the deepening of the body-flesh distinction also highlights what separates them. Falque's critical reading of Henry thus constitutes a relevant propaedeutic of the carnal condition of the human being, often carried out by Nietzsche, post-Nietzschean, and atheist thinkers. Falque suggests that Henry is ultimately led to reject both Hellenism and Judaism in order to defend a dualist conception (the world opposed to life, the body to flesh, the Word became flesh and not body), implicitly criticizing philosophers who have favored a model for seeing a third type of flesh. For Falque, this results only in an "impossible incorporation" of the flesh itself, that is, on an anthropological level, to a negation of man in the true "body," and, on a theological level, a negation in the kenosis of the true body of Christ. We can thus speak of a gnostic position. Henry did not really see, as Merleau-Ponty saw, that the "Incarnation [understood in the material sense of the term] changes everything." It is significant to note that Falque's criticism is of a dual nature, both anthropological and theological. The work of Henry, however innovative and original, does not account for the totality of the incarnation, that of man but also that of God. His reading of the Gospel, however stimulating it may be, radically favors that of John, and offers an interpretation that appears questionably gnostic.

---

17. See Henry, *Incarnation: A Philosophy of the Flesh*.

The Body Otherwise

The Falquian position is both enriching and complex. From a philosophical point of view, it shows a certain evolution which modifies the flesh-body hierarchy. The uniqueness of his position appears particularly in the light of his analysis of the resurrection. Determining a clear view of the body and the flesh, on both a philosophical and theological level (as found in the first two volumes of Falque's triptych), requires us to reflect on the incarnation, the passion, and the resurrection of Christ. Much of this, too, can be found in *The Wedding Feast of the Lamb* and its discussion on the Eucharist, showing that:

> We are of humankind certainly in thinking about death and the anguish of death, whether it be in the Garden of Gethsemane or on Mount Golgotha (*The Guide to Gethsemane*). And we are still of humankind, though transformed and offered divinity, when we accept that finitude can be integrated into God, that we are metamorphosed through birth and resurrection (*Metamorphosis of Finitude*). Again we are of humankind, but taking on our characteristic animality, when, in the act of the eucharist, we communicate through he who recapitulates all in himself, including the Chaos, the passions and drives that also make up our humanity.[18]

We can see that, if it is a question of God, Falque's understanding is made intelligible from a corporeal and carnal dimension, at once authentically human. Just as the concept of "flesh" allows us to understand, as we have seen, the meaning of the resurrection and its "credibility," we also arrive at a new definition of the body for making the Eucharist intelligible too. This, once again, demonstrates the relevance of philosophy, and particularly of phenomenology, to illuminate theological concepts, as well as concretize the experience of Christ as a mode of the human condition. We see that here, too, Falque responds, in a certain way, to a criticism of Merleau-Ponty: "Catholicism finds distasteful a philosophy which is merely a transcription of Christian experience, doubtless because such a philosophy, when carried to its logical extreme, would be a philosophy of man instead of a theology."[19] The Falquian conception of the philosophy-theology relationship overcomes such an opposition. If Falque insists on the need to fully experience the finitude of the human being, it is first of

---

18. Falque, *Wedding Feast of the Lamb*, 66.
19. Merleau-Ponty, *Sense and Non-Sense*, 176.

all because, as a philosopher, he recognizes solidarity with contemporary phenomenology, even though he will criticize some of its developments. Just as with the carnal dimension of the human condition, the same vision is required for the incarnation of God.

Falque, it must be said, is very sensitive to the historical character of philosophical questions. So it is with the old opposition of soul and body, which, at least in the truly philosophical or theological fields, must be reexamined. Additionally, as we have seen, modern thought has substituted another distinction, perhaps more relevant today, that of flesh and body. Phenomenology has pursued it in vivid detail. In this manner, following Falque, once we have accepted the importance of finitude, we will be inclined to recognize that the specificity of this condition lies in its lived, namely, carnal dimension. Such a recognition is decisive in making "the resurrection of the flesh" credible.

Falque refuses a complete identification of the biological body and the resurrected body in favor of showing that "true corporality, today as yesterday, before as after death, is not in our corporal and biological substance—important though that is in our incorporation—but in the way we live, accept, and receive this in our own incarnation."[20] It is the experience of our body, which makes our flesh resurrect. Already, in Falque's *Guide to Gethsemane*, we find the passion of Christ, of his suffering beyond all words, to be a manifestation of this profoundly carnal dimension. The flesh, though a concept that he ultimately intends to surpass, remains deeply instructive for Falque.

A new reversal is necessary, which some, like Didier Franck, have already undertaken, to identify and transcend the limits of phenomenology as well as certain theological discourses. The question is clearly posed by Falque in *The Wedding Feast of the Lamb*: "Has not philosophy forgotten the material and organic body in coming to speak of flesh as lived experience of the body?"[21] At stake is our very existentiality. Some may find such a question paradoxical, from a believing philosopher and theologian. He claims, quite Nietzschean, a larger place for "the great reason of the body" against a certain modern philosophy. With that, we may also dispel reservations that Falque is operating as a crypto-theologian of the body.

The Wedding Feast of the Lamb, which until now we only have mentioned in brief, seems to fulfill the idea of finitude by an idea of "abyss,"

---

20. Falque, *Metamorphosis of Finitude*, 138.
21. Falque, *Wedding Feast of the Lamb*, 1.

that is, a "descent" into not only the limits of philosophy but also to an obscure world of primordial chaos, as illustrated by Merleau-Ponty. It is a question of recognizing in man an existential and indescribable dimension that philosophy cannot easily account for; for this dimension exists in something beyond which escapes all meaning. Whether it is called "Chaos," "Tohu-bohu," or the "Abyss," something Obscure holds us and makes us become more than we are; and the more that we ignore these original gaps or descent the more this path of becoming intensifies.[22] This mêlée of sensations is, like Heidegger, the world of that from which we can no longer articulate, a world of phenomena which cannot fit into an experience, neither lived nor linguistically constructed. Heidegger perceived the existence of such a world, but he could not account for it due to his strict ideality of metaphysics with the phenomenological method of signification.

In response, Falque indicates three forms of the insufficiency of phenomenology which call for its overcoming as well as for the aid of theology and religiously inspired conceptions of the body in the Eucharist: a) the turn of the flesh on the body, b) the hypertrophy of intentional experience on the non-significance of things, c) the uncontrolled primacy of passivity over activity. By resorting to the "experience of consciousness" (i.e., the flesh), phenomenology ironically dismisses "the solidity of the body in its biological dimension and drives."[23] We can observe a certain Gnosticism of phenomenology in the celebration of the "experience" of the body that forgets its organic dimension. Furthermore, the concept of intentionality affirms the priority of meaning, through and against the excess of meaning over non-meaning. The world we perceive always carries meaning. Thus, the initial chaos, which remains in us in a non-signifiable manner, remains foreign to the phenomenological approach. Finally, when phenomenology favors the attitude of reception and passivity of the subject, for example in the excess of intuition over intention, or in the injunction of the face of others, as with Levinas, it obscures the vital push and pull of the subject in the organic impulses of the body. "The limit to the phenomenon because of its abstract and purified character suggests to us that the phenomenon reaches its limit."[24] Such a conception, as we will see, will have theological consequences for the conception of

---

22. Falque, *Wedding Feast of the Lamb*, 17–19.
23. Falque, *Wedding Feast of the Lamb*, 21.
24. Falque, *Wedding Feast of the Lamb*, 23.

a religious ideal of vulnerability and weakness, often invoked today, and usually in critique of a weak or powerless God.

It is, therefore, a question of going towards corporeal life, of returning from the *Leib* towards the *Körper*, of thinking about the organic body which escapes phenomenology in the name of releasing a new idea in the discourse, the "expanded body." Such a work will highlight the strength and activity of the body as such. More broadly, *The Wedding Feast of the Lamb* shows a body through the presence of an initial animality as opposed to a sexual difference underlying the original moment of human conception. This other kind of transformation in the philosophical and anthropological conception of man will be seen, as in the first two volumes of the triptych, by a comparable evolution in the theological analysis of the body of God, namely, Christ. Through his animal dimension of man, we find not only a sense of "incorporation" but also the Eucharist, as famously illustrated in the formulation of "this is my body." Each of the two approaches confirms the truth of each other. And, with it, we have at our disposal principles to make Christianity credible. Then, we may recognize that it has, in itself, the cultural and conceptual means of reaching the depths of humanity as it is lived and thought in the contemporary world. Against a tradition which defines man as a rational animal, or a consciousness without a body, it is thus a matter of being interested in man understood as an animal or as "body without consciousness." As Falque writes: "Flesh is certainly organic, but its matter (organic) and its organicity (functional) are in some way called upon to be saved, according to a form of incarnation that this time (against all Gnostic tendencies) does not scorn the materiality of which we are universally constituted."[25]

Reflecting on the animality of man opens, first, a philosophical and anthropological reading of modernity; and, second, a reading of the Bible and of Christ without leading to a sin of angelism. Moreover, we may note that in *The Wedding Feast of the Lamb* philosophy and theology work together to build a test of the Eucharist that does not dispel the perplexity. *The Guide to Gethsemane* is more theological from the outset due to emotional and affective structures of Christian life. *The Metamorphose of Finitude* seems far more philosophical and patiently rational. *The Wedding Feast of the Lamb*, in contrast, asserts joy and epiphanous celebration. Falque himself considers *The Guide to Gethsemane* as the most existential, *The Metamorphose of Finitude* as the most transformative,

---

25. Falque, *Wedding Feast of the Lamb*, 104.

and *The Wedding Feast of the Lamb* as the most radical. Is this due to the perspective at the end of the triptych enterprise in which he gestures towards Spinoza, Nietzsche, and Deleuze? Or, is it due to the effective union, which seems certain from the beginning of the book, between theology and philosophy? The experience of the body in *The Wedding Feast of the Lamb* is more immediately positive, in its affirmation and power of the organic body as well as in the gift of the body of God. Meanwhile, *The Guide to Gethsemane* describes the suffering of the body, and *The Metamorphose of Finitude* evokes the body as glorious, resurrected, but as something still to come. We must distinguish the Falquian approach from the celebration of the modern and mythical body. The eucharistic body is not reducible to the Dionysian body, as celebrated by Nietzsche.

We can consider that *The Wedding Feast of the Lamb*, as the subtitle illustrates—*Eros, the Body, and the Eucharist*—deepens the analysis of the Eucharist through a Falquian conception of the body grounded in finitude. *The Metamorphose of Finitude* insists on the humanity of man, of man in general, that is, on the necessity to remain here for taking into account the radical transformation of the resurrection. This finitude is found in specific relationship to the constituent components of the incarnation: animality and organic corporeality. As in previous works, there remains a question of metamorphosis, although more profound, since it will not only be that of humanity but also of animality! With regard to the Eucharist, we will also better grasp the dimension of immanence in the figure of Christ.

The Power of the Body Underneath the Flesh

The two essential authors for thinking about the body will be, as one might expect, Spinoza and Nietzsche (in part, that Nietzsche relayed by Deleuze). Spinoza, from the beginning, questioned himself with such a framework: "No one has hitherto laid down the limits [of what the body can do]."[26] Inseparable from the soul, which is only an idea, the power of the body is known as the *conatus*, the "effort to persevere in one's being." This is the ultimate source of animation for all living things, and it is also for all animals a source of joy—at least, for the one who is aware of it. However, the power of this body is unconscious as exemplified by sleepwalkers, those whose body is capable of performing actions of which they

---

26. Falque, *Wedding Feast of the Lamb*, 185; see Spinoza, *Ethics*, pt. 3, prop. 2.

are not aware. As Falque observes, "There is, then, an 'unknown of the body' (Spinoza), even an 'unconscious of the body' (Nietzsche), that in reality goes far beyond the 'psychic unconscious' (Freud)."[27] Our body can do more, and better, than our consciousness; the consciousness of the self, says Nietzsche, is superfluous. "The splendid cohesion of living things, the way in which their superior and inferior activities adjust and integrate one with another, the multiform conformity, not in a blind way and even less in a mechanical way, but critically, prudently, carefully even in a rebellious fashion—all this phenomenon of the body [*Leib*] is, from the intellectual point of view, superior to our consciousness, our spirit, our conscious ways of thinking, feeling and willing, as algebra is superior to the multiplication tables."[28]

Nietzsche, contrary to what has been said, does not simply put the body in the place traditionally occupied by the soul. He puts forward the power of a forgotten biological life, that of a body which has no center, which does not know an orientation a priori, which does not seek to acquire knowledge about itself. Life preserves itself, a force that may be in ignorance of itself, a force from within only waiting to be unleashed. Falque, not necessarily unlike Nietzsche, celebrates the power of this body which manifests itself in a life dedicated to becoming, never definitively fixed.

Power Underneath the Body

Nietzsche, unlike Spinoza, does not make the body a substrate, a substance which would replace another substance, the soul. As Falque writes, "It is a question not of introducing a new preeminence (of the body over the mind, for example), but of thinking in corporal terms, and almost in organic terms, of the nexus, or the bonds, among the whole of living beings, by which they are constituted in their bodies and deploy their corporality."[29] For Nietzsche, this body is the origin of true knowledge. Less familiar as the mind, since we are not conscious of all its mechanisms, though decisive for our survival and perception of the world, it is not, like consciousness, a source of illusions about itself. Only when

---

27. Falque, *Wedding Feast of the Lamb*, 107. For the quotation of Nietzsche, see Nietzsche, *Volonté de puissance I*, §226.
28. Falque, *Wedding Feast of the Lamb*, 107.
29. Falque, *Wedding Feast of the Lamb*, 107–8.

it declines do we seek to flee into a hidden world in order to escape the harshness of our existence. Even before the experience that we have of our body as lived (of the simple experience of our body), a pre-intuited power animates us, of which we are ignorant and into which phenomenology cannot reach. Above all, we have on hand a rich metaphysics of the soul.

We need to specify the nature of the body in modern thought. The return to the organic cannot be identified with neutral biological functions of organicity.[30] The body is not simply a substance. Echoing Nietzsche, the body is the dynamic essence of life made of "the spontaneous, aggressive, expansive, form-giving forces that give new interpretations and directions."[31] As Spinoza saw, it is not the body that deploys force, but forces which seek a body.[32] Falque applies this statement, in a daring way, to the Eucharist. It is not an act by which the body releases a force, but the act by which the force seeks a body. The eucharistic bread is the place where the strength of the Spirit gives itself a body. Eucharistic communion, like erotic communion, demonstrate a sharing of forces. It must be reiterated that "bodies derive from forces or powers—not forces or powers from bodies. It is not substance that exercises power, but first power, which then locates itself in substance."[33] In the Eucharist, as in the resurrection, force gives meaning to substance.

To better describe the strength of this body, Falque uses the expression "body without organs," coined by Deleuze and Artaud. It designates "the inorganic life, that is to say a power of vital individuation which has not stabilized in the form of an organism."[34] As Deleuze suggested, this new conception of the body is "no longer a matter of form and organ, but of speed and slownesses, of a composition of forces and affectivity." It is about challenging the pyramid hierarchy "where the major organ, the brain, regulates and controls the rest of the body."[35] It is also to recognize the strength of this disorganized body where the organic precisely takes hold.

---

30. See Falque, *Wedding Feast of the Lamb*, 100–101.

31. Falque, *Wedding Feast of the Lamb*, 110. For Falque's reference to Nietzsche, see Nietzsche, *On the Genealogy of Morals*, 78–79.

32. Spinoza, *Ethics*, pt. 3, prop. 2.

33. Falque, *Wedding Feast of the Lamb*, 111.

34. See Marzano, *Dictionnaire du corps*, 255.

35. Marzano, *Dictionnaire du corps*, 255.

The Spread Body, or the Hypothesis of a Third Body

Falque intends to overcome the phenomenological, and by extent modern, opposition between the flesh and the body, in order to describe and think of a third body, "spread body." This is neither *Körper* nor the "lived body" (*Leib*). A body that "spreads" more than it "extends" is thus "experienced."[36] This body is distinguished by both the objective body, purely physical, and the subjective body, of a psychological nature. This is "organic flesh." Falque writes: "To repenetrate one's own being is not simply to be incorporated into a physical or objective body (*Körper*), nor to be incarnate in a phenomenological or subjective flesh (*Leib*), but rather to '*se corporéiser*' (roughly, to be embodied) . . . an organic flesh made up of nerves, muscles, digestion, secretion, respiration, . . . things that can, like so much of this is my body, remain foreign to me if I am not fully able to make them my own."[37]

This acceptance of a "third" body (a "spread body") is experienced through an "unconscious" experience, more imposed than voluntarily chosen. To illustrate this complex multi-layering, Falque evokes the situation of the bedridden patient on the operating table:

> We can take as an example the body under anesthetic, something most of us have experienced ourselves and seen in others, both animals and human beings. A doctor, or rather a surgeon, works with or cuts open the body as bodily objectivity (*Körper*). He or she knows that another subject is there, at least as far as they share a hypothetical humanity. And he or she shows respect for the body lying on the operating table, if not as a matter of experience, at least through a professional ethic (isolation of the part to be operated on; prohibition of completely stripping the body to the nude). Nonetheless, the body that doctors work with, and do something to, cannot be called a purely subjectivized flesh (*Leib*). Nor does the encounter with the lived experience of the medical staff constitute intersubjectivity, or a mode of empathy, of the kind that is so often falsely sought.[38]

It is significant to note with Falque that, if philosophers like Nietzsche or Deleuze think of such a body, it is made visible only in the works of painters like Lucian Freud who show this "thickness of the body"

---

36. Falque, *Wedding Feast of the Lamb*, 113–14.
37. Falque, *Wedding Feast of the Lamb*, 113.
38. Falque, *Wedding Feast of the Lamb*, 13.

or the "open organic body." Contemporary painting also communicates this transition from flesh to body: "Body in movement (Bacon), body in bulk (Freud), and the open body (Arickx): painting moves toward the 'incarnating' that philosophy hopes to think through (and theology to recover). The contemporary metamorphosis of art is no longer that of body into flesh—as it would be in a Rembrandt or Roualt of our time—but of flesh into body."[39] Contemporary art does not reproduce forms like figurative art; it does not invent them like abstract art, but captures forces. As Paul Klee says, art is not about "making the visible" but to "make visible," to show what we do not see and which makes precisely what we see.[40] Falque will see the same motive of forces in the Eucharist. It is up to theology to rediscover this original movement. Here, we might ask: What can be said of the body of man in becoming that of the body of Christ?[41] We may recall that, following Balthasar, "God has delivered himself to the senses."[42] Such a rapprochement can appear striking: the most traditional and dogmatic theological references may join with the most modern philosophical positions and even most contemporary aesthetic creations—which certain "believers" often oppose in the name of their faith!

Original Difference

The other essential dimension of human finitude in its corporeality is the immediate link with sexuality, a link that contemporary anthropology highlights but that Gospel texts also illustrate in a dazzling way. Here, the eucharistic Last Supper in its erotic dimensions finds the *hoc est corpus meum* (this is my body).[43] The importance of corporeality is thus attested by a philosophical and anthropological way of seeing through the erotic scene in order to arrive at the theological plane, the Eucharist. This link between the erotic and the eucharistic may be a surprise, but it is well founded on an understanding of the body in two fundamental ways. It is indeed a question of a common experience of the gift of the body, from man to woman and vice versa; and, likewise, a question of the gift of the

---

39. Falque, *Wedding Feast of the Lamb*, 116.
40. Klee, *Creative Confession*, 7.
41. Falque, *Wedding Feast of the Lamb*, 117.
42. Falque, *Wedding Feast of the Lamb*, 129. For the reference to Balthasar, see Balthasar, *Glory of the Lord*, 392.
43. Falque, *Wedding Feast of the Lamb*, 209–10.

body of God to man in the host of the Eucharist. The gift makes the body, and the body to the gift; the gift allows us to affirm the differentiation between man and woman, between God and man, but also manifests a common "love of the limit." Finitude, body, and limit are all terms that play key roles in Falque's descriptions. This is not simply identifying the Eucharist with eros per se. Rather, the gift of God to man in the Eucharist gives meaning to the reciprocal gift of man and woman, and not the inverse.

The erotic experience, which is based on the differentiation between man and woman, is constitutive of the passage from animality (male-female) to humanity (man-woman). If the nonrecognition of the organicity of the body makes us forget its animality, the nonrecognition of eros leads to another forgetting, that of sexual difference. Falque devotes many pages to establishing that original difference. "In the creative fidelity of sexual difference, as also in the unique sacrifice of the eucharistic gift, the abiding—or the imperative that tells us to stay—becomes the condition of our permanence and is the principal requisite of all true fruitfulness."[44] This "erotic imperative" requires rethinking an original Christian hermeneutics of sexual difference based on Christ's words in the Gospel of Mark, "From the beginning of creation, God made them male and female" (Mark 10:6). For Falque, Christ practices here an inversion; for it was only on the sixth day that "in the image of God he created them; male and female he created them" (Gen 1:27).

The specificity of Christianity on this point is also seen in the comparison with Greek thought. The famous myth of the androgyne, attributed in Plato's *Symposium*, poses the question of the original unity of the sexes but later separated. In Christianity, too, it is differentiation that composes true wholeness and originality. We may be surprised, in view of such assertions, that this same Christianity has been able so often, in its history, to devalue sexuality and the image of women. If we could say, in a very schematic and caricatured manner, that for Freud "everything is sex," we could therefore maintain, in an equally schematic manner, that for Christianity—at its origins—everything is body—and, above all, sexual body. In this regard, Falque's approach is instructive, innovative, and much needed.

This sexual difference in the beginning, as affirmed by Falque, will also be transformed after the resurrection. To the question asked in Matt

---

44. Falque, *Wedding Feast of the Lamb*, 228.

22 (will a man recognize his wife once in heaven?), Christ answers that in the resurrection we take neither a wife nor a husband, but we are like angels in heaven. But being "like" angels means precisely that humans will never be angels and the abolition of differences is not the suppression of differentiation. In this sense differentiation refers, more generally, to sexuality more than genitality. Here, Falque reinterprets the Thomist understanding of the procreative body. The organs which serve us, whether or not they are used, will be resurrected in men and women in order to restore the integrity of the natural body.[45] The maintenance of this differentiation is also a satisfaction, as we will see, of the limit at which the condition of man experiences positively the relationship between man and woman, and, moreover, between man and God. "If there is to be a resurrection, or a metamorphosis of finitude, it will never be made at the price of a breaking up of frontiers, but will simply be another way of living within our limited being."[46]

If the figure of Christ illuminates the nature of human sexuality by showing the original character, the Eucharist, the gift of the body of Christ as the manifestation of divine love, also reveals the nature of love. Falque accepts neither the conception of univocity nor that of equivocity. "We cannot be satisfied with the total 'equivocity' of *eros* and *agape* (Nygren), nor accept simple 'univocity' (Marion). The former risks separating divine charity from human love to such a degree that nothing remains in common between the two; the latter considers the modalities of divine love on the model of human love so comprehensively that nothing remains that is particular to God."[47] In this regard, Falque speaks of an "incorporation of erotic union" into the "eucharistic body." Divine love integrates human love and transforms it in the act of the Eucharist. The deep and profound nature of love is revealed in the experience of the gift, that of the body of Christ in the Eucharist and of the body of the spouses in desirous as well as erotic union.

Thus, Falque highlights the existence of desire in both situations. If it seems evident in the union of two human bodies, it is also true in that of the Eucharist. The Gospel affirms that Christ "desired eagerly to eat this Passover" with his disciples.[48] And it is not a question, in the Eu-

---

45. Falque, *Wedding Feast of the Lamb*, 165–66. On the reference to Aquinas, see Aquinas, *Contra Gentiles* 4.88.2.

46. Falque, *Wedding Feast of the Lamb*, 147.

47. Falque, *Wedding Feast of the Lamb*, 134.

48. Luke 22:15.

charist, of only "taking and eating" the body of Christ, but to truly desire it. It is a common motivation of the body, divine body as well as human body, to be longed for. God and human beings experience the desire to encounter a body (for God in the incarnation), that is, the gift of a body in the erotic scene and, theologically, in the eucharistic supper.

They also both experience a common love of the limit as expressed by the story of human and divine solitude in Genesis. The Eucharist summarizes what God has already done in the act of creation. Why, in fact, create man when he could have been satisfied with making a world of self-contemplation? "There is only one answer to these questions: Because of his love and respect for limits, he the Unlimited had need of a different limited one, capable of being itself for him as a face-to-face for his own act of loving."[49] This solitude experienced by God is also felt by Adam before the appearance of Eve, so much so that God eliminated and reversed his loneliness. Here, Falque sees a positive turn in the idea of a limit, as opposed to the experience of limitation as refusal. He writes that "in the double choice of limitation in a body: the decision to bring about incarnation, and the narrowing down as far as the transubstantiated bread in the act of the eucharist."[50]

The transition to theological argumentation may be taken, ironically, by a return to Nietzsche and the role he plays in Falque's approach. At this stage of our interpretation, we can see an evolution in the Falquian conception of corporeality. Taking note of the reversal of the body brought about by modernity, Falque initially resumed the phenomenological distinction between the flesh and the body. However, after having shared, in a way, with Michel Henry the emphasis of the carnal dimension, Falque restored a more specifically corporeal and organic dimension, evoking Nietzsche. We can therefore expect that the theological part of Falque's reflection, in building on this perspective, will demonstrate how and where Christ fully assumes his human finitude. To do so, the analysis of the body must go through a doubly "carnal" and "corporeal" dimension in order to reach an understanding of the resurrection of the flesh. Thus, a double question inevitably arises relating to the confrontation of the human body to the divine body: on the one hand, the consequences of the Falquian conception of corporeality, on the other hand, that of philosophical and theological coherence. Formulated schematically, Falque

---

49. Falque, *Wedding Feast of the Lamb*, 148.
50. Falque, *Wedding Feast of the Lamb*, 149.

intends to clarify the nature of the body of Christ in his incarnation, his passion, his resurrection, and, last, the Eucharist.

The description of the human offered in *The Wedding Feast of the Lamb* seems clear enough: "Certainly the human is not only body, but the human is first body—a body in which Christ's incarnation is different from all other forms of angelic apparition."[51] Falque does not stop there. He announces, further, another transition, from the corporeal to the carnal and from the organic to the phenomenological. Such a development may reassure a particularly attentive reader who, remembering the emphasis placed in the description of the resurrection and on the carnal dimension of Christ, might question the privilege granted in the preceding pages to the organic dimension of man. This last turning point in our philosophical reflections has a strong theological justification. Falque writes: "If the power of the body and the manifesto of the flesh remain undoubtedly the basis on which embodiedness is shown, we might still wonder whether the *conatus* (Spinoza), the creative will (Nietzsche), the Nerve Meter (Artaud), or the body without organs (Deleuze) say all that we need to say about embodiedness. Because, if Christ in his Resurrection appeared in 'flesh and bones' (*sarxa kait ostea*) in the sight of and the understanding of his disciples (Luke 24:39), such an apparition does not signify, retrospectively, that he will be there in the consecrated Host with this 'flesh' or with these 'bones'—as though something physical, even anatomical, or of the cadaver, were to be chewed or crunched."[52] This leads us to a new horizon. But it is, for the moment, interesting to note that this movement, which leads to an apparent suspension of philosophical or anthropological studies, is first provoked by a confrontation with a theological reference, namely, the evocation of the physical nature of Christ. Such an argument is revealing of Falque's own evolution. In recently published texts, he highlights the contribution of theology to philosophy, and the transformation that results from passing from philosophy through theology.

We must therefore move from the "organic of the body" to the perspective of "the flesh." This leads to a new distinction between the "layers of corporeality," already indicated by Husserl, but with a reformulated hierarchy: a) the physical body (*Körper*), "of which the extent marks the main characteristic," b) the biological body (*Leib* or flesh in the ordinary

---

51. Falque, *Wedding Feast of the Lamb*, 117.
52. Falque, *Wedding Feast of the Lamb*, 117.

sense of the term) which, for Falque, finds its meaning in the "expanded" body, c) the lived body (*Leibkörper*), a place of an immanent and pre-reflected knowledge, d) the corporeal and spiritual flesh (*Leib* in the phenomenological sense of the term). The task that presents itself, after we have put the first body in brackets and put it back in honor of the second, is to rethink the last two "within the context of the eucharistic act."[53] As Falque observes: "I am also 'flesh,' not simply in forgetting body or the organic living being this time, but in my perceptive faculty of understanding the world, or of receiving it and relating to it."[54]

We perhaps already suspected, in light of the presentation of the resurrection, the need for such an articulation. It seems that Falque anticipates this already: "As far as theology is concerned, the eucharist cannot be understood independently from the Resurrection, any more than the 'biological body' can be considered independently from the 'phenomenological flesh' in philosophy."[55] Thus, Falque's work is of a dual nature, critically questioning both phenomenology and theology. As we have seen, the insufficiency of phenomenology in its triple hypertrophy, that of "flesh on the body," of "signification in chaos," and "passivity on activity" lead to a pressing concern in theology, namely, to articulate the primacy of the flesh over the body in the act of the resurrection. Such is one of the great insights of *The Metamorphosis of Finitude* and *The Wedding Feast of the Lamb*. For Falque, it is necessary to link the organic body to the experience of the flesh and the Eucharist to the resurrection. We will therefore fill a double gap, that which exists between the Eucharist as body and the resurrection as flesh. This resolution represents more than a vitalist and organicist tradition from the nineteenth century (Schopenhauer, Nietzsche, Feuerbach) as well as a phenomenological and self-affective tradition of the twentieth century (Husserl, Scheler, Henry, Levinas). In this regard, we can appreciate the ambition of Falque's task to locate new foundations for a question that is commonly felt to be beyond theology yet, in fact, remains at the core of its very practice. Falque, it can be said, demonstrates that the essential contribution that theology can make to philosophy and, to a certain extent the person of Christ, depends upon a reliable account of humanity. But, before thinking through this next articulation, it is necessary to deepen the analysis of the act of the Eucharist itself.

53. Falque, *Wedding Feast of the Lamb*, 118.
54. Falque, *Wedding Feast of the Lamb*, 119.
55. Falque, *Wedding Feast of the Lamb*, 119.

SECTION TWO: THE EUCHARIST AND THE THEOLOGY OF THE BODY

We will find an essential reading of Christianity that our "de-Christianized" world has forgotten or simply ignores: the proposed salvation of the Gospels comes from the flesh through the resurrection of Christ with and by the Eucharist. It is the bodily dimension that plays the decisive role. Such an affirmation can be received only on the condition of defining these two terms well. We may ask, does Falque allow us to think about the body, whose "forgetting" would be as decisive as that of the forgetting of Being denounced by Heidegger? We can think of this as one of the most valuable contributions of Falque's work. This direction appears more and more clearly throughout the three volumes of the triptych. We might ask, on a level of narrative, was it already present in his mind, or did its evidence gradually become apparent to him through his reflection and writing? Perhaps he could not really think about it in its Christian and Catholic specificity, so that after having put it in terms of philosophical concepts, he was able to give it fruitful application for a wide audience.

It seems to me that the instrumental philosophical move is initially apparent in the first part of Falque's reflection on the body in *The Wedding Feast of the Lamb*. While the theological content was present, it does not become explicitly pronounced until the analysis of the altarpiece of Ghent. In order to arrive at a productive communion of philosophy and theology, a goal that we have already seen attempted at length, the principles of contemporary anthropology, philosophy, and aesthetic experience must therefore be confronted with those of theology and faith. One would be tempted to say that, for a non-believing reader, the weight of theology is even more immediately significant here. The reasons of such an impression are multiple. The Eucharist is probably even more mysterious than the resurrection for those who experience difficulty in believing. Falque would agree that this is one the greatest oddities of Christianity that, at times, has been the cause of scandal on grounds of cannibalism. Once again, Falque comes forward unmasked. As in the case of the resurrection, he confronts his reader with the "fact" of the Eucharist in all its radicality, seeking to bring out its true nature, without hiding all the difficulties it has given rise to and still arouses today. It is not nothing to want to show that the Eucharist is intelligible according to the criteria of the most modern thought.

Certainly, this reflection on the Eucharist is grafted, again more directly than the philosophical analysis of the human body, on Christ's words: "This is my body." Yet, for Falque, it is more than a theological item, it is an essential cornerstone of our Western culture, beyond or in short of a believing perspective, as Jean-Luc Nancy has also recognized. The latter offers an interpretation, which is certainly not very orthodox. He reads it as a sort of unthought mode of Christianity, but which structures Western thought all the same: "It is our *Om mani padne* . . . , our *Allah ill' allah* . . . , our *Schema* Israel."[56] If this denomination of the body has declined previously, according to Falque, through the Spinozist question (taken up by Nietzsche): What can a body do? It must, now, take another formulation through the analysis of the Eucharist.

"This is my body" covers a conception of the body of God in his *giving* which also translates into a double questioning: first, already contained in the Gospel, concerning the person and the body of Christ ("Who is this man who asks to be eaten?"); second, referring more precisely to the behavior of man (what means "eat this body"?). Note the prosaic and very concrete mode of the question of an act of "eating." It refers to the carnal dimension of the Eucharist and its apparently mysterious and strange character. Falque recalls the possible astonishment of Augustine himself: "It seemed like delirium and madness to give to men his flesh to eat and his blood to drink. . . . Does it not seem like madness to say: 'eat the flesh and drink my blood?' And saying: 'Whoever will not eat my flesh and not drink my blood, will not have eternal life (e.g., John 6). Does Jesus not seem delirious?"[57] As theology takes its point of departure from philosophy, the body of Christ will be understood from the bodily traits discovered in the anthropological and philosophical analysis of the human body. Christ having to assume the entirety of humanity, must also assume our animality and organicity. This double dimension requires more articulation.

In fact, the task at hand is to do many things. It is to define the nature of the body of Christ in the Eucharist as developed in *The Guide to Gethsemane*, and to uncover the passion of Christ in *The Metamorphosis of Finitude*. It is also, from the point of view of Jesus's resurrection, to ground and explore the body of the Eucharist as a testament to a transformation of the body of the finite being. A story of transformation

---

56. Nancy, *Corpus*, 3.
57. Received in conversation with Falque.

and metamorphosis, this approach culminates in the reality of the Risen Christ. And, to reach that level, Falque proposes a passage from transubstantiation (of bread into body and wine into blood), through assimilation (of God into man through consumption), and into incorporation (of man into God through the mystery of the church). Falque calls this last phase an institution, in reference to the body of the church.

Of Transubstantiation

Falque highlights two essential characteristics of this transformation: the assumption by the eucharistic body (of all the components of the human body) and the affirmation of the real presence of Christ in the host and the Eucharist.

The Assumption of the Totality of the Human Body

The Wedding Feast of the Lamb begins with an analysis of the famous Ghent altarpiece, *The Mystic Lamb* by the Van Eyck brothers, where Christ is represented in the form of a lamb—immolated, ready to be seen, adored, as well as eaten. The body of Christ is offered here through the painting of an animal. The organic character is evidenced in this "Lamb of God," which "takes away the sins of the world." Christ, by becoming incarnate, took charge of our humanity, but the assumption broadens the reach of Christ's humanity by also invoking our animality. Christ did not, to be clear, become animal. He simply takes on the care of our animal side (i.e., flesh, passions, impulses, and corporeality). Such is the naked truth behind our humanity. And, such is the mission of Christ to bear it in sacrifice.

We find, here, a recognition of the true nature of man, so often hidden in a tradition which thinks the angel more than the animal, the "consciousness without body" rather than the "body without consciousness." The biblical text, on this point, is rich with teaching. Furthermore, it clearly distinguishes animality from bestiality. Bestiality designates the sinful tendency of man, capable of falling below animality in certain excesses (pornography, lust, etc.), while animality remains an original and founding structure of man (chaos, passions, impulses, etc.). "The paschal lamb sacrificed for us is thus certainly for our salvation (he who takes away the sins of the world) but also an assumption of our Chaos, the

Chaos of our emotions and our drives, in the form of a building block and substructure of our humanity (a conversion of animality into humanity through filiation as recognized by the eucharist)."[58] The fact that Christ assumed this animality helps, in a certain way, to better understand our condition, as Falque alludes to, following Benedict XVI, "if humanity aspires to be pure spirit and to reject the flesh as pertaining to his animal nature alone, then spirit and body would both lose their dignity."[59] This journey consists of a conversion through transubstantiation and the three components of man: animality (eucharistic heritage), corporeality (eucharistic content), and eros (eucharistic modality). Once again theology nourishes philosophy.

The Real Presence of the Body of Christ

The analysis of transubstantiation refers to older issues and interpretations that Falque, for his part, rearticulates with fresh meaning and relevance. To be sure, he does not hesitate, as he did for the resurrection, to expose mischaracterizations of past formulations. A contemporary reader, unfamiliar with old controversies, may be somewhat at a loss, yet he will be able to understand what is at stake in the specificity of Christianity and Catholicism—and the specificity of humanity at large. Let us remember that the eucharistic presence was, according to Aquinas, more miraculous than creation. Pascal, too, saw in it "the strangest and most obscure secret" of the hidden God.[60]

What is this body as announced in the famous declaration, "This is my body," and who is permitted to eat of it? Schematically, we could say that it is not merely a conception that would reduce the body to a state of meat. It is not a question of resorting to interpretations that would make it possible to attenuate the apparently scandalous dimension of "eating" the body of Christ. There is no need to obscure the real presence of the body and blood of God in the bread and wine, post-consecration. By becoming incarnate, Christ became flesh, taking on a true body, as we have seen. He not only had a body; he was this body. In the Eucharist, it is not a question not only of a "becoming body" but of a "becoming

---

58. Falque, *Wedding Feast of the Lamb*, 32.
59. Falque, *Wedding Feast of the Lamb*, 43. On the reference to Pope Benedict XVI, see Benedict XVI, "Deus Caritas Est," §5.
60. See Chauvet, *Corps chemin de Dieu*, 194.

bread." The "this-ness" of the body of Christ illuminates our way of seeing the transubstantiation, a "force of action" which expresses the power of the Spirit. It is, moreover, a force of expression which prohibits seeing in this transformation a reification. We are therefore witness to a transformation of Christ's own body (flesh) into objectified body (bread), then, ultimately, to transubstantiated conditions (body of flesh).

With such a formulation, lingering questions still remain. Is this analysis representative of eucharistic realism or symbolism? Is it a realistic conception in which we place emphasis on the thing as signified, the bread itself which is transformed into a body and the wine into blood? Or, do we favor the sign or the figure in a symbolist grammar according to which the interior disposition of the one who communicates is more important than what is given—more the ideal than what we eat? Falque seems to align with eucharistic realism. The "eucharistic meal" is not constituted only by the guests, but by what is given to eat and drink. "To insist too much on the consciousness of the subject in common . . . , we probably lose the meaning and consistency of that which is eaten, or given to worship."[61] It is the real body and blood which is in question, and is hardly surprising considering the entire approach and weight given to the body. However, to avoid reducing the body to a state of meat, it is still necessary to specify the true nature of this body. As Falque observes, it is "real" body and "true" blood, it is not a "true" body and "true" blood.[62] That ideal that is made to eat is not the body of the incarnated historical Jesus but the flesh of the resurrected Christ. There, we will be freed from the aporias of cannibalism. "If we don't take up the challenge of answering this, the dogma remains so enigmatic that the problem of cannibalism keeps cropping up and the 'truly body' of the Resurrected One (*corpus vere*) becomes confused with the 'true body' of the historic Jesus (*corpus verus*)."[63] We communicate with a resurrected body which does not risk being broken or disappear when we eat it, but which inherits the qualities or pathic forms of the historical Christ. This guarantees that it is indeed the body of Christ that we are eating, thus ensuring a carnal continuity between the biological body and the historical body *within* the eucharistic body.

---

61. Received in conversation with Falque.
62. Falque, *Wedding Feast of the Lamb*, 218–20.
63. Falque, *Wedding Feast of the Lamb*, 200.

Incorporation: The Eucharist Present in the Body of Christ

The two moments that follow, assimilation and incorporation, describe the way in which Christ comes to us—becoming bread, then body. From there, we may incorporate ourselves into him. Through assimilation, God makes himself ours and we can, it seems, digest this presence. The body and blood of Christ strengthen us in a gift from organic to organic. The assimilation of this life to God's makes our body, in a certain way, incorruptible. We can find there the testimony of the power of the body as organic and corporative, which Spinoza and Nietzsche have highlighted. The joining of this divine body strengthens the power of the human body in a sort of hand-to-hand combat, of push and pull between two worlds and two natures. In a theological language, this assimilation marks the completion of the movement of the incarnation of the Word and its kenosis, of this "becoming body from the flesh."

The believer ingests the body of Christ *as* incorporated. "Nobody simply eats God, but we are always in some respect eaten by him."[64] Falque exposes the radicality of Christianity, using a vocabulary that is certainly orthodox and even traditional, and which may even risk offending certain contemporaries. After overcoming the possibility of a discursive dispute over the meat of Christ, that is, cannibalism, we find the real transformation that is at stake, that of our corporeality in the act of Eucharist. After "assimilation" (the descent of God into the world and into ourselves), "incorporation" becomes the "ascent of ourselves integrated into God by forming his body." After eating the body of God, it is then a question of giving an account of that to be eaten by him.

We should certainly not think of this incorporation in the mode of simple digestion. To defend against this risk, Falque compares eucharistic incorporation to the intentionality of phenomenology. To be aware of something is not to internalize it, assimilate it, and digest it. Against an illusion which would pose that to know is to eat, we must note a form of transcendence which takes us out of immanence. Knowledge is not assimilation of another, but a bursting towards another, just as incorporation into the body of Christ is participation in his life. "Making our communion through the flesh of Christ—in being unified with the true body of the Resurrected One (including and going beyond the true body and the history of Jesus of Nazareth)—we take part in the life of the Resurrected One in its otherness; we make our communion with his Life

---

64. Falque, *Wedding Feast of the Lamb*, 205.

rather than focusing on ourselves or confining ourselves solely within our egoisms."[65] We no longer limit ourselves to our flesh. As Falque echoes from Saint Bonaventure, Christ's body, and not simply the ideal of it, is projected into the fullness of the mystical body.[66]

The Eucharist is therefore a gift from the organic to the organic which, like food, is made stronger in him who assimilates it. We approach the communion with our viscera, our whole body. It is not only the soul that is nourished by the Eucharist; we are integrated in God with our bodily passions and whole life-world. Following St. Irenaeus's sacramental theology, Falque shows that it is this authentically human body, composed of "flesh, nerves and bones," which is nourished by the blood of Christ and strengthened by his body.[67] Thus, the reality of the Eucharist appears in its carnal and organic fullness. This is a double movement: the assimilation of the body on the one hand and the incorporation in his body on the other hand.[68] It is the acting of eating and being eaten, of assimilating and being assimilated.

Institution and Adoration

The eucharistic celebration is not only that of a mystery, of a past event, but that of "an act of the past as never exceeded." It is, more specifically, to only a question of memory, but of "with one of life, of body and blood, newly given and shared," and the memory to which the eucharistic celebration calls is of a "carnal" order.[69] There is a memory of the "body of Christ" that we live with and share in by eating him, as there is a memory of our own body; as the Scripture goes, "Do this in memory of me."[70] Moreover, as Falque observes: "A simple act of consciousness is not enough for the memory celebrated in this is my body, nor indeed is the act of will concerning whether or not we attend a Sunday Mass. The memory is inscribed, or should be inscribed, in our own bodies—just as the memory of food leads us always, almost biologically, to look for

---

65. Falque, *Wedding Feast of the Lamb*, 208.
66. Falque, *Wedding Feast of the Lamb*, 179–81.
67. Falque, *Wedding Feast of the Lamb*, 205.
68. Falque, *Wedding Feast of the Lamb*, 205–8.
69. Falque, *Wedding Feast of the Lamb*, 210.
70. See Luke 22:19.

it."⁷¹ The whole body participates, in the sense that all our organs inscribe within themselves the trace of our present and past lives. Once again, the importance of the body is seen in the Eucharist and, by extent, in the life of Christianity.

The final stage in Falque's systematic thinking is that of "Adoration." It is not enough to "eat" the Eucharist body, we must also "see" it in order to love it and worship it as a source of transformation. This "desire to see the host," as Falque shows, corresponds to that contemplation of not only God but also of me as the whole of my interior being, itself made of Chaos, passions and impulses, as if projected and transformed into God.[72] I do not see only God, I see myself in God. Such a perspective passes over a form of abandonment of the self, insofar as it turns towards God and moves, in contemplation, through a conversion of our senses. Like St. Bonaventure's philosophy of adoration, Falque observes: "All the same, the discourse on such frontiers is nothing, or almost nothing, in comparison with the 'silent experience of the flesh' that is told, or rather, that is lived, when the *eros* is transformed into *agape* in the act of the manducation of Christ eucharisticized and in contemplation of his body in the Adoration."[73] The whole eucharistic ceremony is indeed the experience of a "body to body" which thus attests to "the power of corporeality" but—this is an essential point—this power is not only produced by me; it is "impulsed by an Other in me but not reducible to me."[74] It is unlike any experience celebrated by Nietzsche or Spinoza.

This power of the body is also illuminated if we remember what has been said, philosophically, of the relationships between force and the body. In the conception of Spinoza and Nietzsche, the forces do not impact bodies but bodies are the expression of these forces. We could thus read the Eucharist as a balance of power (i.e., forces). It is the forces of vitality which give themselves to another force in Christ, a greater force that seeks to give its body to another body. This also transcends Nietzsche's critique of the idea of the Christian God identified with a principle of ideal or pure spirit, as though it is an obstacle to the expression of the body. On the contrary, Christ represents the strength of the body as a human achievement.

---

71. Falque, *Wedding Feast of the Lamb*, 211.
72. Falque, *Wedding Feast of the Lamb*, 214.
73. Falque, *Wedding Feast of the Lamb*, 233.
74. Falque, *Wedding Feast of the Lamb*, 207.

An equally importance presence of the body is demonstrated in the mystical body of the church. In particular, it can be seen in the episode of the washing of the feet, a reflection of the eucharistic meal from the Gospel of John where the Last Supper is actually absent. Both episodes represent two forms of history arriving in the flesh. Jesus, after having making himself one with the bread, makes himself one here with the body of his disciples, pulled together in solidarity by the same cloth. *The Wedding Feast of the Lamb* ends with that very reading of the eucharistic viaticum. This moment, essential to Falque's conclusions on the body, can take on two different meanings. The viaticum can set us free and save us at the time of our death, represented by the last Christian sacrament. As Christ states: "Amen, Amen I say to you, unless you eat the flesh of the Son of Man and drink his blood, you do not have life within you. Whoever feeds upon my flesh and drinks my blood has eternal life, and I will raise him up on the last day."[75] Falque suggests that our nourishment nevertheless remains with what we are in this life here below. We must also recall, here, Falque's insistence on the idea that we are *in via*, on the way. The Eucharist constitutes our daily food, for us who are attached to life, and whose earthly pilgrimage "does not indicate, in biblical terms, that it is necessary to leave anything, and still less that we have already arrived at that point."[76] We also find, here, a double reading of Heidegger (the "phenomenological finitude") and Aquinas (the "theological limit"). We must remain below, in permanence of our finitude where the permanence of God is manifested in us through the Eucharist. As the Johannine word says, "Whoever eats my flesh and drinks my blood, I will abide in him and he in me."[77]

This permanence, or act of remaining, is exhilarating and euphoric. The Eucharist reveals itself as a source of Christian intoxication in contrast to Dionysian pleasure, as Nietzsche might have it. In this dialogue with Nietzsche, we find yet another firm ground to respond to the criticism that Christianity devalues living in the present. The eucharistic sacrifice is indeed a source of joy; it is not a simple "transit towards another place of existence;" it generates "enthusiasm" in the sense that it is integrated into God *in-theos*. "The true joy is not simply to possess God in himself (assimilation), but to give oneself up to him (incorporation), without ever losing that difference that always and forever forms the site

75. John 6:53–54.
76. Falque, *Wedding Feast of the Lamb*, 223.
77. See John 6:56.

of self-identity as well as the site of pleasure (desire and differentiation)."[78] The Eucharist therefore expresses a logic of permanence and dwelling. It allows you to grasp it, as Stanislas Breton says: "The issue is not to leave (the tendency of Platonism) nor to want to end (the aim of nihilism), but to live according to a mode of 'subsistence' where subsistence is defined this time as 'effort to stay in the presence.'"[79] Falque would probably accept, regarding the Eucharist, what Louis-Marie Chauvet says of the sacraments: "There is a time of an 'already,' yet shot through with a 'not yet,' under penalty of reducing the kingdom of God to a simple 'otherwise' of 'this world.' . . . We are thus witnesses to a God whose coming is just beyond our temporal horizons of understanding."[80] Against the privilege granted to the immediacy of meaning, to the flesh in the celebration of passivity, the apparent meaninglessness of finitude is overcome through the different modes of the eucharistic reality. In particular, it is brought to the fore by the organicity of the body together with the strength of the Spirit.

The previous section devoted to the status of finitude focused on its essential and sustainable dimension. It was positively (i.e., theologically) linked to the status of the creature, as willed by God. The same positivity is now recognized in the body, in the carnal dimension of being human. Working through contemporary thought, we were able to locate distinctions between flesh and body as well as showed theologically its profound relationship to the sacrament of the Eucharist. That weight of the body in its most organic content, which is also the weight of life, is assumed by Christ in the gift of his body at the eucharistic banquet. Each of these moments only confirms the importance of finitude as bodily experience.

In *The Wedding Feast of the Lamb*, we find a celebration of the body in this world, manifested as an affirmation of life. As Falque recognizes, it is a profoundly Nietzschean insight. To be sure, he responds to that challenge of Nietzsche who makes this assertion at the expense of Christian truths. Perhaps, Falque, like Ricœur, productively engages with the "masters of suspicion." For, in a way, Falque evokes a Spinozist and Nietzschean joy. Though seemingly grounded in atheism, it continues to offer a rich existential a priori. Falque is not quick to conceal the tragic nature of the human condition. He might even take up Ricœur's formulation

---

78. Falque, *Wedding Feast of the Lamb*, 231.
79. See Breton, *Vivant miroir de l'univers*, 42.
80. Chauvet, *Corps chemin de Dieu*, 190.

of finding a joy of the yes within a sadness of the infinite. In light of the analysis of the Eucharist, one would be tempted to say that, for Falque, the body is the place of salvation. In contrast to Spinoza and Nietzsche, who defended a conception of salvation closer to health, the body is a sign of salvation through its religious metamorphosis. Man, in Christ, does not resurrect himself; he is raised by another, who is the Father, by the power of the Spirit. This metamorphosis, according to Falque, is that which is offered by the Eucharist. It is made possible by the resurrection—a resurrection that does not disqualify this world (as Nietzsche thought) but makes anew this world through the work of God.

It is through finitude, but also that of its transformation (first and foremost that of the body), that the human condition is truly realized for what it really is. The Falquian project is dedicated to the teachings of Christianity but only in such a way that makes it intelligible to our contemporaries. Christianity ought to express full appreciation of the human being in bodily form, without which the metamorphosis would not be possible.

Epilogue
A Promise Kept?

OUR INITIAL WAGER IN the value of Falque's thought was anchored in the conviction that, independently of any belief, his approach allowed us to "think" God. At the end of our journey, the reader is nevertheless invited to confirm or deny whether that assertion has held true. A clarification may be necessary. "Thinking" God does not mean "knowing" God, that is, reducing God to a static object of knowledge. The first Christians, unlike the pagans who sought to delimit God, argued that God manifested himself through dynamic practices of charity as seen in the gospel message. Pascal, too, noted that a distance exists between the knowledge of God and his love. The conditions of these "thoughts" on God may be more apparent if we take some time, by way of a conclusion, to summarize some points of emphasis.

The Necessity of Thinking

To Think Is to Decide

Falque is a "believing" philosopher, but he often recalls certain ideas of Christianity, or rather dogmas, that structure our culture—believing or not. An atheist like Jean-Luc Nancy also recognizes this last point with regard to the Eucharist. Christianity is much more than a heritage; it is also a promise, and Falque offers a presentation that can be enriching for readers who are doubtful about the nature of this expectation. This Christianity deserves to be thought through in its most fundamental principles. Falque does not see the future of Christianity in an abandonment of speculation in favor of "soft" or "weak" thinking. The essential truth of Christianity is found in the teaching and practice of charity, which now pays little attention to metaphysical questions. The word "metaphysics," the meaning of which would certainly need to be clarified, is understood as something not reducible to problems of onto-theology. For Falque, this task has now been replaced by a more urgent task.

Thinking—thinking with, beyond, and through limits of divinity and humanity—is indeed the task that Falque offers us. It allows the believer and unbeliever alike to plumb the depths of truth in their existence. To think about Christianity is also to struggle, to use the title by Olivier Roy, against "holy ignorance."[1] The conjunction between faith and culture is essential here.

Philosophy and Theology

The More We Philosophize, the Better We Theologize

One of the most original points of Falque's approach is, without a doubt, his conception of the union of theology and philosophy. Against a tradition (ancient and modern) which approaches the relationship between these two disciplines as a framework of smooth continuity and fulfillment, Falque interrogates the conventional boundaries between them while also maintaining their respective autonomy. In many cases where he opts for theology, he also keeps philosophy creatively in play. In *Crossing the Rubicon*, Falque recognizes—having crossed the Rubicon—that there is a certain freedom in being a theologian. He does so in order to liberate theology through philosophy. He also shows how the teaching of theology can overcome and resolve philosophical upheavals too.

We must therefore be able to use both disciplines in a dual framework without confusing and conflating them. It is in fact on condition of avoiding a hasty amalgamation that we will be able to see in this "bi-disciplinarity" a guarantee of openness. Indeed, where certain philosophers have constructed their own approach with reliance on scientific practice, we may reasonably expect a similar partnership in philosophy and theology. It offers a didactic opportunity for mutual contributions in the history of thought. Openness is at the origin of transformations of concepts and issues in both disciplines. It remains, for a contemporary reader, a certain recognition of the philosophical fecundity of theology;

---

1. See Roy, *Sainte ignorance*.

there, Falque may be the most innovative—the crossing of a threshold that is not thought of in terms of a leap nor of mere continuity but rather through retrieval and metamorphosis.

A question inevitably arises: Would Falque fall under the accusation of a "theological turn"? We may notice from the outset that the term "turning point," as far as it concerns him, is inadequate, since he has always defined himself as both philosopher and theologian. He seems to have never changed on this point. His possible accusers should rather speak of a more original fault before any turn. Falque himself has even recognized the merits of Janicaud's criticism of other phenomenologists who mix philosophy and theology without recognizing and reflecting a preemption of the infinite. For Falque sought to be, first, a philosopher. The weight and the place he gives to finitude suggest, if anything, a turning point within phenomenology as a matter of method, that is, on the pure and simple question of horizons of existence. Theology, in its time, will shed light on the philosophy (and metamorphosis) of finitude, but the reader will initially share with philosophers, seemingly fixed in immanence, an appreciation for the radicality of the experience of living a fully human life.

Emmanuel Tourpe, a theologian, despite his favorable reading of our author's works, once criticized Falque for being too loose with the concept of finitude. He accused Falque of pressing too hard against transcendence while granting too important a role to atheism as an existential a priori. To my mind, the fact that such a criticism may come from within Catholicism seems only to demonstrate the very uniqueness and broadness of Falque's approach. Ultimately, the legitimacy of the philosophy-theology rapport finds its basis in their interaction. Beyond epistemological questions, it is indeed in the light of their co-fertility that one may merit importance for scholarship today. Falque shares, with Hannah Arendt and Levinas, a reading of philosophy organized around its Greek and biblical sources.

Tradition and Modernity

One Must Interrogate a Newness in the Tradition

Do we say that theology seems to hearken back to a bygone era of outdated ideas and practice? It is the unique specificity of our thinker at hand that in relying on this tradition he is able to nourish a contemporary world of thought and culture, to keep alive the projects of tradition and modernity. Christianity cannot hope for survival with a mere return to the past, hence Falque's enthusiasm to bind medieval thought with phenomenology. These two disciplines, when brought in conversation, provide fertile grounds of possibility for future work.

Medieval thought, so present in Falque's work, effectively illuminates contemporary thinking. As Falque reminds us, "Why should we work on the Middle Ages if we do not let the Middle Ages work on us?"[2] Modern philosophy, in the form of phenomenology, makes it possible to identify the potentialities and riches of medieval theology due to the fact that the very practice of medieval thinkers, in many aspects, is akin to the phenomenological method. These thinkers of the past teach us how to "inhabit the world," as does phenomenology, for the sake of building a manner and style of thought (i.e., Merleau-Ponty). A double richness is thus promised: for medieval philosophy in seeing the same things differently; for phenomenology in opening one's horizons to experience that which has not yet been described or anticipated. Thus, it is not a question of trying to relive and think in the confines of the Middle Age, but rather to bring it to life in a fresh context of new epistemic and cultural possibilities.

Bringing medieval thought into conjunction with phenomenology has, at times, been the subject of reservations and criticisms (from medievalists or phenomenologists). We will simply recall that Heidegger himself had insisted on the importance of such a confrontation, for example, when he devoted his habilitation to Duns Scotus. We can certainly understand that any intellectual pursuit develops out of a given tradition with its own historical conditions. That being said, our audience is the contemporary world, with its own language, idiom, and preconceptions. Aquinas makes this perfectly clear in the *Summa* on that question of the gentiles. It is not a goal of Aquinas to reject Muslim and pagan thought, but rather to discuss, with them, the commonalities that persist in a model of natural reason. In a similar manner, with the concept of finitude, we have at hand another place of dialogue with our own contemporaries. Thinking God should never be disembodied from dialogue and exchange. The Western tradition is, of course, not solely philosophical in nature. Theology and religion have played a prominent role too. Falque, through his writings, offers a much-needed rereading in order to close any interpretive gaps between the two. Perhaps he can claim, like Péguy,

---

2. Cited in Falque, *God, the Flesh, and the Other*, 5. Also, see Libera, *Penser au Moyen Âge*, 25.

that revolution represents a "call from a less perfect tradition to a more perfect tradition."³

Life and Thought

"To Die Is to Not Write."⁴

The incarnation of thought seems to be true of Falque in a very personal way. If his triptych has a properly theoretical development, it finds its sources in the events of his own existence which, at times, have nothing to do with the academic world of professional scholarship. Like Nietzsche, he writes many of his books from the experience of his own flesh. Beyond the erudition of his books, there is a quest for wisdom that is not Greek per se. Thinking is indeed a way of living. If thinking is a task, it cannot develop against life. (Here is, once again, a lesson from medieval thinkers.) At its core, Falque's writings bear the mark of a deeply existential dimension, that is, a lived dimension of writing that cuts through any abstract model. It is life, not theory, that Falque intends to demonstrate. Such an observation is evident from his work on *God, the Flesh, and the Other*. The list of references is impressive, especially for a reader unfamiliar with medieval thought. We can even find an erotic dimension that some may correlate to theology. The reader may see himself as a fellow author in a theological discourse that may appear to be archaic but in fact nourishes a collective project of finitude. By offering a philosophy of theological concepts, we are able to productively invert a superiority from one side or the other.

The relationship between life and thought is equally true in the conception and act of writing. It is not immediately apparent that the style of Falque reveals his personality, but we may lean on his article "To Die Is to Not Write," where he distinguishes three types of his own writing practices: "academic," "debate," and "the joint practice of philosophy and theology."⁵ He recognizes, evoking Rilke, that "nothing is falser than the ideal of transparency, even of the light of *alêtheia* that it would supposedly suffice to let unveil itself . . . no longer being able to depend on the pneuma (or the 'breath') that alone can inspire it. . . . No one writes to

---

3. Péguy, *Portal of the Mystery of Hope*, xii.
4. See Falque, *By Way of Obstacles*, 159–60.
5. For the English translation of this originally French text, see Falque, *By Way of Obstacles*, 159.

gaze at himself, and still less to congratulate himself, but to open onto other worlds that are always 'possible' and still 'unsuspected.'"[6] His writing is driven by a passion to render the truth of experience without leaving it behind when the pen is taken up.

Confrontation and Dialogue

"It Is a Body-to-Body Confrontation That Christianity Would Be Wrong to Ignore."[7]

The union of tradition and modernity, of thought and life, rings truest in Falque's interest in the *disputatio*. This kind of thought is not new in itself, but it is a practice that remains at the core of Falque's work. With it, we make new encounters, locate new voices, and aspire to reach beyond static presuppositions. Thinking God differently, beyond a mere deepening of belief, means to debate with those who doubt his existence, that is, to arouse interest in the question of God among those who are indifferent or hostile to the stakes. This dimension of confrontation persists in culture, past and present. While Falque would probably not reduce Christianity to a counterculture, it is telling that the triptych, for example, opens with a contemplation of medieval paintings and later proceeds into comments on contemporary works; for Falque, the two speak to each other. Moreover, references to Nietzsche, Artaud, or Deleuze, to the painters Bacon and Lucian Freud, bear witness to an ongoing evolution within Falque and the wider religious discourses of today.

Specificity and Radicality

"This Is . . . Not a Quarrel Between Confessions, Even Less Between Religions."[8]

To think about God through Christianity, and even more so Catholicism, is to claim from the outset a *particular* conception. Religion requires specificity. Falque does not intend to advance with a mask. He makes his assertions not on the basis of "philosophy of religion" but on a "religious

---

6. See Falque, *By Way of Obstacles*, 160.
7. Falque, *Metamorphosis of Finitude*, 51.
8. Falque, *Crossing the Rubicon*, 30.

philosophy"; in his latest works, this opens into a "philosophy of religious experience." For the reader, this should be seen as an attempt to not hide or remain content with inherited presuppositions and convictions. At the same time, we see that he does not claim to be only Christian but Catholic (as seen in his differences with Ricœur). To be sure, this decision is fraught with consequences and holds the crux of the wager within Falque's overall project. Is it true to say that Christianity is more admissible if more masks are removed as to what Christianity does not and cannot pursue; does it make it more paradoxical, more radical? To claim to be a religious philosopher is in fact to attach oneself to a specific faith. A question thus arises: What place should be reserved for other beliefs if we recognize their legitimacy? This manner of thinking God is fundamentally in accord with a syncretic approach that strives to find a form of christological truth in all religions (even if nothing is said explicitly in Falque's texts on the merits of dialogue between religions). There is little doubt that Falque will take up this question more fully in the coming years.

As for the radicality of the Christian message, it is clearly visible in the place that the triptych reserves for the resurrection, the Eucharist, and the role played by the Trinity. This radicality, seen in the choice of concepts and realities less and less familiar to our modernity, indicates that Falque's approach is not really (not directly at least) apologetic. It would be somewhat imprudent to try to convince a reader of another faith commitment; if anything, it would risk dissuading or discouraging. Nevertheless, adhering to a certain Christian tradition allows us to offer our contemporaries a presentation of these realities which, through the mediation of philosophy, gives them a real and thoughtful intelligibility. The Christian doctrine, as Falque observes, is only placed before the reader. The choice to listen and participate ultimately rests with them.

Finitude and Universality

"We Have No Other Experience of God Than That of Man."[9]

The reader may well assert that Falque's approach seems to detach Christianity from other religious beliefs, and some will even think that it detaches them from the very spirit of philosophy. To be sure, as soon

9. Falque, *Metamorphosis of Finitude*, 63.

as the content is clarified, the universality of the approach emerges in the foreground. One of the major lessons, in fact, is to demonstrate the weight that Christianity gives to lived finitude and, moreover, how the incarnation can help us to reconstruct this dimension of life. Another major insight is the place reserved for that version of the finitude of man that thinks of his life without God. Falque preserves this space too. It is a paradox made possible only by Christianity. We can think of God only through the experience we have of him, which may very well be that of his absence. To think of God is first to think of human finitude. As we have amply seen, this is a necessity: "We have no other experience of God than that of man." It is an anthropological observation as much as a theological affirmation that the word was made flesh. By incarnating himself in human finitude, Christ attests to the essential character of this finitude, here and now. This remains a teaching specific to Christianity, as opposed to other religions and ancient philosophy. One of the contributions of the Falquian approach is to establish to what extent this importance granted to finitude by Christianity, to the point of making it a matter of specificity, ensures its modern existence and therefore its admissibility—all of this on the condition of thinking of finitude in a radical way, that is, without seeking to surpass it immediately but letting it come to life on its own terms. This acceptance of the limit has deep links to philosophy, by recourse to contemporary thought such as Heidegger and Foucault. On the other hand, the believing thinker can also pursue it theologically through the status of the creature where finitude becomes the very condition of man, and not the consequence of a sinful fall. Sin lies precisely in refusing the limit. The acceptance of finitude is confirmed, as we have seen, through a love of the limit, an incarnation that expresses a good anthropomorphism.

Love of the Limit

"A 'Love in Common of Limits' of God for the World and of Eve for Adam, and Vice Versa."[10]

Falque shows that the love of the limit is specifically an experience that God shares with man. He, the Unlimited, created man to be able to meet him. He created Eve to enable this man, his creature, to bear

---

10. Falque, *Wedding Feast of the Lamb*, 153.

his limit with others. This progression of creation is itself composed of limits and differentiation: of God and man as well as of man and woman. Both remain after the resurrection, which does not remove limits but rather transforms them. God himself experiences the limit through his incarnation, expressed by the limit crossing in the humanization of the divine. Before the divinization of the human, Falque first emphasizes the humanization of the divine. The "impossible God" is not the God who surpasses us in the ineffable (Dionysius), but the one who discovers himself hidden in the deepest of limits of man. This is, above all, the specificity of Christianity in relation to other religions. While there is no question of diminishing the importance of the Christian God or of the resurrection which manifests the force of the Holy Spirit, it is through kenosis, which we may read as an overcoming of transcendence to reveal a positive status of immanence.

This is why Falque reflects on the transformation of finitude and the passage from philosophy to theology, not in terms of a leap, but as a metamorphosis. This sharing, in some way, of the finitude and the limits between God and man, explains why we can say that "we have no other experience of God than that of man." This is Falque's response to Bultmann's assertion according to which "the being-aware of God is first a being-aware that man has of himself, of his limits."[11] We can thus speak of a "good anthropomorphism" and the criticism of "bad anthropomorphism." Anthropomorphism properly construed is the idea that "God himself, in his incarnation, takes on our part of animality and transforms it into a humanity recognized in its filiation, in that nothing of that which is human must or can be strange to him in his incarnation, apart from sin."[12] Feuerbach accused religion of alienating man, of dispossessing him of his essence by transposing him into a God who would be only a projection of his desires and unsatisfied ideals. Such a God is indeed "human, all too human." In the true light of the incarnation, the humanity of God is no longer the expression of the weakness of man, but that of the strength of a God who humanizes himself. According to Falque, this acceptance of finitude counters Nietzsche's accusation that Christianity gave rise to a flight from existence. Falque, in *The Wedding Feast of the Lamb*, presents a God who totally assumes finitude, in its most tragic, carnal, corporeal, and organic dimensions.

11. See Falque, *Metamorphosis of Finitude*, 63. Also, see Bultmann, *Historicité de l'homme et de la revelation*, 466.

12. Falque, *Wedding Feast of the Lamb*, 65.

The Possibility of an Ethic

Man Tout Court?

God is known to us through man (philosophy, anthropology), but also to the extent that God actually became man through the figure of Christ (theology). Here, we can see the possible foundation of an ethic that may ensure respect for human dignity against certain contemporary excesses of a trans-humanism, where man seeks to go beyond his limits without respect for the limits as they exist. To be sure, Falque does not reduce Christianity to humanism, religious ethics to anthropology. Rather he draws attention to how rarely contemporary authors pull from Christianity a moral or metaphysical teaching for today's context. In one pressing respect, Falque seems to establish a link between the limits of identity and sexual differentiation by suggesting a reevaluation of the resurrection—body and soul. His recognition of finitude prohibits him from judging the limits of life in the name of mere theoretical and categorical principles. He is probably one of those who, like Péguy, would reproach Kant for wanting to have pure hands with regard to thought. Sin, for Falque, is based upon a refusal to accept one's own limits—to refuse to live with limits.

It would be interesting to deepen the analysis here to a debate that today is perhaps already a little dated and on which Falque has never spoken. The debate concerns the morality of faith versus autonomous morality. Which would Falque choose? Would it even be possible to compare the status of the "limit" in Falque to that of the "Other" in Levinas, as a criterion of moral determination? How would he create a lived practice out of this debate?

Flesh and Language

"The Word Became the Flesh . . . the Flesh Became the Word."[13]

The reader who gradually discovers Falque's triptych will be struck by the prominence of reflections given to the body. The body is an object of phenomenological analyses, of aesthetic illustrations, and of essential theological insights. Many over the years have maintained a simple ignorance of Christianity, believing that it held a certain hatred of the

---

13. Falque, *Guide to Gethsemane*, 83.

body and sexuality. Ironically, it is the body that serves as a reference for identifying the specificity of Christianity and, even more, of Catholicism. Incarnation (God became flesh), resurrection (transformation of the flesh), Eucharist (gift of the body of God); all three refer to the central role of the body. The finitude of man and his metamorphosis are also matters of the body. Christianity, from this point of view, is not a spiritualism; it is a fleshly realism expressed by a carnal human condition. Falque thus articulates a theology of the body as manifested from the incarnation, from the resurrection of Christ and the Eucharist. From there, he attempts to convey an equally powerful philosophy of the body with phenomenology, with *philosophèmes* (physical body, biological body, lived body, corporeal flesh), to which is added the "expanded body," to make intelligible the *théologoumènes*. The divine body is illuminated and revealed by that of the human body from which it reveals. Here, a further connection is made with Merleau-Ponty, for whom incarnation changes everything. As Emmanuel de Saint-Aubert writes: "God is thus clothed with a condition which man cannot achieve to recognize and assume. As if it took an incarnate God to teach man what he is, and help him live it. As if it had taken a carnal God for man to content himself to be flesh."[14]

The insistence on the role of the body, a role recognized by modern philosophy, entails a certain distancing of ourselves from a theology that favors text and speech. This is neatly illustrated by Ricœur.[15] As Falque would suggest, the Word was made flesh so that the flesh becomes Word. The truth of Christ is revealed in his carnal and active experience and not only in his words. From this point of view, phenomenology is more relevant than hermeneutics. To be sure, in his more recent work Falque has recognized the importance of speech, precisely for accounting for the fullness of the carnal experience. In *The Wedding Feast of the Lamb*, this comes forth in the concept of "this is my body" as well as "the flaws of the flesh" in the erotic dimension. Even more so, in the incarnation, the Word plays an essential role. The links between speech and the flesh are promising avenues for future debate and insight.

---

14. See Saint-Aubert, "Incarnation change tout."
15. See the appendix found at the end of this book.

Metamorphosis of Trinitarian Action

"God is the One Who Begins, Not Us."[16]

Perhaps it is the case that Christianity proposes the acceptance of finitude as well as its metamorphosis. To be fully efficacious, the Christian life must necessarily pass through finitude, because, in the manner of Gregory of Nazianzus, only what is assumed will be truly saved. One essential element in this proposed schema is that the metamorphosis of finitude is made possible only by the Trinitarian action of God. In this, too, lies the specificity of Christianity. It is not merely man's desire for eternity which grounds his resurrection but also the action of the Father, who resurrects Christ. There is nothing in man to overcome death, if not for the force of God to raise him up. As Irenaeus asserts (and as is often quoted by Falque), "Our bodies must be resurrected not by virtue of their substance, but by the power of God." We may try to establish a rapprochement with Péguy, who shows that the feelings we experience are first and foremost those that God has sent towards us. We can hope only because God hopes in us. "We had faith in God; for He certainly had faith in us."[17]

Here, the recourse to the Trinity, which may surprise contemporaries, takes on an anthropological sense. This is in no way a matter of denying the moment, as though a naïve revolt against death. Man himself cannot escape his finitude. The radical specificity of Christianity consists in fully assuming one's humanity as well as proposing a metamorphosis made possible by the incarnation and resurrection of Christ, through the action of the Father and the Holy Spirit. On this point Falque clearly shows that the Christian metamorphosis is distinct from that proposed by Nietzsche, since it is not the work of man but of God. From this angle, the Christian is in no way in flight from the world; our very condition is to remain with the earth; it is willed by God, who designated us to this world as our home and the place of realization of our humanity. Nor is Christianity an idealism or a spiritualism, both of which would disqualify the body and sexuality. The rapprochement between the Eucharist and the erotic, the gift of the body of Christ and that of the partner, illustrates this in a striking way. Recognized in this way, Christianity is "in the world but not of it." It is creatively universal.

---

16. See Falque, *Saint Bonaventure and the Entrance of God into Theology*, 63–64.
17. Péguy, *Portal of the Mystery of Hope*, 67.

The Method of Phenomenology

To Return to the Things Themselves

Throughout his approach, Falque remains faithful to the method and style of phenomenology. Even in *The Wedding Feast of the Lamb* when he denounces its total sufficiency, it is difficult to imagine another approach that may bring us closer to the truth. Falque's criticism of it attests to a certain mark of respect. His writings bear the mark of phenomenology for its challenges, questions, and prevailing force. Such a pursuit would be the result of a certain philosophical education received in a given era of French thought. For Ricœur, at least, we might remark: "This decision in favor of phenomenology could certainly be questioned in the name of other philosophical enterprises and as a testament to a commitment to its basic presuppositions. A young philosopher did not hesitate to see in the phenomenological reduction, and the rejection of the natural attitude, a 'nihilism of a higher power.'"[18] Some might argue that the philosophical choices and foundations of Falque are resigned to the limits of his approach. Limits and foundations, as in all human endeavors, are never far from each other. Falque would likely respond to this criticism by evoking Augustine and Aquinas: they both appealed to the philosophy available to them, in their own time, in order to ensure their own approach. Aquinas, for example, drew on a model of rationality that was dominant at the time, namely, Aristotle's discovery of metaphysics. It cannot be ignored that phenomenology is indeed one of the essential contributions of twentieth century philosophy.

The Method of Revelation in Relationship to Phenomenology

"The Experience of Transcendence First and Foremost Lives Within Immanence."[19]

It is interesting to recall how Falque's choice in favor of phenomenology allows for a specific approach to thinking God. This may no doubt cause a certain frustration in the reader; yet, in a way, it also makes his argument more acceptable to contemporaries. Schematically, one would say that his approach, in its philosophical and especially phenomenological

---

18. Citot, *Condition philosophique et le problème du commencement*, 97.
19. Falque, *Loving Struggle*, 123.

dimension, remains at the level of possibility and does not reach that of effectiveness of God or faith within the framework of theology alone. We must "return to things themselves," as the Husserlian precept goes. Rejecting the natural attitude, we must apprehend not things, but those acts of consciousness in experiences. Phenomenology seeks to describe the way in which these things appear to us, which means that we cannot grasp them independently of consciousness. One can say nothing about reality in itself apart from the experience we have of it. So, it is the same for God. An attempt to demonstrate the existence of God would be a vain and meaningless enterprise if all we aimed for was effectiveness. What philosopher today would dare to engage in such a project? Merleau-Ponty already said it: "In truth, the question for a philosopher is not so much whether God exists or does not exist, if the proposition 'God exists' is correct or incorrect, than knowing what we mean by God, what we mean when we speak of God."[20] Describing the experience that may be had is reasonable, but it will prove nothing regarding the status of the existence of the object of this experience. To argue that God is present in me says nothing of his presence outside of me; this, so long as we remain at the philosophical level. As others have said before, how could it be understood not as an object among other objects, or not as the supreme being of an onto-theology?

We mentioned the possible frustration of a reader faced with the noneffectiveness of God. But remaining with the theological possibility may also prove fruitful for present purposes. From this point of view, the limits of phenomenology may attest to its effectiveness. They guarantee a certain admissibility, which an apologetic thinker would risk compromising. This is not to say, however, that Falque's choice is wholly appropriate here. Rather, for his part, to the extent that he seeks to be a theologian, and not only a philosopher, he may assert a profoundly creative distinction: "We concede, of course, that 'revelation' is not denied here, but it is only envisaged as a 'possibility' of the saturated phenomenon, independently of all actuality: 'the phenomenon of revelation remains a mere *possibility*.'"[21] It is certainly up to us to make a choice; to believe is to decide.

In fact, as we have seen, one of Falque's objectives is to make Christianity "credible" and intelligible for those for whom it is "incredible" and without forgetting those who consider it "believable." As Falque observes

---

20. Cited by Saint-Aubert, "Incarnation change tout," 147.
21. Falque, *Loving Struggle*, 133.

concerning St. Anselm, by reinterpreting the famous "hermeneutical circle," there can be an "understanding without believing" which is not content to merely reflect on God, but is oriented towards the common experience of "man in general," whether believer or unbeliever.[22] Taking up an Anselmian distinction compared to Spinoza, Falque shows that believer and unbeliever share two modes of knowledge-granting sources, faith and reason. The believer, like any other, also benefits from knowledge by experience. We thus find an idea of non-believing philosophers like Jean-Luc Nancy who write that Christianity, through some of its dogmas, is still constitutive of culture, even if atheism is often kept as an existential a priori. This makes, all the more urgent, the larger question of "making the terms of a 'credible' and not merely 'believable' Christianity" for it appears that "Christianity harbors in itself the cultural and conceptual resources for reaching the very core of the human and for transforming it from the inside."[23]

The Nature of Christianity: The Force of the Spirit

"God Raised the Lord and Will Also Raise Us by His Power." (1 Cor 6:14)

Suffering, birth, body, passion, resurrection, and Eucharist—these terms all occupy a determinant place in the Falquian approach. They mark the specificity of Christianity as well as the conceptual importance of the metamorphosis of finitude. We have demonstrated the condition of man, as in the conception of the nature of God. Falque reacts strongly against the representation, common in theology today, of a "weak" God who is reduced in his incarnation and kenosis to the dimensions of man only to suffer and die powerlessly on the cross.[24] Against this "weak" God, it is appropriate to claim the strength of God, that is, the force of the Spirit which allows for the resurrection of Christ in transforming all things. Let us also not forget that the Eucharist is an expression of a divine force which seeks to animate, in bodily form, a transformation.

The Wedding Feast of the Lamb highlights the strength of the organicity of the body by attesting to the animality in humanity. There, the

22. Falque, "Argument théophanique," 92.
23. See Falque, *Emmanuel Falque Reader*, 143.
24. As Hans Jonas developed it in another context; see Jonas, "Concept of God After Auschwitz."

Nietzschean reference appeared particularly relevant. Theology and philosophy both celebrate the power of the incarnation, and Christianity, in this consideration of the reality of human finitude, testifies to a realism distinguished from the spiritualism to which it has often been reduced. The Christian spirituality is an incarnate spirituality. One of the more powerful analogies has come from Mounier in *The Christian Confrontation*. In it, Mounier questions those criticisms addressed by Nietzsche against Christianity. Mounier, in contrast, showed how Christianity, in confronting human finitude, does not flee from it to another world but celebrates it. This is the virtue of Christian strength. But insisting on strength alone does not satisfy the test of finitude. Falque describes at length the tragedy of the human condition, in its psychic and physical form, as well as in *The Guide to Gethsemane*. Perhaps he would take up the assertion of his friend and colleague, Jérôme de Gramont: "We are not born in joy or bliss. We are perhaps born to joy, from its other side: suffering, in history and its trials."[25]

The Perspective of a New Anthropology?

"The Being-Aware of God Is First a Being-Aware That Man Has of Himself, of His Limits."[26]

The evolution manifested by the volumes of the triptych is significant in more ways than one. First, more and more space is given to authors like Nietzsche, Artaud, Deleuze, to Greek myths, biblical Chaos, and even Tohu-bohu. Second, and related to the first, a certain religious and philosophical tradition is interrogated based on such nuanced perspectives. A new figure of man is implicitly and progressively drawn up. *The Wedding Feast of the Lamb*, in particular, guides the reader towards developments that will necessarily engage Christianity and postmodernism, towards principles of traditional humanism along with contemporary social theory.

As we have seen, Falque emphasizes the need to resort to anthropology to make theological concepts truly intelligible. This recourse is visible throughout the triptych (and, once again, is particularly significant in

---

25. Jérôme de Gramont, "L'entre-deux," in Falque and Zielinski, *Philosophie et théologie en dialogue*, 81.

26. Falque, *Metamorphosis of Finitude*, 63. Also, see Bultmann, *Historicité de l'homme et de la revelation*, 466.

The Wedding Feast of the Lamb). In addition to the theological analysis of the divine body, Falque makes it possible to question certain philosophical representations of the human body which, ultimately, are in need of redefinition. Here, Falque would implicitly wager that some theological concepts may prove perfectly operational for thinking new perspectives in anthropology.

Emmanuel Falque and Dietrich Bonhoeffer

Living *"Etsi Deus Non Daretur"*

The importance given to finitude, in recognition of the weight of atheism, may prompt us to question a possible relationship with the perspectives developed by Dietrich Bonhoeffer in *Resistance and Submission*.[27] A set of letters written in prison, Bonhoeffer strives to think through Christianity from a world that has become autonomous and dangerously secularized. Falque and Bonhoeffer both insist on the same ideality within the earth, namely, the world that Christ assumed in his work.

Nietzsche is, for both, an author with whom debate is necessary. Falque inevitably makes one think of the "nonreligious" Christian of Bonhoeffer, like an atheistic existential a priori found in the saying "etsi Deus non daretur" (as if God were not given to us). As Bonhoeffer writes: "Being a Christian is about tempering one's passions (where is there any such tempering in the Old Testament)."[28] Being Christian is to be, in a certain way, human. Likewise: "Whoever wishes to be and perceive things too quickly and too directly in New Testament ways is to my mind no Christian. We have already, of course, discussed this a few times, and every day confirms for me that it is right. One can and must not speak the ultimate word prior to the penultimate. We are living in the penultimate and believe the ultimate, isn't that so?"[29] These very same sentences could be taken up by Falque. Both are not satisfied with human self-sufficiency. As Bonhoeffer continues: "It's possible for a human being to manage dying, but overcoming death means resurrection. It is not through *ars moriendi*, but through Christ's resurrection that a new and cleansing wind can blow through our present world."[30] These words

---

27. See, for example, Bonhoeffer, *Letters and Papers from Prison*.
28. Bonhoeffer, *Letters and Papers from Prison*, 394.
29. Bonhoeffer, *Letters and Papers from Prison*, 213.
30. Bonhoeffer, *Letters and Papers from Prison*, 333.

would suit Falque. But we also have the feeling that Falque's position on metamorphosis corresponds to a moment that Bonhoeffer would not be willing to totally yield to. Here we find, as with Ricœur, a certain confessional divergence between Catholicism and Protestantism.

Their difference can also lead to a reflection on the relationships between Christianity and humanism in Falque. To be a Christian, does this mean to fully realize the humanity of man? Is this really Bonhoeffer's position? Falque's recognition of the positivity of human finitude, assumed by Christ, can certainly lead to the affirmation of a "Christian humanism," concretized in the *humanization* of man (e.g., found in liberation theologies) or his *hominization* (e.g., Teilhard de Chardin). For Falque, we can be fully human without being Christian. To maintain the opposite would be to return to the necessary God, denounced by Eberhard Jüngel, a God who would fulfill our shortages and would fall under need. The fact remains that, for Falque, it is not enough to conform all things to Christian dogma. Rather, Christianity seeks only to call man to recognize himself as created, and that this creation may be integrated into an understanding of Christ. Moreover, such a humanism is inseparable from the actions of the Trinity.

Emmanuel Falque and Other Theologians

"Why Will the Philosopher Not Earn His Keep in Service to Theology?"[31]

Our study has tried to avoid any superfluous erudition with regard to the objectives of Falque. We can, however, shed light on Falque's approach by situating him, very briefly, in relation to great theologians—ancient, medieval, and modern. Falque himself acknowledges having undergone various influences and having used a wide array of references at different stages. In terms of his strict academic training, he devoted his doctoral thesis to Bonaventure. The title is perhaps revealing: "Saint Bonaventure and the Entrance of God into Theology." It evokes, one could say, a certain privilege of faith over reason, of theology over philosophy. But it remains, also, a Thomist model that links philosophy and theology, reason and faith; granting them, like the Angelic Doctor, the same dignity to both domains in order to reach after the importance and richness of human

---

31. See Falque, *Crossing the Rubicon*, 138–39.

finitude. It is precisely in the metamorphosis of it that we rediscover him as Bonaventurian. This similarity between the two authors is further found in the reconciliation that he recognizes between the two great contemporary theologians Hans Urs von Balthasar and Karl Rahner. Falque seems, in the first place, to be a Balthasarian by insisting on the figure of the Trinity and the force of revelation. Later, we may say that he then became a Rahnerian by emphasizing the conditions of reception of the Word that ever presupposes humanity. In Falque's project, these two approaches, which appear to be mutually exclusive, seem complementary. We can first be Rahnerian, if it is a question of how to listen to man in the same way as we listen to the word. And, then, we may be a Balthasarian, if we assert the Trinity as the place of incorporation and transformation of humanity. One further point remains essential. Falque will also defend Rahner against Balthasar's accusation of anthropological reduction. The revealed cannot be independent of the conditions of its revelation. God gives himself through human language, passing through the channels of his creation. It is not a question of reducing God to man, but rather seeing God accepting this reduction through kenosis.

Emmanuel Falque and Blaise Pascal

Is the God of Abraham, the God of Isaac, and the God of Jacob a Philosopher?

Falque places Pascal among the religious philosophers who have influenced him the most. He recognizes the role of Pascal in seeing existence for what it is. Pascal's description of a human condition unenlightened by faith, as seen in his *Pensées*, evokes a similar definition to that of Falque. And, yet, Falque's anthropology never mentions "the misery of man without God." Atheism is not necessarily a "drama," and finitude is not the consequence of sin. The anguish that accompanies it comes from the weight of existence itself, as Falque tries to show with Saint Augustine. With regard to Pascal, Falque recognizes in him a means by which philosophy liberates theology. Both thinkers find no difficulty in moving from philosophy to theology, as opposed to Descartes—the opposite of Pascal. To be sure, Pascalian thought implies a jump or break between the orders, whereas Falque speaks of a metamorphosis of finitude. It remains a "building with" of philosophy by theology, without breakage or rupture. In this way it is more faithful to the Catholic tradition as inherited from

Aquinas than other contemporary models that insist on the separations of orders.

Metamorphosis of Finitude

"The Experience of Thought as the Thought of Experience"[32]

The title of the second volume of the triptych—*The Metamorphosis of Finitude*—seems to best summarize the journey proposed here to the reader, whether believer or unbeliever. In a way, the title captures the essentials of the Christian message as Falque understands it. Apologetics is not about conversion per se, nor even a matter of reason. It comes down to recognizing that nothing in man will be "metamorphosed" if he is not first sanctified by the Son of Man.[33] It is not simply a contemporary thought to radically combine finitude and humanity. Christianity pursues the same task through the incarnation of Christ, who, like us, has fully assumed finitude. It follows, for the Christian as for the human being in general, to embrace this experience in its entirety, both the tragic and joyful dimensions, and not simply to take refuge in the background of the world. This amounts to accepting limits, no longer as a limitation per se, but as a condition for realizing one's vocation.

The description that Falque offers of this finitude fits well into a common space of thought that he wishes to create. He is further unique in the sense that he brings forth Nietzsche as a partner in matters of finitude—however tense this relationship appears. Falque also never quits the aims of the theologian who stands in contrast to Nietzsche's celebration of Zarathustra. The term of metamorphosis is itself very revealing if we juxtapose it with that of a leap, so often used to account for certain ruptures from reason to faith, or from philosophy to theology. To make a conversion, a metamorphosis, is to remember its expression as a form of continuity between the transformer and the one who is transformed. Falque, as we have seen, neatly illustrates this with the role he grants to the Trinity.

---

32. See Falque, *Crossing the Rubicon*, 122–24.
33. See Falque, *Emmanuel Falque Reader*, 142–44.

Humanity and Belief

"Nothing Is Harder to Believe Than the Absence of Belief."[34]

A reader who may share with Falque the experience of finitude may not feel the same kind of experience with regard to metamorphosis. They may not have the knowledge from experience, as proposed by Saint Anselm; they may not even conceive of that perspective in general. In this regard, the reader may discover a certain solitude, perhaps that of thought itself, which Plato calls a silent dialogue that the soul talks with oneself. He may also remember Heidegger's observation that to think is to decide. Falque knows full well that the Christian teachings, found here, do not relate to knowledge alone; they call for a decision. Is this decision only the work of one's will or does it belong to the sphere of hope? As Kant reminds us, what can one hope for? Perhaps a metamorphosis that, like a gift, the exact nature and premises remain unknown? Or must the human being will his choice by coercion? It is a delicate matter.

Falque, as we have said enough, does not seek to convert his reader, but to show him how Christianity can appear credible, that is, intelligible, even if others may consider Christian teaching incredible. We thus find the old problem which has spanned centuries of theology, namely, how to make faith intelligible. To the one who judges Christianity as incredible, Falque wishes to show that the teaching of Christ offers a relevant description of man as well as a heritage that our society may lean on for insight. In doing so, he emphasizes the need to fight against a "holy ignorance" against crossing religion and culture today; this ignorance refuses the constitutive dimension of intelligibility without which Christianity cannot even stand on "believability." We thus recognize here the double-sided exigency placed on the believer and unbeliever—to meet each other in productive and open dialogue.

Can and should we be satisfied with Falque's framework of "credibility"? Are the effects of his work limited solely to this one objective? No, first of all since it is also a question of the living bonds between faith and decision-making. Falque warned his reader as early as *The Guide to Gethsemane*: "Christian faith is not what Christians give themselves, but what they receive. According to Karl Barth, who follows on here from Kierkegaard's ideas, anyone who would claim to have faith, to be capable of believing, would certainly not believe. In the same way that anxiety

---

34. See Falque, *Crossing the Rubicon*, 80.

leads Christians to a kind of abandonment of the self as a condition of their faith, so treatment of death is an index among contemporary philosophers of the extent to which they hold on to or abandon the self."[35]

In *Crossing the Rubicon*, Falque analyzes the relationship between faith and decision. Chapter 3, in particular, expresses a suggestive title: "Always Believing." Belief appears constitutive, in some way, of humanity; however, it is not reducible to its traditionally conceived religious definition. As Falque creatively shows, there are three types of belief: philosophical, religious, and confessional. Moreover, each of these is based on a "common humanity."[36] The first translates the original and more primitive perception of faith that we have in the world. Any doubt facing it, as exposed in the philosophical presentations of Cartesianism or the phenomenological *epoché*, arises from a bracketing of theoretical suspensions; yet, it does not alter, in reality, our confidence which, for Falque, remains irreducible. "If we can doubt the existence of the world, along with Descartes, or yet 'place in parentheses' any judgment about the world, following Husserl, are we truly capable also of freeing ourselves from 'our belief in the world,' as Husserl indicates or instead as Merleau-Ponty debates?"[37] This perceptual faith, not unlike Merleau-Ponty's phenomenology, means that "it is true that we naturally live in the mode of trust rather than distrust, whether it is a question of philosophical belief in the world or theological belief in God, a matter of a same 'perceptive faith' or 'believing certainty' such that we consider and rightly believe in being rather than nonbeing."[38] This observation thus seems to offer a nobility to the attitude and lived practice of belief.

The two other forms of belief are, one would be tempted to say, more familiar: religious and confessional. With "religious faith," we shift from "joining the world" to a "decision to trust ourselves to another (God?) who would have come into our world."[39] More deeply, this linkage also indicates and opens up "a possible relation to transcendence, whether or not it is named."[40] As for confessional faith, it expresses "an act of faith,

---

35. Falque, *Guide to Gethsemane*, 30. On the reference to Barth, see *Evangelical Theology*.

36. Falque, *Crossing the Rubicon*, 77.

37. Falque, *Crossing the Rubicon*, 81.

38. Falque, *Crossing the Rubicon*, 88.

39. Falque, *Crossing the Rubicon*, 89.

40. Falque, *Crossing the Rubicon*, 90.

no longer beginning with the sole self but also with an 'other' who lives in me."[41] This is the Christ.

The intention behind these distinctions is to show that man, in general, does not escape from belief. Falque emphasizes this common space between believers and unbelievers. Confessional faith should not be the order of the strange or the incomprehensible. In contrast, it ought to presuppose those other creative forms of belief. "There would be no decided faith in God—for example, in the kerygma—without an always-presupposed faith in the world."[42] Thus, there is no theology without anthropology. We have knowledge of God only through the experience of man. By recognition of this common foundation, Falque concludes:

> If it is necessary to find and propose a "perceptive faith" at the foundation of "religious faith," does the former exclude the latter, or rather, is it not its condition of possibility as its transcendental structure? There would be no decided faith in God—for example, in the kerygma—without an always presupposed faith in the world, since we are always there beforehand, or are even always "the world." In excluding perceptive faith, as indefectible belief that we are in the world, from religious faith as an act of confessional faith, the very believers have sometimes excluded themselves from the "always believing" human community. In the same way, in denouncing confessing religious faith in the name of a presumably independent perceptive faith, atheists or nonbelievers do not or no longer imagine the ties that bind the profane world to the sacred world as if religious belief must necessarily detach itself from humanity.[43]

Decision and Faith

"The Non-Choice Is a Choice."[44]

It remains for us to question more precisely the specificity of the confessional belief in comparison with the Christian belief that Falque holds. It is an unavoidable question. Does this faith belong to the order of a decision, does it come from voluntary will, or is it a gift? The chapter

41. Falque, *Crossing the Rubicon*, 90.
42. Falque, *Crossing the Rubicon*, 79.
43. Falque, *Crossing the Rubicon*, 79.
44. See Falque, *Crossing the Rubicon*, 108.

"Kerygma and Decision" in *Crossing the Rubicon* offers a strong example in reference to Bultmann and Kierkegaard. It reveals the specificity of the decision from a theological point of view as well as clarifies Falque's more "Catholic" approach. In some ways, it is akin to the approach of Claude Romano. As Falque observes, the decision to transform "does not go without the necessary transformation of the concept of decision."[45]

The importance of the decision is based, first of all, on the nature of the kerygma. Here, Falque quotes Ricœur in relationship to Bultmann: "The *kérygma* is not primarily an interpretation of a text, but an announcement of a person; in this sense it is not the Bible which is the word of God but Jesus Christ."[46] Stated another way: "The decision takes precedence over interpretation."[47] We can recall here, as Joseph Pieper shows in *Of the Faith*, that religious faith is not a sum of dogmas but a relationship to persons. It is certainly based on a revelation of and from God. However, the decision to believe is less about believing that God exists than believing in God as a living and creative force in the world.[48] In Christianity, the decision is relative to that person. From this observation, from a believing perspective, Falque states the question this way: "If in Christianity specifically it is not a matter of deciding for oneself but also and especially of deciding with and through another or others, 'I no longer live, but Christ who lives in me,' is it not appropriate in light of the Christian structure of eschatology, as suggested, to transform the concept of decision in making the decision to transform oneself?"[49] From there, Christianity may produce a "conversion" within the act of deciding because "the one in whom one believes theologically transforms the object of the very belief and even the access to it."[50] Let us clarify this a bit more.

Above all, Falque analyzes, with Kierkegaard, a transformation of the concept of the choice: not choosing this or that (i.e., the ontic choice), but choosing to choose or not to choose and choosing oneself by choosing one's self (i.e., the ontological choice). In this regard, Falque posits, we may reach the heart of the nature of choice. We move from the decision as choice of some "thing" to the decision to participate in choice

---

45. Falque, *Crossing the Rubicon*, 102.

46. See Ricœur's preface to the French edition of Bultmann, *Jésus, mythologie et démythologisation*.

47. Falque, *Crossing the Rubicon*, 102.

48. See Pieper, *De la foi*.

49. Falque, *Crossing the Rubicon*, 102. Also, see Gal 2:20.

50. Falque, *Crossing the Rubicon*, 102.

itself. Thus, Falque's disposition towards his readers is not to lead them to choose for or against Christianity but rather to choose to choose, to make a decision. To the extent that Christianity has been made credible, it is up to the individual to decide, which is ultimately that of deciding to make a choice at all. Echoing Pascal, we have no choice not to make a choice.

Yet, another conception of the decision can be traced in Heidegger. In response, Falque proposes a religious framework where it is no longer a question of starting from the decision of man before God but of God's decision with a view to man. Deciding is not simply choosing but, more so, responding. To illustrate his point, Falque draws on the analysis by Marion of "the call" as illustrated by Caravaggio, who paints Matthew responding to the call of Christ. There, we may see the fusion of call-and-response, that is, an incorporation of the believer's decision in God.[51] From this perspective, the election becomes the name of the decision where man is placed second. And it is not a question of deciding between possibilities, but of deciding on the great Possible. By exposing yourself to possibility, as Kierkegaard's and Heidegger attempt, we find that "possibility" is now replaced with "passibility," through the power of an unknown gift.[52] "Becoming what you are" turns into "Be what you become." It marks "the transformation of the advent receiving." Moreover, Falque continues, "The novelty consists not only in the opening or creation of a horizon by the decision but in the fact that this horizon of the decision is not first of all mine, but an Other's."[53] The claim of faith expressed in the call-and-response paradoxically resembles a pure phenomenology of the gift and the given.

This double transformation in the conception of the decision, however informative for the dimensions of faith, does not fully satisfy Falque. In a way, it seems to renounce the subject's power of the decision, as though it is a celebration of passivity, a new kind of activity, that is, "a possible cooperation between humans and God."[54] Falque recognizes that we are not masters but rather active participants. "If the force comes from an Other and will be shared, I am not reduced to exposing myself to it but to participating in it."[55] If we follow Aquinas and his distinctions of the first cause and second causes, God remains the first cause, "the cause

51. See Marion, *Being Given*.
52. Falque, *Crossing the Rubicon*, 112.
53. Falque, *Crossing the Rubicon*, 111.
54. Falque, *Crossing the Rubicon*, 114.
55. Falque, *Crossing the Rubicon*, 115.

of the operation of everything that operates" but he does not operate for us. Rather, "He cooperates, strictly speaking, in our operation."[56] The mark of true power consists in deciding with the other.

Thinking God Otherwise?

It is certainly not a foreign God who appears at the end of this approach. Many aspects in Falque's work connect to fundamental dogmas of Christianity: the christological dimension as well as the insistence on the role of the Trinity are perhaps the two most central examples. He does not hesitate to reference pontifical texts too. Theologians will certainly be surprised by some of his analyses, perhaps appearing questionable. Nevertheless, his entire approach is far from heterodox. If anything, it is bold and illuminating.

The brilliance of certain hypotheses, in fact, leads to what I see as a very basic—dare I say—convenient—truth. It seems to me that Falque invites us simply to think God differently, to think God otherwise. This formulation, like Marcel Neusch, and as cited in *God, the Flesh, and the Other*, underwrites the novelty of a project that reads "philosophically" those texts that were "theological" to the medieval era. Indeed, this observation of medieval thought has even greater implications: thinking God otherwise today involves a continuity between concepts used with experiences lived. Is this not the task of any theological enterprise that wants to be received by its contemporaries?

For the sake of ultimate clarification, Falque's project must be recalled in final summary. To think God, as Falque proposes, is not to offer a new conception of God but to read in a new way a God proposed by a Christianity of old. It is to articulate in a unity those often-opposed realities: theology and philosophy, tradition and modernity, past and present, divine revelation and human experience. The timely relevance of Falque's project can be appreciated in its intent to un-conceal any and all presuppositions, to lay bare the curiosities, prejudices, and aspirations of the Christian in the world today. To reiterate: "We have no other experience of God than that of man."[57] The work of Falque, and especially the triptych, motivates us to better approach God through human experience. It aims to ground God in lived realities of suffering, death, birth, and eros.

---

56. Falque, *Crossing the Rubicon*, 114.
57. Falque, *Metamorphosis of Finitude*, 63.

It seeks to know more fully the conditions of man through a rereading of the passion, death, resurrection, and Eucharist. It is certainly a challenge to think more creatively about God, an unthinkable mark of human reality. It is equally challenging to reach into the unthought dimensions of divine revelation. But, if done in the right way, it will no doubt lay fertile grounds of possibility. The insights will surely survive the test of time.

Appendix

Paul Ricœur—Emmanuel Falque

A Symbolic Confrontation?[1]

ANY CONTEMPORARY THINKER, IN France at least, who reflects on religion and Christianity could not and cannot do without the work of Paul Ricœur. We cannot escape his influence, however direct or indirect. Historically, Ricœur always denied being a "Christian philosopher," but this is often how he was described in many cases by those who did not share his faith commitment. While he never denied that religious beliefs were at the origin of his philosophical enterprise, there remained a certain autonomy with regard to religion when the philosophical work itself was actually carried out. How could Emmanuel Falque deny this heritage? Let us clarify right away: if numerous references to Ricœur's corpus pepper Falque's work, they essentially serve as an opportunity for Falque to affirm and strengthen his own approach.

The generational difference immediately prevents us from talking about a possible patricide on the part of Falque. Such an accusation would be in any case inadequate, since Falque was never a doctoral student under Ricœur. Can we go so far as to evoke, according to Karl Jasper's expression, a *Liebeskampf* (a loving struggle) between the two philosophers? The reader may come to realize that the presumed differences between the two thinkers actually represent subtle similarities. We could begin, at a superficial level, by observing an admiring tribute from Falque to Ricœur, as a thinker from another time who has satisfied the tasks that

---

1. This text comes from a lecture given on December 15, 2011, at the Pontifical Gregorian University in Rome on the occasion of the "Genèse d'un triptyque," a thematic conference dedicated to the work of Emmanuel Falque.

Falque has deemed important. This historical dimension is particularly important for Falque, who often recalls that philosophical debates always bear the mark of their era. We, therefore, must be mindful to write today with the concern of being heard by our contemporaries. Of course, such assertions are entirely compatible with Ricœur's enterprise, which also had the concern to self-reflect about his own era and its specific issues.

But beyond the change in times, which brings a certain historical relativity to theoretical issues, other productive oppositions are revealed. I will limit myself to three. The initial two oppositions emerge around two pairs of related terms: philosophy and theology, Word and flesh (or hermeneutics and phenomenology). A third opposition could be constituted by two conceptions of the resurrection. This latter theme is more present in Falque than in Ricœur. (In the latter, a posthumous and unfinished work proposes an approach which has sometimes been harshly judged.)

Some methodological clarifications are also necessary. We will consider the confrontation of the two philosophers based on the critical positions taken by Falque with regard to Ricœur. Furthermore, we are well aware of the artificial nature of the connection of a work completed versus another still in progress. Moreover, the proposed confrontation presents yet another problematic dimension: if Falque cites Ricœur, the latter wrote nothing of Falque. We know, however, through testimony, that Ricœur had read, shortly before his death, *The Guide to Gethsemane*. He expressed his agreement with the content, going so far as to say that he would have liked to have written it himself.[2] For now, let us remain with a presentation of Falque's remarks on Ricœur's work. I would argue that the unity, or driving force, of my presentation is found more simply in the experiences I myself lived as a personal disciple and reader of Ricœur, now today captivated by Falque's approach. I do not feel totally captive to it, but it resonates with me greatly. So, I wonder, is it we who have changed the times, or is it the times that have changed us? Or, are we encountering the same questions but in different form?

Philosophy and Theology

The difference between our two authors seems particularly significant on the point of philosophy and theology. Ricœur categorically refuses to associate theology and philosophy together, whereas Falque, who tries to

---

2. This testimony was received in conversation with Falque.

maintain their respective autonomy, seeks to be a philosopher who can also perform theology. Ricœur never denied extra-philosophical motivations, i.e., religious sources at the origin of his work and convictions. He recognized a double allegiance, yet remained firm to distinguish them from his philosophical argumentation. Seeing himself as a philosopher without absolutes he chose a philosophy where "all my philosophical work, leads to a type of philosophy from which the actual mention of God is absent and in which the question of God, as a philosophical question, itself remains in a suspension that could be called agnostic."[3] Even Janicaud spared him of the more intense criticisms and accusations of theological deviation which he launched at several other phenomenologists.

To be sure, the philosophy-theology distinction, or philosophy-religion, was not always so obvious. Ricœur wrote a great number of texts on religious themes, and analyzed numerous passages from the Bible. He has often been seen as a confessional thinker, accused of favoring "conviction" to the detriment of "criticism." He always said that he "walked on two legs."[4] As he put it: "The philosopher that I am acts upon the apprentice theologian that moves within me."[5] Falque does not really oppose Ricœur on his conception of philosophy-theology relationships. It is helpful to explain this by recalling the ideological and academic contexts that Ricœur experienced, at least in France. If the image of theology has changed since then—even atheist thinkers today devote themselves to the study of theology and Scripture—it now seems archaic or threatening. Additionally, Falque would no doubt judge that Ricœur's position comes from his belonging to a Protestant tradition that may be reticent against large theological systems. To Ricœur's imagery of walking on two legs, we might even add an observation from Henri Matisse: "You always have to do two things at once," and not simply walk on two legs. The choices are surely complex for those caught between both worlds.

The religious philosopher like Kierkegaard or Pascal, and the philosopher of religion who studies religion (whether a believer or not), may try to suspend his beliefs. Yet, this qualification does not really suit Ricœur. He would certainly join Falque in his criticism of the expression "Christian philosophy," but not necessarily for the same reasons. This reason is much deeper. For Falque, such an expression does not sufficiently recognize the place of philosophy, whose role is to patiently account for

3. Ricœur, *Oneself as Another*, 24.
4. Ricœur, *Critique and Conviction*, 139.
5. Ricœur, *Critique and Conviction*, 152.

human finitude and, if necessary, respect the methodological import of an a priori atheism. Furthermore, someone such as Falque who has carefully studied the patristic and medieval thinkers has no reason to shrink from the prospect of a union between philosophy and theology. Here is another difference between the two philosophers. Medieval thinkers, with the exception of Augustine, did not particularly inspire Ricœur. On the other hand, Falque has devoted numerous writings to them, not least of which is *God, the Flesh, and the Other*.

The close union between theology and philosophy seems justified by an observation that Falque frequently recalls: "We have no other experience of God than that of man."[6] Passing through philosophy is essentially based, for Falque, on the status that he reserves for the finitude of man. This was described by contemporary philosophy, in particular by Heidegger as well as Foucault. It is also justified theologically in the act of creation, that is, to be a creature on earth. As Falque has noted, "*Théologoumènes* are also translated into a number of *philosophèmes*."[7] The three examples of Falque's triptych illustrate this well. Christ's passion is made intelligible by human suffering, the resurrection is understood from the experience of birth, the Eucharist in the light of marital eros. For Falque, philosophy and theology can deal with the same objects, but according to different methods: didactic and dogmatic for theology, heuristic for philosophy. The passage from one to the other is not a jump but a continuity; it is most fruitfully seen in a creative reimagining of method.

If theology is made intelligible by philosophy, it, in turn, is enriched. Falque summarizes this in a striking formulation: "The more we theologize, the better we philosophize."[8] As *God, the Flesh, and the Other* has shown, through a study of medieval thinkers, concepts of theology can contribute to philosophy. *The Wedding Feast of the Lamb* analyzes at length the contribution of theology to philosophy, through a triple maneuver of phenomenology for locating sense over nonsense, flesh over the objective body and passivity, weakness over strength. Now, it is the study of the body of Christ that renews our philosophical conception of the human body and relativizes the privilege that phenomenology has granted to the flesh. In *The Wedding Feast of the Lamb*, Falque distinguishes between

---

6. Falque, *Metamorphosis of Finitude*, 63.

7. Falque, *God, the Flesh, and the Other*, xxi.

8. This theme was taken up at a conference given under a title which can resonate particularly only in Rome: "Finally Theology, or the Crossing of the Rubicon" (Paris, November 26, 2011).

the "extended body" and the "lived body," thus showing "a body below all meaning and, in its chaos, where Christ in his Eucharist comes to dwell."[9] We can thus speak of a double liberation of philosophy through theology and of theology through philosophy. Yet, such a liberation would not have taken place with Ricœur.

Word and Flesh, Hermeneutics and Phenomenology

The meeting point between hermeneutics and phenomenology revolves around two formulas: one philosophical, from Husserl ("to go to the things themselves"), the other theological, from John 1:14 ("And the Word became flesh"). It also reflects two other important criteria, that of ideality in Husserl, on the one hand, to the nature of human experience, on the other hand. Falque would probably criticize Ricœur for breaking away from the Husserlian premise of phenomenology. Husserl dreamed of a first science to grasp essences in a direct and intuitive way versus the "short way," a path that Ricœur judges unattainable and impractical; he replaces it with the "long path," which seeks to reach things, indirectly, through words and the mediation of signs. Ricœur therefore proposes a hermeneutic bridge on phenomenology. Such a formulation, as Falque recognizes, has the advantage of being explicit.

In a way, Ricœur proposes a "hermeneutic variant" of Husserlian phenomenology by asserting that "phenomenology, generally speaking, is the sum of Husserl's work and the heresies resulting from Husserl."[10] If he implicitly recognizes himself on the side of heresy, he affirms that the evolution of Husserl himself attests to a project of radical self-foundation. More dramatically, "it is phenomenology's paradise lost."[11] Phenomenology would therefore call for a passage through hermeneutics. But this passage from phenomenology to hermeneutics is first, for Ricœur, the result of an experience. His initial phenomenological work on the will had nothing strictly hermeneutical about it, but his later reflection on evil led him to discover that it could not be analyzed and understood without going through the study and interpretation of the great symbols of experience which sought to account for it. As he writes: "There is no self-understanding that is not mediated by signs, symbols and texts; in

---

9. Falque, *Wedding Feast of the Lamb*, 3.
10. Ricœur, *À l'école de la phénoménologie*, 9.
11. Ricœur, *From Text to Action*, 14.

the last resort, understanding coincides with the interpretation given to these mediating terms."[12] Against the immediacy of intuition of oneself by oneself, "we appropriate to ourselves the meaning of our desire to be."[13] Hence, we find the original linguistic condition of all human experience.

Even Ricœur claims that "what hermeneutics has ruined is not phenomenology, but one of its interpretations, namely its *idealistic* interpretation by Husserl himself."[14] As Jean Grondin similarly questions: "1) The Husserlian ideal of scienticity 2) the primacy of intuition as a means of access to phenomena 3) the Cartesian and Husserlian primacy of an immanence of the subject in itself 4) the status of ultimate principles which is found then recognized in the subject and finally 5) the conception still too theoretical of self-reflection within Husserlian phenomenology."[15]

We know that the development of Ricœur's work went through diverse phases of reflection, and thus broadened the meaning of his hermeneutics as no longer interested only in symbols but "in everything as a set of meaning capable of being understood and which can be called a text."[16] This hermeneutics thus became "the theory of operations of understanding in their relationship with the interpretation of texts."[17] Understanding the human experience requires a use of text—including even the Self. The interpretation of text by Ricœur recognizes a methodological fecundity between the phenomenological method and theoretical or ontological assertions behind the surface. Ricœur will also emphasize, as we know, the autonomy of the text in relation to its referent. It is a methodological decision, but one that will help define the conditions for a certain apprehension of reality and experience.

Falque's criticism is not necessarily based on the concern for ideality with regard to Husserl, but rather on the nature of references pointing to human experience. Here, we could distinguish three examples: the condemnation of the pretension of hermeneutics, the definition of a "good" Catholic hermeneutics, and the recognition that hermeneutics and phenomenology both call for a mutual exceeding. In "The Visitation of Facticity" (dedicated to Jean Greisch), Falque contests the existence of an immediate connection between hermeneutics and phenomenology

12. Ricœur, *From Text to Action*, 15.
13. Ricœur, *Conflict of Interpretations*, 21.
14. Ricœur, *From Text to Action*, 25.
15. Grondin, *Herméneutique*, 79.
16. Ricœur, *From Text to Action*, as originally cited by Grondin, *Herméneutique*, 85.
17. Grondin, *Herméneutique*, 86.

which would imply that hermeneutics and phenomenology necessarily go hand in hand.[18] He thus opposes hermeneutics which "appears to work exclusively on texts, which, though said to be grounded fundamentally in experience, are always mediated by language (hermeneutics and Ricœur, in particular); the other, by contrast, seems to be based on a radical method, whose object is none other than pure experience—'so to speak, still dumb . . . which now must be made to utter its own sense.'"[19]

Falque further contests the role that Jean Greisch commits to language in Husserl and Heidegger, as well as responds to Ricœur's assertion that Heidegger also carried out a hermeneutical "graft of phenomenology."[20] Phenomenological description and hermeneutical interpretation must be carefully distinguished. "Nevertheless, I will say both have consequences, which are not necessarily good, whether or not one holds the Ricœurian meaning of hermeneutics as the reader's self-transformation in and through investigation and interpretation of the world of the world. The excessive attention paid to the medium oftentimes kills what it supports or conveys: the often *inarticulable* meaning of experience, which it nevertheless seeks to describe."[21]

In "Is Hermeneutics Fundamental?" (in tribute to Ricœur and later republished in *Crossing the Rubicon*), Falque introduces a criterion of distinction between the "Protestant" hermeneutics of the "meaning of the text" and a so-called "Catholic" hermeneutics, that is, a hermeneutics of the body.[22] For Falque, Scripture is an incorporation of the logos, a life which addresses a life, a body to a body. We must therefore "go to the body without staying at the text," to develop a hermeneutics of the body rather than a hermeneutics of the text. Consequently, one may achieve an incorporation of oneself into Scripture, an incorporation into the body of another which is not me. The argument further contends a "detour" through the text and the development of a hermeneutic of "corporeality rather than textuality."[23]

The contention above seems to justify Ricœur's approach, while also finding a reason to distinguish itself from its "Protestant" character. The confrontation, in a way, develops on theological and philosophical

18. See "The Visitation of Facticity," in Falque, *Loving Struggle*.
19. Falque, *Loving Struggle*, 243.
20. Falque, *Loving Struggle*, 243.
21. Falque, *Loving Struggle*, 246.
22. See Falque, *Crossing the Rubicon*, 30.
23. Falque, *Crossing the Rubicon*, 40.

levels. The affirmation, essential to Protestantism, of *sola scriptura* and the return to Scripture as "text," is opposed to the conception of "the body—as really present in the bread in the Eucharist," as well as to tradition and the magisterium, the twin pillars of Catholicism for building up and interpreting the biblical message.[24] Thus, as Falque observes, a choice is carried out by Ricœur, to see the text as a medium (and not speech), including setting forth "both philosophical reasons—dumb and silent experience—and theological reasons—the primacy of the book of the world over the book of scripture."[25]

Falque's criticism is therefore of a dual nature. On a philosophical level, against the underlying assertion, according to Claude Romano, to Ricœur's approach: "It is no longer because we are at the world that we have language, it is because we have language that we are in the world." Rather, he reaffirms: "Indeed, there exists an autonomy of the prelinguistic order, of pre-predicative experience with regard to superior forms of thought and language."[26] As for the theological argumentation, Falque recalls that God did not first give Scripture to Adam, but on the basis that he needed it as a result of sin to portray through text the experience of this world. This privileging of a book of the world is affirmed by Saint Bonaventure as an aid to decipher not simply texts, but also the presence of God in the world. In *God, the Flesh, and the Other*, for example, Falque contrasts the founding experience of the flesh in Saint Bonaventure with the original experience of speech in Saint Dominic. Should we therefore speak of an evolution in Falque, to the extent to which hermeneutics has, this time, reached full display? Recall: "Authentic hermeneutics is phenomenology and phenomenology is accomplished only as hermeneutics . . . which would render superfluous the 'graft' of the one on the other, to pick back up Ricœur's famous image. Hermeneutics and phenomenology would be the flowering of a same 'essence,' of a same bud."[27] So, is the conception of the body really a turning point in Falque?

To specify the features of a "good" hermeneutic is to indicate that it is no longer a deciphering of textuality, but an experience of the world and the body. "I come not only to the world but also to the text with my flesh and body. Moreover, the text only becomes incorporated in me when I

---

24. Falque, *Crossing the Rubicon*, 40.

25. Falque, *Crossing the Rubicon*, 44.

26. Falque, *Crossing the Rubicon*, 35. Cited from the original French: Romano, *Au coeur de la raison*.

27. Falque, *Crossing the Rubicon*, 35. Cited from Romano, *Au coeur de la raison*.

also become capable of incorporating myself in it, in the same way as we become incorporated in Christ or in the church."[28] Furthermore: "'What is to be believed' is first of all 'a real presence.'"[29] In this hermeneutic of facticity, I do not understand myself at first in front of the text, but the text stands there before me. It is less me who reads the text, and more the text which reads me; it is not so much conscious as it is carnal. As Falque writes: "In reality, what matters is the kind of relation that grounds the interpretation of the message—mediation of the text or exposition of the body."[30] The voice of God refers to the presence of a body. It is, ultimately, an inter-corporeality.

Thinking Death and Resurrection

The different ways to read language, text, and body may also be used to read the resurrection. At first glance, the connection may seem a little superficial. Ricœur, for example, addressed the theme only in a posthumous and unfinished, fragmentary book, *Living Up to Death* (as well as in an interview found in *Critique and Conviction*). Falque devotes the entirety of *The Metamorphosis of Finitude* to those texts. Whereas the Falquian conception seems to be consistent with the spirit of his other texts, certain commentators have questioned the coherence of Ricœur, such as Xavier Tillette, SJ.

Ricœur's intentions are expressed in a letter to a friend in which he mentioned a "late apprenticeship" consisting of a necessity and perhaps difficulty of mourning a desire to exist after death, "joy—no, instead, cheerfulness joined to a hoped-for grace of existing until death."[31] The words are simple enough but deserve to be commented on at length. Ricœur's project seems to join, here, a certain philosophical tradition of wisdom, at times Epicurean and other times with Spinozist connotations. Ricœur, moreover, does not play the theologian; instead, we may see him as a new Montaigne who speaks freely. In brief, we may summarize the argument in three points: being alive before death (not imagining my death in front of death of the other), being alive at the moment of death (agonizing and not dying), and, last, experiencing death or fighting to

---

28. Falque, *Crossing the Rubicon*, 48.
29. Falque, *Crossing the Rubicon*, 49.
30. Falque, *Crossing the Rubicon*, 30.
31. Ricœur, *Living Up to Death*, 7.

stay alive until the last moment (thanks to the help of others). Life, in this way, seems to elicit a certain strength over death in which I can experience joy. Although I die, death does not have the last word.

Liberation from fear of death also involves criticizing false images and representations. Only then can we encounter the prospect of the resurrection that Ricœur interprets. For him, we carry out a dismantling without restriction of survival through the accomplishment of self-detachment, which leads to the renunciation of a self-enclosed survival identity. We survive by acting for others. This is how the death and resurrection of Christ may be interpreted. Ricœur insists on this point. He evokes the memory of God in which "God remembers me." The belief in such a salvation reflects a kind of wager and self-less abandonment to God. What it does is bring into play the idea of grace, a certain confidence in grace in which little is owed to me. "To use a language that remains quite mythical: Let God, at my death, do with me as he wills. I demand nothing. I demand no 'after.'"[32] Should we see in this an opposition to an entire religious tradition, or a stimulating new reading? The question remains open.

Falque, for his part, does not hide from thinking about the resurrection; though it is a difficulty of a dual nature: "On the one hand, there is a hesitation on the part of theology to believe that it should be concerned with what happened to the resurrected Christ. On the other, there is a burden of philosophical finitude that probably we cannot overcome and even less can hope to transform. . . . The contemporary theologian, like the philosopher, needs to take finitude as the first given. Finitude doesn't summarize a doctrine, but simply sums up the most ordinary existence of all human beings, including that of the Son of God, who was exactly 'made man' (*et homo factus est*)."[33] It is necessary to delve into "the theological dimension of that other experience, of the resurrection of the body, lived through so far (at least according to Catholic dogma) by Christ and by Mary his mother."[34] Falque does not hesitate to confront the teaching of tradition; he wants to render it "credible." The prospect of resurrection is never called into question; rather, it is merely set up for newer and richer interpretation for contemporary eyes.

The Falquian reflection on the resurrection differs from Ricœur. First of all, it develops out of collective practice of both theology and

32. Ricœur, *Living Up to Death*, xvi.
33. Falque, *Metamorphosis of Finitude*, 13.
34. Falque, *Metamorphosis of Finitude*, 6.

philosophy. On a second level, it asserts itself as a "phenomenology of resurrection" through a reading of the evangelical texts which does not solely cling "to their hermeneutic but that opens up on a descriptive and phenomenological experience."[35] Here we find the essential distinction in Falque between "the hermeneutics of texts" and "a true reflection on the sense of our own corporality, as on that of the corporality of Christ."[36] The resurrection of Christ is understood from the consideration of his body, in the same way that the Word can be grasped from human experience. This dimension of corporeality expresses a radical novelty that Ricœur may have inspired but did not pursue himself.

The understanding and presentation of the resurrection is performed by Falque from an existentialist view of carnal birth, that is, a heuristic and philosophical approach which sees man crossing his finitude, not as a being for death but a being for beginning. Yet, this is not fully realized through the phenomenological description of experience alone; it must also reveal the action of the Father and the strength of the Spirit in that very resurrection. *The Metamorphosis of Finitude* defines, in a certain way, the transcendental conditions of this resurrection. The argument is developed in four major moments: the analysis of what is to be transformed, the finitude of the human being, the strength of the one who transforms in intra-Trinitarian action, and the description of what is resurrected (the experience of the body, the flesh as not simply bodily substance). This flesh, through resurrection, does not leave this world.

The relationship between philosophy and theology regarding the resurrection illustrates the two theses essential to Falque: "We have no other experience of God than that of man" and "*Théologoumènes* are also translated in *philosophèmes*." These are not only philosophical arguments; they also remind us that Christianity forges a path towards the divine from the human. The Falquian perspective, in contrast to Ricœur, does not envisage a mastery over death. Resurrection and birth both escape our power. The metamorphosis, as Falque understands it, is not the continuation of life but the creative result of divine action. Falque, at least in the heuristic moment of his analysis, does not seek to conceal the tragic nature of the human condition. "Finitude is not simply derived from the infinite but is the end-stopped horizon of our existence and so also of his, the Son's."[37] He does not propose remaining "alive until death" (i.e., Ricœur). This cannot

35. Falque, *Metamorphosis of Finitude*, 9.
36. Falque, *Metamorphosis of Finitude*, 148.
37. Falque, *Metamorphosis of Finitude*, 66.

be the work of the human will but of hope based on the words of Christ and his carnal experience on earth. "We can't have recourse to God through a simple will to last, to go on and on, even supposing that were required by the rebellion of our own bodies (health as opposed to sickness). The resurrection is then not principally an affair for human beings, even though it is also for human beings: It is an affair of God's—of him, in him, and by him."[38] There is no question of desire for eternity, of an openness to transcendence and of a desire for God. "The metamorphosis of the world is the metamorphosis of God."[39] As Falque draws on Irenaeus: "Our bodies must be resurrected not in terms of their substance [*non ex sua substantia*] but through the power of God [*sed ex Dei virtute*]."[40] We must, therefore, distinguish the action of God in us from his recollection of us, a point posed throughout Ricœur's work.

Conclusion

I will limit myself to a brief judgment of this productive confrontation between Falque and Ricœur. To begin, I want to raise a question: Does Falque take sufficient account of the evolution of Ricœur? In his reflection on language, Ricœur, at the time of the "linguistic turn," defended the importance of "the meaning," of "the reference," of "the subject," all against the closure of a certain structuralism and infinite interpretation (e.g., Foucault). It perhaps goes without saying that, for Ricœur, mediation through language always aims to recover the experience of the subject. Without side-stepping Ricœur's achievement, Falque's fundamental criticism amounts to an opposition between a hermeneutics of body and voice to a hermeneutics of text and writing. The opposition, more specifically, refers to the status of language and the body, to the relationship between words and carnal things.

A second question necessarily arises: What would Falque have done if he worked within the same generation as Ricœur? Would he not also have sought to assume the consequences of the "linguistic turn" which, mutatis mutandis, could thus be considered as the analogue of a sort of carnal turn that we can identify in his work at present? The

---

38. Falque, *Metamorphosis of Finitude*, 65.

39. Falque, *Metamorphosis of Finitude*, 73.

40. Falque, *Metamorphosis of Finitude*, 79–80. On the quotation from Irenaeus, see Irenaeus, *Adversus haereses* 5.6.2.

task now appears to be taken within the philosophical challenge of thinking through the body, as it was formerly a challenge to think through language. And we can say that, each in their own way, both Falque and Ricœur strive to find a path that goes beyond antinomies: beyond a philosophy of consciousness against the death of the subject (by Ricœur), beyond a dualism of the soul and the body (by Falque).

We might add that Falque once contrasted himself against a "fox," as the adage goes, which traverses many paths and pursues several ideas at the same time. Rather, Falque sees himself as a "hedgehog": reducing everything to a single mosaic in constant association between phenomenology, medieval philosophy, and the reception of revelation. Following this picture of philosophy, one could even evoke the owl (Ricœur himself liked to collect figurines of this animal)—that Hegelian creature which wakes at nightfall to meditate on the work of the day. Yet, I propose that the Falquian hedgehog is the most authentic model. The Falque of *The Wedding Feast of the Lamb* is a case in point. In it, he raises a criticism of phenomenology's insufficiency on questions of meaning, flesh, and passivity. To succeed, like Ricœur, in his own time, he urges for a hermeneutical bridge with phenomenology. It seems that Falque is recognizing a greater place for hermeneutics as well as for language, as demonstrated in his reflections on the flesh and the Eucharist.

Can we not find an analogy between the increasing place given to Nietzsche by Falque and that reserved by Ricœur for Spinoza? Identifying these figures with our two authors perhaps allows us to highlight a common dimension between them: the need to confront new forms of thought in unconventional ways. Yet another question may be addressed directly to Falque, especially since I made only a minor allusion to it earlier. It refers to the status of finitude, a topic of importance for both thinkers. For instance, how can we explain the fact that the author of *The Metamorphosis of Finitude* never confronted, in relation to this finitude, even partially Ricœur's *Finitude and Guilt*? Was it the reference to guilt that dissuaded him? We have seen Falque describe this finitude in a much more carnal and existential way, in particular, in *The Guide to Gethsemane*. Ricœur also reflected on it at length, for example, in *Living Up to Death*. He certainly privileged finitude in his early works, in a way speaking to a phenomenology of the ordinary; and, on this point, he would be closer to Falque than to Marion (whom Falque, as with other phenomenologists, reproaches for a "preemption of the infinite").

We could consider that the most relevant element of distinction between our two authors lies in a choice relating to the articulation of the Word and the flesh. On more than one occasion, Falque evokes the privilege granted to the Word or to the flesh, through the antagonistic figures of Saint Dominic and Saint Francis, or even that of Aquinas and Saint Bonaventure. We constitute the world by our body rather than by speech, in its hermeneutic and verbal meanings. "Our world becomes birth, sexuality, and death."[41] *God, the Flesh, and the Other* already seems to indicate the solution that Falque, unlike Ricœur, assumes as a philosopher who also wishes to be a theologian: that "absence of a word without flesh" which is to say hermeneutics without phenomenology or, conversely, a "blindness of flesh without word" (i.e., phenomenology without hermeneutics) in order to respond to "the emergence of the Word made flesh in original unity" as the two profound lineages of contemporary philosophy.[42] It is not certain if Ricœur, the author of Hegelian condemnation in *Time and Narrative*, would volunteer such a reconciliation so willingly. It is significant to note that Falque's recent texts prioritize the analysis of the body through language, in a perspective convergent with theology, as if it could resolve or reduce the antagonisms taking place within philosophy. That seems to be his ultimate aim of juxtaposing Word and flesh together.

Does the confrontation of these two authors leave us in the face of a stark opposition? For example, on the one hand, there is the thought of the "or": philosophy *or* theology, phenomenology *or* hermeneutics, life *or* death. This seems to appear to be Ricœur's approach. In contrast, Falque adopts the thought of the "and": philosophy *and* theology, phenomenology *and* hermeneutics, finitude *and* resurrection?[43] Yet another interesting distinction can be made between our two authors. Falque does not hesitate to evoke Ricœur's Protestantism, which may explain the privilege granted to Scripture and the text over the body and the flesh—in other words, the privilege of exegesis over theology. It reminds us of a clear separation between theology and philosophy, a philosophy without absolutes. This Protestantism also accounts for a concept of finitude that Ricœur associates with the guilt of fallible man. Falque, in contrast, prefers to describe finitude in a more flexible way, emphasizing suffering rather than willful guilt. The differences between the proponent of a philosophy "without absolutes" (on one level, "agnostic") and a "religious

---

41. Falque, *Metamorphosis of Finitude*, 135–36.
42. See Falque, *God, the Flesh, and the Other*, 167–75.
43. Emphasis is made by the translator.

philosopher" (not a "philosopher of religion") reflects a fundamental choice in the attitude of the philosopher who recognizes himself as a believer and who may proceed either masked or unmasked. This choice is particularly clear in Falque, whose objective is to make "credible" (i.e., the domain of the believer) what for many of our contemporaries remains "incredible" (i.e., "the domain of the unbeliever"). To do so requires the foresight and honesty to un-conceal one's own intentions. Only then may we hope to reach a universalizable rationality and philosophical fertility for all to share in. In this way, a common space can be established where believers and nonbelievers can meet in celebration of one another. For Falque, in a clever reorientation of the hermeneutic circle, it is possible to understand without believing, to meet without masking differences.

Falque's way of responding, though different from Ricœur, perhaps lingers—though nuanced—with Maurice Blondel's older assertion to inspire belief in those who do not believe. The important thing is not to speak for the souls that believe, but to say something that counts for the minds that do not believe.[44] Prudence and temperance, boldness and assertiveness—which attitude is most relevant and legitimate to transmit the Christian message today? This unique confrontation between Ricœur and Falque may yet help us to resolve those age-old questions that confront Christianity. At the very least, these two thinkers, when seen side by side, bring us closer to grasping the true stakes at hand.

---

44. See Blondel, *Letter on Apologetics*, 134–38.

Acknowledgments

THE TRANSLATOR WISHES TO thank Alain Saudan for his permission to translate and republish this text in English. The translator is also grateful for the support of Wipf and Stock Publishers, including Charlie Collier, Matt Wimer, George Callihan, Zechariah Mickel, and Stephanie Hough, as well as the support of those in France, including William Connelly and Emmanuel Falque, especially for his philosophical guidance on the creation of the translated text.

Books by Emmanuel Falque Translated into English

The Metamorphosis of Finitude: An Essay on Birth and Resurrection. Translated by George Hughes. Perspectives in Continental Philosophy. New York: Fordham University Press, 2012.

God, the Flesh, and the Other: From Irenaeus to Duns Scotus. Translated by William Christian Hackett. Evanston, IL: Northwestern University Press, 2015.

Crossing the Rubicon: The Borderlands of Philosophy and Theology. Translated by Reuben Shank. Perspectives in Continental Philosophy. New York: Fordham University Press, 2016.

The Wedding Feast of the Lamb: Eros, the Body, and the Eucharist. Translated by George Hughes. Perspectives in Continental Philosophy. New York: Fordham University Press, 2016.

The Loving Struggle: Phenomenological and Theological Debates. Translated by Bradley B. Onishi and Lucas McCracken. New York: Rowman and Littlefield, 2018.

Saint Bonaventure and the Entrance of God into Theology. Translated by Brian Lapsa. Revised by William C. Hackett. St Bonaventure, NY: Franciscan Institute, 2018.

The Guide to Gethsemane: Anxiety, Suffering, and Death. Translated by George Hughes. Perspectives in Continental Philosophy. New York: Fordham University Press, 2019.

BOOKS BY EMMANUEL FALQUE TRANSLATED INTO ENGLISH

Nothing to It: Reading Freud as a Philosopher. Translated by Robert Vallier and William L. Connelly. Leuven: Leuven University Press, 2020.

By Way of Obstacles: A Pathway Through a Work. Translated by Sarah Horton. Eugene, OR: Cascade, 2022.

The Book of Experience: From Anselm of Canterbury to Bernard of Clairvaux. Translated by Georges Hughes. Explorations in Philosophy and Theology. London: Bloomsbury Academic, 2024.

The Emmanuel Falque Reader: Key Writings in Phenomenology and Continental Philosophy of Religion. Edited by Nikolaas Cassidy-Deketeleare. London: Bloomsbury, 2024.

The Flesh of God. Translation by Georges Hughes. Perspectives in Continental Philosophy. New York: Fordham University Press, 2025.

Spiritualism and Phenomenology: The Case of Maine de Biran. Translated by Sarah Horton. The Things Themselves. Eugene, OR: Cascade, 2025.

The Extra-Phenomenal: At the Limits of Phenomenality. Translation by Nikolaas Cassidy-Deketeleare. London: Bloomsbury, forthcoming.

Bibliography

Albertson, David. "The Limits of Earth: The Question of Finitude in the Young Marx and Two Popes." *Crossing: INPR Journal* 4 (forthcoming).
Arrien, Sophie-Jan. "Penser sans Dieu, vivre avec Dieu: Heidegger lecteur d'Augustin." *Esprit* 391 (2013) 68–80.
Balthasar, Hans Urs von. *La Gloire et la Croix III*. Paris: Desclée de Brouwer, 1990.
———. *The Glory of the Lord: A Theological Aesthetics I*. Translated by Erasmo Leiva-Merikakis. San Francisco: Ignatius, 1982.
———. *The Theology of Karl Barth: Exposition and Interpretation*. Translated by Edward T. Oakes. San Francisco: Ignatius, 1992.
Barth, Karl. *The Epistle to the Romans*. Translated by Edwyn Hoskyns. 6th ed. New York: Oxford University Press, 1933.
———. *Evangelical Theology: An Introduction*. Translated by Grover Foley. Grand Rapids: Eerdmans, 1979.
Benedict XVI, Pope. "Deus Caritas Est." Vatican, December 25, 2005. https://www.vatican.va/content/benedict-xvi/en/encyclicals/documents/hf_ben-xvi_enc_20051225_deus-caritas-est.html.
Berger, Gaston. *Un philosophe dans le monde modern*. Paris: Presses Universitaires de France, 1961.
Blondel, Maurice. *"The Letter on Apologetics" and "History and Dogma."* Edited and translated by Alexander Dru and Illtyd Trethowan. New York: Holt, Rinehart, and Winston, 1964.
Bonhoeffer, Dietrich. *Letters and Papers from Prison*. Translated by Lisa Dahill et al. Minneapolis: Fortress, 2010.
Breton, Stanislas. *Le vivant miroir de l'univers: Logique d'un travail de philosophe*. Paris: Cerf, 2006.
Bultmann, Rudolf. *L'historicité de l'homme et de la revelation*. Vol. 1 of *Foi et comprehension*. Paris: Seuil, 1970.
———. *Jésus, mythologie et démythologisation*. Paris: Seuil, 1968.
Chauvet, Louis-Marie. *Le corps chemin de Dieu*. Paris: Bayard, 2010.
Citot, Vincent. *La condition philosophique et le problème du commencement*. Paris: Cercle Hermeneutique, 2009.
Derrida, Jacques. *Given Time: 1. Counterfeit Money*. Translated by Peggy Kamuf. Chicago: University of Chicago Press, 1992.

Descartes, René. *Descartes' "Meditations."* Edited by David B. Manley and Charles S. Taylor. Translated by John Veitch [English] and the Duc de Luynes [French]. Trilingual ed. Dayton: Wright State University Press, 2013.

Falque, Emmanuel. "After Metaphysics? The 'Weight of Life' According to Saint Augustine." In *Philosophies of Liturgy: Explorations of Embodied Religious Practice*, edited by J. Aaron Simmons et al., 207–20. Expanding Philosophy of Religion. London: Bloomsbury Academic, 2023.

———. "L'argument théophanique." In *Saint Anselme: Un penseur et un saint pour notre temps*, edited by Abbaye Bec-Hellouin, 63–118. Bec-Hellouin, Fr.: Ateliers du Bec, 2009.

———. "Athéisme moderne et puissance de la resurrection." Lecture given at the Sorbonne, December 9, 2007. Later printed in *Revue Résurrection* 122 (2007). https://www.revue-resurrection.org/archives_revue-resurrection/Atheisme-moderne-et-puissance-de.html.

———. *By Way of Obstacles: A Pathway Through a Work*. Translated by Sarah Horton. Eugene, OR: Cascade, 2022.

———. *Crossing the Rubicon: The Borderlands of Philosophy and Theology*. Translated by Reuben Shank. Perspectives in Continental Philosophy. New York: Fordham University Press, 2016.

———. "The Debt for the Gift." In *The Book of Experience: From Anselm of Canterbury to Bernard of Clairvaux*, translated by George Hughes, 49–67. Explorations in Philosophy and Theology. London: Bloomsbury Academic, 2024.

———. "Dieu nous éprouve-t-il ou faut-il sauver la providence?" *Vie spirituelle* 734 (2000) 71–89.

———. *The Emmanuel Falque Reader: Key Writings in Phenomenology and Continental Philosophy of Religion*. Edited by Nikolaas Cassidy-Deketelaere. London: Bloomsbury Academic, 2024.

———. "God Extra-Phenomenal: For a Phenomenology of Holy Saturday." *Journal for Continental Philosophy of Religion* 4 (2022) 1–28.

———. *God, the Flesh, and the Other: From Irenaeus to Duns Scotus*. Translated by William Christian Hackett. Evanston, IL: Northwestern University Press, 2015.

———. *The Guide to Gethsemane: Anxiety, Suffering, Death*. Translated by George Hughes. Perspectives in Continental Philosophy. New York: Fordham University Press, 2019.

———. *Hors phénomène: Essai au confins de la phénoménalité*. Paris: Hermann, 2021.

———. "Limite théologique et finitude phénoménologique chez Thomas d'Aquin." *Revue de sciences philosophiques et théologiques* 92 (2008) 527–56.

———. *The Loving Struggle: Phenomenological and Theological Debates*. Translated by Bradley B. Onishi and Lucas McCracken. New York: Rowman and Littlefield, 2018.

———. *The Metamorphosis of Finitude: An Essay on Birth and Resurrection*. Translated by George Hughes. Perspectives in Continental Philosophy. New York: Fordham University Press, 2012.

———. "Michel Henry théologien (à propos de *C'est moi la vérité*)." *Laval théologique et philosophique* 57 (2001) 525–36.

———. "Mystique et modernité: Aspirations spirituelles de notre temps et mystique chrétienne." *Études: Revue de culture contemporaine* 394 (2001) 785–92.

———. "Penser, c'est décider: Entretien avec Franck Damour." *NUNC* 19 (2009) 76–84.

———. "Philosophie et théologie: Nouvelles frontières." *Études* 4042 (2006) 201–10.
———. *Saint Bonaventure and the Entrance of God into Theology*. Translated by Brian Lapsa. Revised by William C. Hackett. Ashland, OH: Franciscan Institute, 2018.
———. *Triduum philosophiques*. Paris: Cerf, 2015.
———. "Les trois modèles philosophiques du rapport entre foi et raison." *Esprit* 333 (2007) 279–81.
———. *The Wedding Feast of the Lamb: Eros, the Body, and the Eucharist*. Translated by George Hughes. Perspectives in Continental Philosophy. New York: Fordham University Press, 2016.
Falque, Emmanuel, and Agata Zielinski, eds. *Philosophie et théologie en dialogue: 1996–2006; Lipt une trace*. Collection Ouverture Philosophique. Paris: Harmattan, 2005.
Fisher, Simon. *Revelatory Positivism? Barth's Earliest Theology and the Marburg School*. Oxford: Oxford University Press, 1988.
Fœssel, Michaël. "Trois modèles philosophiques du rapport entre foi et raison." *Esprit* 333 (2007) 279–81.
Forte, Bruno. *À l'écoute de l'autre*. Paris: Cerf, 2003.
Foucault, Michel. *Les mots et les choses*. Paris: Gallimard, 1966.
Franck, Didier. *Nietzsche and the Shadow of God*. Translated by Bettina Bergo and Philippe Farah. Evanston, IL: Northwestern University Press, 2012.
Gachoud, François. *Par-delà l'athéisme*. Paris: Cerf, 2007.
Gauchet, Marcel. *The Disenchantment of the World: A Political History of Religion*. Translated by Oscar Burge. Princeton, NJ: Princeton University Press, 1997.
Greisch, Jean. *Le buisson ardent et les lumières de la raison II*. Paris: Cerf, 2009.
Grondin, Jean. *L'herméneutique*. Paris: Presses Universitaires de France, 1993.
Heidegger, Martin. *Being and Time*. Translated by John Macquarrie and Edward Robinson. Cambridge, MA: Blackwell, 1962.
———. *Duns Scotus's Doctrine of Categories and Meaning*. Translated by Joydeep Bagchee and Jeffrey D. Gower. Bloomington: Indiana University Press, 2022.
———. *Identity and Difference*. Translated by Joan Stambaugh. New York: Harper and Row, 1969.
———. *Kant et le problème de la métaphysique*. Paris: Gallimard, 1953.
———. *The Phenomenology of Religious Life*. Translated by Matthias Fritsch and Jennifer Anna Gosetti-Ferenci. Bloomington: Indiana University Press, 2004.
Henry, Michel. *Barbarism*. Translated by Scott Davidson. New York: Continuum, 2012.
———. *I Am the Truth: Toward a Philosophy of Christianity*. Translated by Susan Emmanuel. Stanford, CA: Stanford University Press, 2003.
———. *Incarnation: A Philosophy of the Flesh*. Translated by Karl Hefty. Evanston, IL: Northwestern University Press, 2015.
———. *The Michel Henry Reader*. Edited by Scott Davidson and Frédéric Seyler. Evanston, IL: Northwestern University Press, 2019.
———. *Phénoménologie et christianisme chez Michel Henry*. Edited by Philippe Capelle. Paris: Cerf, 2004.
Husserl, Edmund. *The Crisis of European Sciences and Transcendental Phenomenology: An Introduction to Phenomenological Philosophy*. Translated by David Carr. Studies in Phenomenology and Existential Philosophy. Evanston, IL: Northwestern University Press, 1970.
———. *Ideas I*. Translated by F. Kersten. Vol. 2. Boston: Nijhoff, 1983.

Janicaud, Dominique. *Phenomenology and the "Theological Turn": The French Debate*. Translated by Bernard Prusak. Perspectives in Continental Philosophy. New York: Fordham University Press, 2000.

John-Paul II, Pope. "Address of His Holiness John Paul II to the Bishops of Western Canada on Their 'Ad Limina' Visit." Vatican, October 30, 1999. http://www.vatican.va/holy_father/john_paul_ii/speeches/1999/october/documents/hf_jp-ii_spe_30101999_ad-limina-west-canada_en.html.

———. "Discours du samedi 30 octobre 1999 aux évêques du Canada." *Osservatore Romano* 46 (November 16, 1999).

Jonas, Hans. "The Concept of God After Auschwitz: A Jewish Voice." *Journal of Religion* 67 (1987) 1–13.

Jüngel, Eberhard. *God as the Mystery of the World: On the Foundation of the Theology of the Crucified One in the Dispute Between Theism and Atheism*. Translated by Darrell L. Guder. Eugene, OR: Wipf & Stock, 2009.

Justin Martyr. "First Apology." In *The First and Second Apologies*, translated by Leslie William Barnard, 23–72. New York: Paulist, 1997.

Kierkegaard, Søren. *Discours édifiants à divers points de vue*. Ouvres complètes 13. Paris: Orante, 1966.

———. *Fear and Trembling*. Edited by C. Stephen Evans and Sylvia Walsh. Cambridge Texts in the History of Philosophy. Cambridge: Cambridge University Press, 2006.

Klee, Paul. *"Creative Confession" and Other Writings*. Edited by Matthew Gale. London: Tate, 2013.

Léon-Dufour, Xavier. *Dictionnaire du Nouveau Testament*. Paris: Seuil, 1975.

Libera, Alain de. *Penser au Moyen Âge*. Paris: Seuil, 1991.

Lubac, Henri de. *The Drama of Atheist Humanism*. Translated by Edith Riley. New York: Meridian, 1967.

———. *The Mystery of the Supernatural*. Translated by Rosemary Sheed. New York: Herder and Herder, 2016.

Marcel, Gabriel. *Being and Having*. Translated by Katharine Farrer. London: Dacre, 1949.

Marion, Jean-Luc. *Being Given Toward a Phenomenology of Givenness*. Translated by Jeffrey Kosky. Stanford, CA: Stanford University Press, 2002.

———. *Believing in Order to See: On the Rationality of Revelation and the Irrationality of Some Believers*. Translated by Christina M. Gschwandtner. Perspectives in Continental Philosophy. New York: Fordham University Press, 2017.

———. *In Excess: Studies of Saturated Phenomena*. Translated by Robyn Horner and Vincent Berraud. Perspectives in Continental Philosophy. New York: Fordham University Press, 2002.

———. *Revelation Comes from Elsewhere: A Contribution to a Critical History and a Phenomenal Concept of Revelation*. Translated by Stephen E. Lewis and Stephanie Rumpza. Stanford, CA: Stanford University Press, 2024.

Marzano, Michela. *Dictionnaire du corps*. Paris: Presses Universitaires de France, 2007.

Mauss, Marcel. *The Gift: The Form and Reason for Exchange in Archaic Societies*. Translated by W. D. Halls. Routledge Classics. London: Routledge, 1990.

McCormack, Bruce L. *Karl Barth's Critically Realistic Dialectical Theology*. Oxford: Clarendon, 1997.

Merleau-Ponty, Maurice. *"In Praise of Philosophy" and Other Essays*. Translated by John Wild and James Edie. Evanston, IL: Northwestern University Press, 1988.

———. *The Phenomenology of Perception*. Translated by Colin Smith. New York: Routledge, 1958.

———. *Sense and Non-Sense*. Translated by Hubert Dreyfus and Patricia Dreyfus. Evanston, IL: Northwestern University Press, 1964.

———. *Signs*. Translated by Richard McCleary. Evanston, IL: Northwestern University Press, 1964.

Milbank, John. "Can a Gift Be Given? Prolegomena to a Future Trinitarian Metaphysic." *Modern Theology* 11 (1995) 119–61.

Moltmann, Jürgen. *Le Seigneur de la danse: Essai sur la joie d'être libre*. Translated by A. Liefooghe. Paris: Cerf, 1977.

Nancy, Jean-Luc. *Corpus*. Translated by Richard A. Rand. Perspectives in Continental Philosophy. New York: Fordham University Press, 2008.

Nédoncelle, Maurice. *Existe-t-il une philosophie chrétienne?* Paris: Fayard, 1961.

Neusch, Marcel. "Dieu, pour penser autrement: Un remède nécessaire devant l'affaissement spirituel contemporain." *Maurice Zundel*, May 31, 2008. https://mauricezundel.com/31-05-2008-dieu-pour-penser-autrement-un-remede-necessaire-devant-laffaissement-spirituel-contemporain/.

Nietzsche, Friedrich. *The Gay Science*. Translated by Walter Kaufman. New York: Vintage, 1972.

———. *On the Genealogy of Morals*. Translated by Walter Kaufmann. New York: Vintage, 1969.

———. *La volonté de puissance I*. Paris: Gallimard, 1942.

Péguy, Charles. *Dialogue de l'histoire et l'âme charnelle*. Paris: Gallimard, 1992.

———. *The Portal of the Mystery of Hope*. Translated by David Schindler. New York: Continuum, 1996.

Pieper, Josef. *De la foi*. Paris: Ad Solem, 2011.

Ricœur, Paul. *À l'école de la phénoménologie*. Paris: Vrin, 1986.

———. *The Conflict of Interpretations: Essays in Hermeneutics*. Edited by Don Ihde. Evanston, IL: Northwestern University Press, 1974.

———. *Critique and Conviction: Conversations with François Azouvi and Marc de Launay*. Translated by Kathleen Blamey. European Perspectives. New York: Columbia University Press, 2006.

———. *From Text to Action: Essays in Hermeneutics II*. Translated by Kathleen Blamey and John Thompson. Evanston, IL: Northwestern University Press, 1991.

———. *Hermeneutics and the Human Sciences*. Translated by John Thompson. Cambridge: Cambridge University Press, 1981.

———. *Living Up to Death*. Translated by David Pellauer. Chicago: University of Chicago Press, 2009.

———. *Memory, History, Forgetting*. Translated by Kathleen Blamey and David Pellauer. Chicago: University of Chicago Press, 2004.

———. *Oneself as Another*. Translated by Kathleen Blamey. Chicago: University of Chicago Press, 1992.

———. *Thinking Biblically: Exegetical and Hermeneutical Studies*. Translated by David Pellauer. Chicago: University of Chicago Press, 1998.

Romano, Claude. *Au coeur de la raison: La phenomenology*. Paris: Gallimard, 2010.

———. "Le possible et l'événement (I)." *Philosophie* 40 (1993) 68–95.

Roy, Olivier. *La sainte ignorance*. Paris: Seuil, 2008.

Saint-Aubert, Emmanuel de. "'L'incarnation change tout': Merleau-Ponty critique de la 'théologie explicative.'" *Transversalités* 112 (2009) 147–86.
Sockness, Brent W. *Against False Apologetics: Wilhelm Herrmann and Ernst Troeltsch in Conflict*. Beiträge zur historischen Theologie 105. Tübingen: Mohr Siebeck, 1998.
Spinoza, Benedict de. *The Ethics*. Translated by R. H. M. Elwes. 1677; Project Gutenberg, 2009. https://www.gutenberg.org/files/3800/3800-h/3800-h.htm.
Stein, Edith. *Phénoménologie et philosophie chrétienne*. Paris: Cerf, 1987.
Thévenaz, Pierre. *L'homme et sa raison*. Neuchâtel: Baconnière, 1956.
Valéry, Paul. *Poésies. Mélange. Variété*. Edited by Jean Hytier. Vol. 1 of *Œuvres*. Paris: Pléiade, 1957.
Zachhuber, Johannes. *Theology as Science in Nineteenth-Century Germany: From F. C. Baur to Ernst Troeltsch*. Changing Paradigms in Historical and Systematic Theology. Oxford: Oxford University Press, 2013.

Index

Adoration, 124, 125
Anselm, Saint, xiv, xxiii, 21, 143, 149
Anxiety, xv, xxi, 40, 42–43, 55, 57–62, 68, 71, 85, 149
Aquinas, Thomas, xx, 10, 12, 19, 21, 26, 28, 48, 50–52, 66, 71, 79, 114n45, 121, 126, 132, 141, 148, 153, 170
Arendt, Hannah, 141
Atheism, 1, 33–34, 36, 39, 44–46, 49, 67, 79, 92, 127, 131, 145, 148, 160
Augustine, Saint, 12, 17–18, 26, 67, 72, 73, 82, 84, 85, 119, 141, 147, 160

Badiou, Alain, xii–xiii, 1
Balthasar, Hans Urs von, xxiii, 16, 27, 34, 62, 112, 147,
Barth, Karl, xxiii, 12, 80, 149, 150n35
Believability, ix, xiii, 4, 15, 82, 87, 142, 143, 149
Blondel, Maurice, xiii, 3, 8, 13, 24, 26, 28, 31, 32, 48, 171
Bonaventure, Saint, 10, 12, 26–28, 32n72, 50–53, 66, 124–25, 140, 146–47, 164, 170
Bonhoeffer, Dietrich, xix, 2, 34, 46, 47, 145, 146
Bultmann, Rudolf, 67, 80, 137, 144n26, 152
Breton, Stanislas, 127

Call, the, 26, 37, 38, 153

Chrétien, Jean-Louis, xiii, 2, 26, 68, 69
Conversion, 26–30, 34, 84–86, 88–89, 102–3
Credibility, 23, 74, 77, 104, 149

Deleuze, Gilles, xiii, xxi–xxii, 48, 108, 110–11, 116, 134, 144
Derrida, Jacques, xii, xxiiin27,
Descartes, René, 9, 21, 25, 26n52, 98, 102, 147, 150
Duns Scotus, 10, 12, 26, 39, 52–53, 132

Extra-phenomenal, xiv–xv, 64n95

Face, the, 44, 58–59, 69, 96, 106
Flesh, xv, xix, xxiii, xxv, 26, 54, 58, 61–62, 68, 75, 80–82, 87–92, 95, 97–106, 108, 111, 115–19, 121–23, 125–27, 138–39, 160, 164, 167, 169, 170
Foucault, Michel, xiii, 42, 136, 160, 168
Franck, Didier, 90–91, 105
Freud, Sigmund, 99, 109, 111–13

Gift, the, xiii, xvii, xxii–xxv, 20, 26, 48, 68, 108, 112–15, 127, 140, 153
Gilson, Étienne, xiii, 12–13
Greisch, Jean, 17, 69, 162, 163

Hegel, Georg Wilhelm Friedrich, xi, xii, 43, 169, 170

INDEX

Heidegger, Martin, xix, xxi–xxiii, 11, 17–18, 21, 28, 38, 39, 40–44, 46, 49, 50–52, 55–61, 64–65, 67, 68, 70–74, 84, 99–102, 106, 118, 126, 132, 136, 149, 153, 160, 163

Henry, Michel, xiii, xxii, 2, 26, 54n52, 68–70, 100–103, 115, 117

Husserl, Edmund, xxiii, 20, 25, 50n37, 54, 83, 88, 100, 103, 116–17, 142, 150, 161–63

Immanence, 13, 21, 37, 38, 42–44, 50, 53, 68–69, 82, 95, 108, 123, 131, 137, 142, 162

Incarnation, x, 14, 16, 23, 26, 28–30, 32–34, 38, 44, 47, 52–55, 57, 62, 65, 67, 74–77, 87, 89–90, 92, 93, 98, 102n15, 103–5, 107–8, 115–16, 123, 133, 136–40, 143–44, 148

Irenaeus, xx, 10, 26, 96, 124, 140, 168,

Janicaud, Dominique, xiii, 9, 68–70, 131, 159

Jonas, Hans, xii, 92, 143n24

Jüngel, Eberhard, 2, 3, 156

Justin Martyr, xvii, xviii, xix-xx, xxiii–xxv

Kant, Immanuel, xxii–xxiii, 6, 34, 63, 70n106, 79, 138, 149,

Kierkegaard, Søren, xix, xxvn35, 16–17, 43, 72–73, 149, 152–53, 159

Klee, Paul, 112

Lack, 3, 13–14, 43, 61, 78, 87, 95, 101

Lacoste, Jean-Yves, xiii, xxii, 2, 26, 45, 48, 67, 71

Leap, the, 8, 91, 131, 137, 148

Levinas, Emmanuel, xiii, 26, 68, 69, 103, 106, 117, 131, 138

Lubac, Henri de, xiii, 38, 39, 44, 45, 48

Moltmann, Jürgen, xiii, 2, 3n7, 60

Marion, Jean Luc, xiii, xxii, xxiii, xxiv, 2, 6–9, 20, 23, 26, 53, 68, 69, 114, 153, 169

Marcel, Gabriel, xiii–xxiii, 37n3

Mask, the, 9, 118, 134–35, 171

Meister Eckhart, 26, 89

Merleau-Ponty, Maurice, xix, 14, 20, 21–22, 23n43, 32, 33n75, 45, 69, 75, 76, 99, 100n10, 103–4, 106, 132, 139, 142, 150

Mysticism, 6, 16, 39, 87, 120, 124, 126

Nancy, Jean-Luc, xiii, xxv, 1, 94, 95n3, 119, 129, 143

Neusch, Marcel, 3, 154

Nietzsche, Friedrich, xxi-xxii, 1, 3, 33, 37, 44, 57, 61, 64–65, 84, 90–92, 98, 99, 103, 105–8, 117, 119, 123, 125, 126–27, 128, 133–34, 137, 140, 144–45, 148, 169

Organic, the, xix, 54, 68, 96–97, 105–13, 115–17, 119–20, 123–24, 127, 143

Other, the, 16, 68, 80, 92, 154, 165

Pascal, Blaise, xix, 6, 16–17, 27, 41, 71, 121, 129, 147, 153, 159

Paul, Saint, 1, 17, 76, 82

Péguy, Charles, 55, 132, 133n3, 138, 140

Philosophème, 23, 25, 31, 32, 77, 86, 139, 160, 167

Pieper, Josef, 152

Pope Benedict XVI, 121

Pope John-Paul II, xxii, 34, 46

Rahner, Karl, xiii, 26, 34, 147

Ricœur, Paul, ix, xi–xiii, xvi, xx, xxiii, 6–9, 15, 17, 19, 23–25, 49, 78, 94, 127, 135, 139, 141, 146, 152, 157–71

Romano, Claude, 58n68, 152, 164

Saint-Aubert, Emmanuel de, 139, 142n20

Spinoza, Benedict de, xi, 3, 6, 108–10, 116, 123, 125, 128, 143, 169

Stein, Edith, 50

Tertullian, xx, 26, 54

Théologoumène, 25, 31–32, 77, 86, 139, 160, 167
Tiling, 27, 30n68, 31
Transcendence, 21–22, 36–37, 43, 50, 67, 69, 123, 131, 137, 142, 150, 168
Trinity, the, 10, 26, 28, 32–33, 47, 66, 77, 80–81, 85, 98, 135, 140, 146–48, 154

Threshold, the, xxiii, 7, 8, 31, 37, 42, 131

Universality, xx, 14–15, 135–36, 171

Valéry, Paul, 100